WORLD HISTORY

World History

Ideologies, Structures, and Identities

EDITED BY

Philip Pomper, Richard H. Elphick, and
Richard T. Vann

Copyright © Blackwell Publishers Ltd 1998, except Chapter 10 © Rowman and Littlefield Publishers Inc., and Chapters 1, 3, 4, 8, and 9 © Wesleyan University

First published 1998

2 4 6 8 10 9 7 5 3 1

Blackwell Publishers Inc.
350 Main Street
Malden, Massachusetts 02148
USA

Blackwell Publishers Ltd
108 Cowley Road
Oxford OX4 1JF
UK

Library of Congress Cataloging-in-Publication Data
World history: ideologies, structures, and identities / edited by Philip Pomper, Richard H. Elphick, and Richard T. Vann.
      p. cm.
   Includes bibliographical references and index.
   ISBN 0-631-20898-4. – 0-631-20899-2 (pbk.)
   1. History – Philosophy. 2. Historiography. 3. History – Methodology. I. Pomper, Philip.
II. Elphick, Richard. III. Vann, Richard T.
D16.8.W73 1998
901–dc21   97-45817
                                                      CIP

British Library Cataloguing in Publication Data
A CIP catalogue record for this book is available from the British Library.

Typeset in 10pt on 12pt Goudy
by Brigitte Lee, redshoes cooperative, Worcestershire, UK

Printed in Great Britain by MPG Books Ltd, Bodmin, Cornwall

This book is printed on acid-free paper

Contents

Contributors

The contributors are the authors and editors of numerous books. Only some of their more prominent works (not more than two) are listed below.

Professor **Janet Lippman Abu-Lughod**, Center for Studies of Social Change, New School for Social Research, 64 University Place, New York, NY 10003. *Before European Hegemony: The World System AD 1250–1350* (New York: Oxford University Press, 1989); *Cairo: 1001 Years of the City Victorious* (Princeton, NJ: Princeton University Press, 1971).

Professor **Michael Adas**, Department of History, Rutgers University, PO Box 5059, New Brunswick, NJ 08903-5059. *Machines as the Measure of Men: Science, Technology, and Ideologies of Western Dominance* (Ithaca, NY: Cornell University Press, 1989); *Prophets of Rebellion: Millenarian Protest Movements against the European Colonial Order* (Chapel Hill, NC: University of North Carolina Press, 1979).

Professor **Shmuel N. Eisenstadt**, Rose Issacs Professor Emeritus of Sociology, Faculty of Social Sciences, The Hebrew University of Jerusalem, Mount Scopus, Jerusalem 91-905, Israel. *Patrons, Clients, and Friends: Interpersonal Relations and the Structure of Trust in Society* (New York: Cambridge University Press, 1984); *Revolution and the Transformation of Societies: A Comparative Study of Civilizations* (New York: Free Press, 1978).

Francis Fukuyama, George Mason University, Institute of Public Policy, MS 3C6, Fairfax, VA 22030-4444. *Trust: The Social Virtues and the Creation of Prosperity* (New York: Free Press, 1995); *The End of History and the Last Man* (New York: Free Press, 1992).

Professor **William A. Green**, Brooks Professor, Department of History, College of the Holy Cross, Worcester, MA 01610. *History, Historians, and the*

Dynamics of Change (Westport, CT: Praeger, 1993); *British Slave Emancipation: The Sugar Colonies and the Great Experiment, 1830–1865* (Oxford: Clarendon Press, 1976).

Professor **William H. McNeill**, Robert A. Millikan Distinguished Service Professor Emeritus, Department of History, University of Chicago, School House Road, Colebrook, CT 06021. *The Pursuit of Power: Technology, Armed Force, and Society since A.D. 1000* (Chicago: University of Chicago Press, 1982); *A World History* (New York: Oxford University Press, 1979).

Professor **Bruce Mazlish**, Massachusetts Institute of Technology, School of Humanities and Social Science History Faculty, Cambridge, MA 02139-4307. *The Fourth Discontinuity: The Co-Evolution of Humans and Machines* (New Haven: Yale University Press, 1993); *The Revolutionary Ascetic: The Evolution of a Political Type* (New York: Basic Books, 1976).

Ashis Nandy, Fellow and Director, Center for the Study of Developing Societies, 29 Rajpur Road, Delhi 110054, India. *The Illegitimacy of Nationalism: Rabindranath Tagore and the Politics of Self* (New York: Oxford University Press, 1994); *The Intimate Enemy: Loss and Recovery of Self under Colonialism* (Delhi: Oxford University Press, 1988).

Professor **Philip Pomper**, William F. Armstrong Professor and Professor of History, Wesleyan University, Middletown, CT 06459-0002. *Lenin, Trotsky, and Stalin: The Intelligentsia and Power* (New York: Columbia University Press, 1990); *The Structure of Mind in History* (New York: Columbia University Press, 1985).

Professor **Lamin Sanneh**, Yale University, The Divinity School, 409 Prospect Street, New Haven, CT 06511-2167. *Encountering the West: Christianity and the Global Cultural Process* (Maryknoll, NY: Orbis Books, 1993); *Translating the Message: The Missionary Impact on Culture* (Maryknoll, NY: Orbis Books, 1989).

Professor **Theodore H. Von Laue**, Clark University, Department of History, 950 Main Street, Worcester, MA 01610-1477. *The World Revolution of Westernization: The Twentieth Century in Global Perspective* (New York: Oxford University Press, 1987); *Sergei Witte and the Industrialization of Russia* (New York: Columbia University Press, 1963).

Dr **Lewis D. Wurgaft**, 35 Wendell Street, Cambridge, MA 02138. *The Imperial Imagination: Magic and Myth in Kipling's India* (Middletown, CT: Wesleyan University Press, 1983).

Acknowledgments

The editors wish to thank the contributors to this volume for their willingness to shape their ideas to fit our conception of a conference and then a book on ideologies, structures, and identities in world history. Not least of all, we thank them for their readiness to meet deadlines. We are also indebted to Gary Yohe, our colleague at Wesleyan University, who administered the grant for the World History Conference held at Wesleyan on March 25–6, 1994. The conference received support from the Pew Charitable Trusts as part of the University's International Program at the John E. Andrus Public Affairs Center.

The conference and book are products of the joint labors of the staff of *History and Theory*. The editors of this volume are especially grateful to Brian Fay, Executive Editor of *History and Theory*, and Ann-Louise Shapiro, Associate Editor, for their contributions to the World History Conference and to the realization of the project. Julia Perkins, Administrative Editor, played an important role at every stage and the quality of the finished product owes much to her vigilance and skill at preparing manuscripts.'

Introduction:
The Theory and Practice of
World History

Philip Pomper

The authors contributing to this collection have played and continue to play a major role in shaping the writing of world history. They engage historiographical and theoretical issues, present exemplars of their craft, and discuss the evolution and current state of the field. The authors vary considerably. Some of them affirm systemic, structural approaches, such as world-systems and liberal modernization theory. Others radically criticize or reject such approaches, whether from postmodern viewpoints, which call into question the scientific, "totalizing" character of the project of world history; or from radical, third-world positions that repudiate Western ideas of history in favor of myth. Readers will in addition find a great many dialogues and debates other than those touched upon in this introduction.

The contributors acknowledge the influence of figures and traditions whose ideas they have either amended or repudiated. They recognize, for example, the importance of Oswald Spengler and Arnold Toynbee, who were heartily rejected by most professional historians of their time. In his overview of the field, William H. McNeill notes the retrograde features of Toynbeean world history, but recognizes a debt to Toynbee. Bruce Mazlish argues that Spengler and Toynbee were, each in his own way, in the prophetic tradition, anti-modern and thus unsuitable models for professional historians; and that Marx, one of the most powerful influences on modern thought, also belongs to a discredited prophetic tradition. However, the broad current of Marxian analysis, which used economic systems to explain a vast array of historical data, strongly influenced "dependency" and "world-systems" analysis of sociologists André Gunder Frank and Emmanuel Wallerstein during the 1960s and 1970s. World-systems analysis, too, has been found wanting, as Michael Adas demonstrates in his critique of systemic models. Yet Adas shows the influence of another thinker in the Marxian tradition, Antonio Gramsci.

An extremely influential rival of Marxian analysis, modernization theory, preceded the neo-Marxist schools of the 1960s and 1970s. Inspired by the sociology of Max Weber and Talcott Parsons, and sometimes integrated with Freudian psychology, modernization theory had, from the 1950s, a powerful and continuing impact on the writing of world history, significantly shaping the outlook of several of the contributors to this volume. Francis Fukuyama regrets its "collapse" in the 1970s, although practicing modernization theorists might quip that the rumor of their demise has been greatly exaggerated.[1] The articles of Shmuel Eisenstadt, Mazlish, and Theodore Von Laue exhibit several of the main themes of modernization theory, although creatively amended.

The *Annales* school, another rich source of inspiration for structural approaches to history, encouraged "history from below," a perspective which grew apace among historians beginning in the 1960s. As Adas suggests, to a new generation of historians history from below rectified the traditional preoccupation with elites and "great men." Together with neo-Marxian schools, the *Annales* school attracted historians of the 1960s and 1970s to social history and to the history of everyday life; by directing close attention to the physical environment it also encouraged an ecological perspective. Some *annalistes*, most notably Fernand Braudel, took the path of regional and world history, influencing McNeill, among others. However, as Adas points out, several of these systemic or structural approaches of the 1960s and 1970s tend to remove both collective and individual agency from history. Structures evidently generated their own changes, and seemed to be immune to human action. Historians immediately reacted against this *reductio ad absurdum* of the "structural," "systemic," or "holistic" tendency in the social sciences. Most preferred a richly varied approach, in which structures and agents interact, and in which neither economic, nor social, nor political, nor cultural, nor psychological factors can be ignored.

"Holism," a term embracing features common to modernization theory, Marxism, and the *Annales* school, has been under theoretical attack since the 1940s. In *The Open Society and Its Enemies* (1945) and *The Poverty of Historicism* (1957), Karl Popper argued that the holistic tradition was based largely on a false analogy of societies with organisms. During the roughly half-century since Popper's opening round, others joined the attack on holism and systemic theory in the social sciences. Some critics associated holistic theories of progress with the historical behavior of imperial Western democracies, others with the catastrophic costs and utter failure of communism. In short, an increasing array of critics found in holism the theoretical adjunct to various forms of oppression. The anti-holistic mood continued to grow after the 1970s, most notably under the spur of poststructuralist and postmodern critiques sometimes called "the linguistic turn." By the 1980s this generally anti-scientistic, anti-holistic, and constructivist movement had won over significant intelligentsia constituencies, who spoke for women, non-Westerners (many of whom had experienced Western imperialism), and other groups that felt "marginalized," insulted, and injured by the norms of "scientific" Western doctrines.

Neither theory alone nor criticism from within the academy stimulated reshapings of world history. The contributors to this volume have witnessed and participated in some fashion in a rapidly accelerating global transformation. Political transformations alone have been vast: empires have disappeared and former colonial subjects have become citizens of nation-states; hundreds of millions of women, as well as men, now cast ballots in elections to representative institutions; the most democratically inclined nations legislate new civil rights (some of them still contested) to assure greater inclusion of formerly degraded and disadvantaged groups. Alongside the expansion of civil rights within the boundaries of ever-proliferating nation-states, world historians detect other global trends, sometimes grouped under the term "identity politics," undermining national or transnational politics.[2]

Bruce Mazlish (along with many others) believes that such vast transformations call for a new approach to world history, even for a new nomenclature for the field. Mazlish distinguishes prophetic varieties of *ecumenical* history (whether issuing from religious prophesies or secular ones, like those of Hegel, Marx, Spengler, and Toynbee), from more recent varieties of *world* history which are soberly systemic – for example, McNeill's and Janet Lippman Abu-Lughod's – and in turn distinguishes *global* history from world history. A genuinely global history, in his view, must historically trace "factors of globalization" such as new technologies that alter our sense of space, the rise of consumerism and multinational corporations, and the spread of popular culture by the new technologies. Mazlish's felicitous distinctions among global, world, and ecumenical histories, however, have not yet come into general use, and even those who apparently share his views about globalization find it difficult to dispense with the term "world history." No attempt will be made to resolve the terminological quandary in this introduction and throughout the volume readers will find "world" and "global" used in tandem.

World historians have long appreciated cultural difference and the historical contributions of non-Western peoples. As McNeill points out, Spengler and Toynbee, though repudiated by guild historians for good reasons, tried to understand non-European historical civilizations and placed them analytically on a level with Europe. By the 1950s Toynbee's popular *A Study of History* had established civilizations as the accepted units for the study of world history. Both McNeill's and Eisenstadt's contributions show that "civilization" remains a useful concept for world historians, although they have modified the monolithic character ascribed to it in earlier definitions. Whatever their failings from the point of view of contemporary historiography, as world historians Spengler and Toynbee far outpaced their more provincial colleagues, who still tended to see the world from Eurocentric and nationalistic points of view.

Other world histories, whether expressing a sense of Western superiority or deploring colonial victimization, organized world-historical time-space accordingly. They declared some areas advanced and others backward, some peoples modern and others traditional; and they assigned some regions to the core and others to the periphery. Organic metaphors (growth and development or their opposites) and spatial ones (higher and lower, core and periphery, center and margin) pervade such texts. Contemporary world historians often try to avoid such metaphors and replace them with "metaphors of movement, flow, circuitry ... and images in motion."[3] Those attuned to constructivist approaches eschew "essentialist," structural images. Critiques of historians' discourse and representations confront the ideologies inspiring the language and images, and the group projects and identities associated with the ideologies.

METAPHORS, ARCHITECTONICS, AND IDEOLOGIES

Rejection of the metaphor of development and "scientific" labeling of groups carries significant consequences, not just for ideology and identity, but for the shaping of world histories. The old Western notion of development provided a useful architectonic to those with both progressive and holistic visions of history.[4] However, the metaphor of development in itself did not furnish a satisfactory explanation of historical change. Philosophers of history made use of another old notion – that one arrived at the truth dialectically, by stating a proposition, negating it, then arriving at a synthesis, in a continuing process. German idealist philosophers, particularly Hegel, transposed the dialectic to history and described progress as a process of development in which later stages sublated earlier ones. Violent moments and wrenching discontinuous changes punctuated the process. For Hegelians, progress thus occurred dialectically and sometimes catastrophically under the spur of "negation." Supplanting religious doctrines of the Fall and God's Grace, a secular European intelligentsia used dialectic as a historical method for bridging the ontological gap between the transcendental and the mundane referred to in Eisenstadt's discussion of axial-age civilizations.

Dialectic was not so much a precise method as a stimulus to interpret history. Practitioners used it to identify progressive and reactionary forces in a modern world changing too quickly for some and too slowly for others. For Marx and Engels, dialectic represented conflict, struggle, crisis, and revolutionary change. Thinkers on the Left provided the first fully secular theory (however shaped by Judeo-Christian culture) combining the metaphor of development and the dynamic and hopeful dialectical principle of change, and produced earthly variations of "heavenly cities." For Marx and Engels, the world progressed systematically, though sometimes catastrophically, toward a benign unity. Most important of all, they grounded their hopeful prophecy in mundane economic and social data, and tried to distinguish what was basic to historical change from what was secondary.

In distinguishing their "scientific" theory from other theories of progress, Marx and Engels usually used the term "ideology" to signify "false consciousness" – a set of illusions and consolations preventing exploited peoples from understanding their real interests and from acting rationally to further them. For them, ideology supported the status quo, the system, the structure of domination. Twentieth-century thinkers in the Marxian tradition elaborated the concept of ideology. In particular, Michael Adas points out that Antonio Gramsci's notion of cultural hegemony contributed to some of the creative contemporary versions of world history. Gramsci and others took as their point of departure the agents whose actions maintained or altered the hegemonic system; and an understanding of agents entails an investigation of their ideologies and self-identities. Thus, in any satisfactory analysis ideology, structure, and identity interpenetrate.

Disagreements over the definition of "ideology" have vexed philosophers since Marx and Engels gave it common currency and the Marxian definition is far from the only one.[5] For our purposes, the plain but practical and capacious definition given by Janet Lippman Abu-Lughod in chapter 4 serves well. Ideology, for her, is "a deep set of beliefs about how the world works."[6] On this definition, both religious creeds and secular theories that organize the cosmos, create meaning, and give human groups a place in a greater scheme of things qualify as ideologies. Different groups contest what belongs at the center, what is higher or lower, more advanced, and so on, depending upon the terms of their ideologies. Disagreements among world historians often reflect ideological differences, although ideological opponents sometimes share basic assumptions.

Whether inspired by a liberal vision and modernization theory, or by a more radical Marxian theory of progress, world historians generally both predicted and affirmed the universal spread of a way of life emerging in the West. Many Western historians have assumed that Europe created the modern world; and that despite the immense suffering caused by European expansion and domination and the process of industrialization, it is better to modernize than not to modernize.

This is the familiar Eurocentric and optimistic narrative of world history derived from European philosophies of history, most notably Hegel's. According to this vision, in McNeill's words, "Freedom was uniquely at home among the states of Europe ... and the entire globe became a theater for the advance of human Freedom."[7] A widely used text first published in 1950 in the United States and still in print calls itself *A History of the Modern World*, but, as the authors confess in the prefaces to the various editions, the book is mainly about Europe.[8] By contrast, McNeill's *The Rise of the West* (1963) placed Europe's modern global ascendancy in a temporally extended and fully articulated world context and – before the surge of criticism decrying Eurocentrism – changed the direction of the field.

The idea of progress has not disappeared, nor has the notion that the West is the vanguard. Traditional liberal ideals, democratic institutions, and the liberal culture of criticism unleashed by the Enlightenment thrive and continue to spread. In this volume Francis Fukuyama defends his argument, set forth at length in *The End of History and the Last Man* (1992), that liberal democracy is indeed advancing globally. In light of the collapse of Soviet communism in 1991 it seemed reasonable to reaffirm the prediction of modernization theorists that the entire globe would converge toward the modern West's civilizational norm.

Yet several contributors to this volume suggest that the theory of convergence contains snares and illusions. Von Laue hypothesizes that durable structural factors (geography, culture, and power based upon them) underlie stubborn global inequalities. Geography favored Europe, as did culture, and European power grew ineluctably. Resentment of Western power and hegemony produced, and still produces, counter-movements of various sorts in non-Western intelligentsias.[9] Culture and power flowed from England and France "downslope" to fragmented Germany where fear, resentment, and envy of Western power in Central Europe produced Romantic nationalism, a precursor of third-world intelligentsia visions of indigenous virtue compared to Western malaise. Not just resentful intelligentsias rejecting Western cultural hegemony, but ordinary people at the "ground floor" of culture remain resistant to change "from above" imposed by Westernizing elites.

Eisenstadt, working in a much broader temporal framework than Von Laue, similarly shows how local elites throughout history resisted centers of power; how heterodoxy flourished; how centralizing trends typically generated dispersive ones. Culture flows not only from the core to the periphery and from upslope to downslope peoples, but the other way around (in the latter case, unhappily for the metaphor), something that Von Laue, too, recognizes in his contribution to this volume. Several other contributors show how a great variety of factors affects the imposition of one culture on others, or complicates processes of cultural exchange.

Such observations about the blurred, ragged, uneven, and (from the point of view of modernization theory) sometimes retrograde processes of cultural transformation show how unprecedented and counter to human experience it would be for a single ideology, whether religious or secular, to prevail. Moreover, in an age of resurgent nationalism and identity politics it is hard to imagine many people embracing a universalistic ideology.

The latest proponents of modernization theory have nonetheless not surrendered to their critics. Fukuyama, for example, claims that modern natural science and economic modernization give democratic and capitalist institutions a unique advantage. Moreover, he presents theoretical grounds in Hegel and Plato for a human nature whose drive for recognition will be satisfied with nothing less than liberal democracy and the market. He does not, however, celebrate the historical victory of liberal democracy or claim to know whether reason alone will prevent the human drive for recognition from producing massive violence. It is thus possible to believe in the victory of modernization (Westernization) without confidently asserting a benign outcome. In his contribution Fukuyama confronts questions that vexed Enlightenment thinkers and continue to trouble their heirs: Can we rely upon Reason to bring about universal cooperation? Can we do without spiritual, religious foundations for social order, whether local or international?

Von Laue, for one, answers firmly in the negative. He finds a universal human power motive behind the dynamics of history, surveys the complex interactions among different regions with quite different cultures, and sees dangerous forms of disorientation emerging. Only religion, which Von Laue regards as a means for shaping "the innermost core of human behavior," can direct our energies toward peaceful cooperation. Without a transcultural spiritual discipline such cooperation on a global scale would be impossible. Otherwise, the dynamics of Westernization, which have already produced the catastrophes of the twentieth century, might produce increasing disorientation, anarchy, and violence. Von Laue offers an uncompromisingly austere moralism and suggests that historians have an obligation to promote universal spiritual values furthering human cooperation. Yet Von Laue and other contributors recognize the role played by religion in parochial identities and clashes. The adherents of modernization theory contributing to this volume thus present neither a united front nor unambivalent, triumphal attitudes.

Marxism, the other major historiographical tradition that affirmed modernization as a benign global phenomenon, accepted as inevitable historical crises and catastrophes. For Marxists modernization under capitalism yielded not a steady (with some disturbances to the system) march toward convergence, as "backward" or "underdeveloped" regions of the globe modernized, but a succession of exploited proletarian groups, some in the European core, others in the colonial periphery, as capitalism pursued its self-destructive logic to the ends of the earth. For orthodox Marxists, rescue of the global victims of capitalism required a revolutionary transformation of the system. The failure of earlier twentieth-century revolutions to achieve their goals generated, in parallel to amended versions of modernization theory, a variety of neo-Marxist theories and syncretic radical doctrines that abandoned the vocabulary of revolution and shifted focus to identity politics and cultural transformation.

Like their Marxist and anarchist predecessors, the radical ideologies of the late twentieth century demand, on new terms, inclusion of history's victims in social, political, economic, and cultural systems. Such ideologies sometimes reject not only Eurocentric approaches to world history accepted by earlier radicals, but also the "scientific" attitudes of the Enlightenment. The contrast between Ashis Nandy's approach and Frantz Fanon's suggests the richness of the third-world intelligentsia's range of responses to European hegemony. Fanon had been inspired by Hegel's doctrine of recognition, but like his mentors in the French intelligentsia, he saw in it a useful addendum to revolutionary Marxism rather than to liberal modernization theory, as Fukuyama does. Combining Hegel with existentialism, psychoanalysis, and Marxism, in *The Wretched of the Earth* (1961), Fanon prescribed violent revolution as a therapy for the victims of Western power. Fanon, of course, prescribed what a great many political leaders had already done and continue to do without the inspiration of Hegel's master–slave dialectic or any psychoanalytic notion of therapy. The appalling results of therapeutic violence (understood here as violence inflicted on scapegoats to salve wounds to group narcissism) have contributed to the postmodern intelligentsia's effort to remove targets of aggression of any sort by subverting the scientific and philosophical discourses that "constructed" them. It is rather difficult to justify killing in behalf of mere constructions, and pointless to train one's sights on a transitory cloud of signifiers.

Unlike Fanon and earlier generations of colonial or postcolonial thinkers who decided to fight the West on its own terms, contemporary non-Western intelligentsias sometimes combine their critique of world history with a general critique of scientific history. Like Fanon, a psychiatrist, Nandy proclaims both the ethical and therapeutic benefits of rejecting history, a discipline tainted with Western scientism. He thus echoes Western radical thinkers who have described Western scientific discourse as an instrument for the labeling and domination of the many by the few, of women by men, of people of color by whites, of "backward" peoples by "developed" ones, of "abnormals" by "normals."

Working within a framework partly defined by Gandhi's *Satyagraha*, Nandy calls for cultural pluralism grounded in prescientific traditions. In place of Western-style history, he proposes ahistorical myth as an appropriate cultural-political therapy. Although he does not count himself one of them, Nandy shares the postmodernists' rejection of the Enlightenment, of Western "scientific" norms, of binary definitions leading to rigid and destructive behavior in the name of masculinity, the nation, or the scientifically defined cause of the moment. He seeks to counteract harmful forms of Western holism and scientism, but not universalism as such. Nandy offers as an antidote the fluidity and androgyny that he finds in traditional Indian culture.

In his trenchant studies of cultural encounters, Nandy probes the psychology of both English intelligentsia figures, who identified themselves with the victims of European power, and educated Indians, who sometimes formed identifications with the aggressors and tried to transform their own culture accordingly.[10] Nandy and other radical third-world critics encourage groups everywhere to assert their identities on their own terms, in therapeutic "mythographies" that defy the Western tradition of scientific history. But do these apparent self-affirmations and rejections of Westernism express the ambivalence of groups undergoing balky conversions to the West's implacably spreading way of life, as is suggested by Fukuyama? Do they presage the benign, multicultural universalism promoted by Nandy? Or are they symptoms of the anarchy feared by Von Laue? Will some new ideology join all of the dissident voices into a chorus, or will the consequence of the postmodern critique be, instead, cacophony?

STRUCTURES, THEIR CRITICS AND PROPONENTS

Combining dissident psychoanalytic, linguistic, and philosophical currents, leaders of the postmodern intelligentsia of the 1970s found paranoia and power motives everywhere in Western thought. Prominent critics in the new generation followed Roland Barthes and Michel Foucault and dissolved into "discourse" the substantial world of "structures" and "systems" described "scientifically" by the vast majority of those engaged with such matters. Of the practitioners of world history included in this collection, Abu-Lughod and Adas most clearly reflect the impact of the linguistic turn and the search for middle ground between traditional, realistic structural approaches and postmodern constructivism. The new emphasis on language and representation makes perfect sense to many scholars who define themselves as social scientists. For some of them the linguistic turn simply licenses chronic heterodoxy and elevates to a more prominent position the readily acknowledged interpretive aspect of history; for others it sanctions an instrumental approach to knowledge long held by philosophical pragmatists; and for still others it serves the moral and political purpose of exposing relationships of power contained in systems of knowledge. But the commitment to realism remains strong. Abu-Lughod, for example, concedes much to constructivist approaches but draws a rather firm line between the narratives of historians and those of fiction writers. The "synthetic imagination" operative in the writing of world history is fully compatible with the practice of social science. In her investigation of the "metatheoretical dilemmas" of world history and investigation of her own creative process, Abu-Lughod acknowledges perspectival limits without surrendering to cognitive pessimism. She affirms systemic projects and investigates how historians "catch" (or are caught by) the shape of the whole.

On the other hand, in his critique of the world-systems school to which Abu-Lughod belongs, Adas shows how one-sided attention to structures, particularly economic and social ones, drove the study of systems to an absurd extreme. At the other extreme, postmodern critiques emphasizing language, discourse, and text denied the reality of structures, and banished the human subject from the text. While acknowledging the importance of discourse and representation, Adas seeks a middle way between the excessively structural and the extravagantly postmodern. His critique of the books that dominated the field of world history in the 1970s, such as Emmanuel Wallerstein's *The Modern World System* (the first volume appearing in 1974) and Theda Skocpol's *States and Social Revolutions* (1979), reflects the current concerns of sociologists as well as of world historians. Adas remains committed to investigating structures, but treats human agency, ideas, discourse, and representations as causes.

A world history genuinely attentive to "peoples without history" or those labeled inferior in some fashion requires careful attention to representation. Adas brings to the fore the problem of cross-cultural representation of gender for practitioners of world history, and the importance of studying Western binary formulations that represented dominant groups (Europeans, men, whites, the upper classes) one way, and "inferior" groups another way. Here Adas seconds Nandy's investigations of the ways in which rigid Western notions of masculine and feminine identity affected both colonizers and colonized in India. Unlike Nandy, however, he does not see a rejection of the scientific approach and its replacement by therapeutic mythography as the solution. Rather, he tries to find the methodological ground on which social

scientists can stand. Adas calls for "contextualized investigation of social relations, symbolic systems, hegemonic and counter-hegemonic discourses, and
subjective identities."[11]

Several practitioners of world history contributing to this volume deal not so
much with identity politics and the therapeutic consequences of holistic and
scientific visions as with the practical problems of shaping a world history.
They are aware of the interplay between the transcendental and mundane
that partially shaped a variety of ecumenical histories. Like most historians
(or historical sociologists), they are conscious as well of the politics of group
identity affecting historiography, past and present; and they acknowledge the
relativizing and interpretive aspects of the historian's craft. McNeill has used
the word "mythography" to describe what historians do, but unlike Nandy, for
him it connotes not so much group self-therapy as worthy efforts at cognitive
mastery that inevitably become obsolete. World historians, though apprised
of all of this, continue to look for the nourishing grains of knowledge amid
the chaff of culture-laden motives and emotions. Knowing in advance the
limitations of their vision, they continue to act as if they can advance knowledge, and as if there is a real, unitary world for them to comprehend. In this
respect they do not differ significantly from scientists who hope that their
hypotheses will be confirmed, but expect them to be falsified eventually.

Among world historians, a robust spirit of self-criticism and openness to
criticism from others sometimes leads to revisions, but never to abandonment
of a macrostructural approach. William Green, for example, presents an array
of reasons for abandoning an "integrationist" approach and any hope for consensus about periodizing world history, but resists disintegrative critiques,
pleading that "It makes no more sense endlessly to disassemble our subject
than it does to erect unities where they may not exist" (64). As noted earlier, McNeill finds problematic earlier definitions of civilization and notes the
considerable diversity subsumed under that spacious but imprecise structural
unit. However, he does not abandon the term; he revises it. "Civilization" to
him now denotes a variety of groups with quite different sociocultural characteristics flourishing within boundaries set by agreements about the legitimacy of rulers and the terms of trade. Even the discovery of new groups, new
sociocultural elements functioning within a civilization, and shifting relationships among them, would not endanger the basic project of a unitary
world history.

World historians investigate on a global level how diverse groups
rearranged boundaries by expanding contacts, tolerating outsiders, and engaging in mutually beneficial arrangements of various sorts. McNeill is willing to
debate the relative virtues of macrostructural terms such as "interactive zone,"

"ecumene," and "world system," so long as historians continue the project of identifying the structures that prefigure our present globalism. Green, McNeill, and other world historians thus remain dedicated to systemic approaches, to the integration of parts into wholes, and to the investigation of patterns.

In presenting his program for an adequate world history Adas suggests an integrative approach in which collective and individual agents interact with structures at many levels, from macro to micro. He also advocates the use of primary sources in world history. Lamin Sanneh in his contribution to this volume clearly meets Adas's requirements, showing by means of primary sources how agents caused structural change in the Muslim world. Sanneh illustrates a phenomenon prominent in the long history of Islam as well as axial-age religions. Religious movements inspired by autonomous intellectuals (in Eisenstadt's terms) lose their momentum and stagnate. "Marginal groups," however, keep the activist teachings alive and, when contingencies permit, transform them into a force for change. Sanneh understands marginality as "a process that implants minority groups and communities in mainstream societies without weakening or threatening their identity or that of their hosts" (127). Sanneh does note, however, that rulers might sense danger and expel such groups (129).

Religious minorities throughout history and revolutionary intelligentsias in the early modern and modern era have had enormous impact on structural change and at times have aspired to power themselves. In promoting activist versions of religion or secular theory, they have often redefined collective identity, thus threatening the sometimes oppressive structures that depend upon quiescent religions (or ideologies in the Marxist sense of false consciousness) and uncontested collective identities. Eisenstadt's and Adas's comparative approaches and Sanneh's study of Muslim Africa show quite clearly the interaction of ideology, structure, and identity, and also illustrate the historical spaces in which groups, sometimes marginal ones, exercise agential power to change structures.

The prophets of axial-age religions and Islam created movements with vast demographic bases in the contemporary world and the potential for continual revitalization. It remains to be seen whether modern secular ideologies can achieve similarly enormous and continuing historical impact on collective identities and cultural, political, social, and economic structures. Although liberal democracies have shown some resiliency and success at exporting liberal ideology to new nation-states, successful liberal experiments remain relatively recent and sparse in world-historical time-space. Marxian ideology in its activist phase served as a stimulus for enormous structural changes, but after several decades ruling Communist elites remained unsupported either by a unified intelligentsia or by a "ground floor" collective identity embracing all of the ethnic groups of the Soviet Union. The efforts of Marx's interpreters failed to create a heroic, proletarian, or Soviet collective identity, even though they transformed Marxian theory, in Eisenstadt's terms, into the "hegemonic premises" of ruling groups in a large part of the globe. In this respect, Marxian movements resembled earlier religio-political ones. First serving a liberating function, the movements then changed into something quite different. After constructing an oppressive power structure, Communist establishments produced their own "marginal groups" – dissident intelligentsias and political leaders promoting the ideology of liberal democracy, the market, and nationalism – who won out in 1991.

Two interlinked macrostructural developments, the collapse of the old multiethnic and multinational empires, including the Soviet Union, and the emergence of the nation-state as the preeminent political structure of the modern world, have undermined secular ecumenical prophecies. Moreover, the endurance and revitalization of axial-age and Islamic religions and collective identities in a great variety of settings have shown strikingly how competing and coexisting ideologies and identities threaten political structures everywhere in the modern world. The historical proliferation of religious diversity and, in the modern era, of secular theories or ideologies with their own prophets and sects, creates the potential for strife in a great many "arenas of salvation."[12]

While dissident intelligentsias compete in arenas of salvation, social scientific proponents of a holistic approach pursue the more modest goal of shaping an adequate world history. Their systemic visions sometimes radically depart from those of earlier philosophers of history or world historians relying upon dialectic and metaphors of growth and decay. Although Green still sees the need for "organic theories of change,"[13] he does not present any sort of metatheory. McNeill offers a sober ecologically inspired picture of a human community expanding or contracting within limits set by fluctuating systemic equilibria. One would be hard put to find there either the optimism of the dialectically driven systems or Spenglerian gloom. Green's, McNeill's, and Abu-Lughod's quest for cognitive mastery and their relative optimism about finding connections, patterns, and system in the data of history do not imply totalistic projects or consolatory accounts of the human condition. They rather search for patterns and integrative periodizations, and aim at cognitive mastery with a less than utopian hope that superior historical knowledge may prove useful.

IDENTITIES: CRISES, CONFLICTS, AND DISSOLUTIONS

World historians unavoidably study the consequences of encounters among different peoples and cultures under conditions of unequal power. Psychoanalysis has important things to say about the human tendency to form distorted images of outsiders in such conditions. Yet historians steer clear of psychoanalysis for a host of reasons. One may say of psychoanalysis what Pareto said of Marxism when comparing it to a bat: it looks like a mouse to some and a bird to others. No less than Marxism, psychoanalysis has taken a great variety of forms, from Freud's grimly deterministic views to the postmodern ones presented by Lewis Wurgaft. Postmodern psychoanalysis prescribes more fluid and capacious selves, and psychoanalytically minded historians generally hope for a time when group identities cease to depend upon paranoid projections. Nandy and Wurgaft in careful studies of the sort applauded by Adas discuss the rigid and static identities that have been responsible for great human pain and for destructive conflicts, large and small. They show how the defense mechanisms of identification and projection affect the way in which groups define themselves and other groups. Such useful forms of psychoanalytic criticism permit us to distinguish the defensive distortions of destructive and sometimes paranoid forms of holism from the benign system-building to which world historians aspire.

As Wurgaft shows, the notion of identity gained currency in the 1950s, when psychohistorians used it as an adjunct to modernization theory. In Erik Erikson's theory of psychological development, during adolescence the ego integrates identifications, identity elements, and other psychological "fragments" into a whole. Because this integration depends upon a sociocultural setting, Erikson calls it "psychosocial identity." It is the "accrued confidence that inner sameness and continuity prepared in the past are matched by the sameness and continuity of one's meaning for others."[14] However, this definition of identity does not imply historical permanence. Erikson rather assumes that psychosocial identity has to change historically in order to satisfy the requirements of modernizing societies. Wurgaft points out that for Erikson, "a mature psychosocial identity incorporated a notion of wholeness elastic enough to maintain a complex, interactive system."[15] Historical change forced transformations of identity, both individual and collective, but these did not happen automatically. Erikson believed individual agents, "heroes of the inner frontier," to be the vanguard of change. He popularized the idea of the "identity crisis" by portraying figures like Martin Luther, who, by resolving their own identity crises, created new therapeutically beneficial ideologies (in this case, religious) suitable for modernizing cultures undergoing collective identity crises. Carried to its absurd extreme, this approach encouraged modernization theorists influenced by psychoanalysis to write of the "adolescent" growing pains of emerging nations, thus continuing the Western practice of seeing "natives" as childlike.

Erikson, like Freud before him, assumed the existence of cultural super-egos. These were presumably shaped by charismatic religious leaders and, once institutionalized, stubbornly persisted despite a great many historical changes on the "outer frontier." Outdated cultural superegos lay behind rigidities and failures to adapt to changing historical circumstances. Religions (or ideologies) serving as adaptations to past (sometimes very distant) circumstances thus become restraints on the formation of modern identities. In keeping with liberal modernization theory, Erikson advocated a generic "protestantism" as the appropriate ideology for modernizing peoples. Von Laue maintains a similar point of view, though without the psychoanalytic inspiration, in his quest for a transcultural spiritual discipline appropriate to global forms of cooperation. Several of the contributors to this volume believe that reformulations of religion will be crucial for the transformations of narrow and rigid collective identities. Others, however, assert that the notion of identity itself has to be transformed.

Like Wurgaft, psychoanalysts influenced by postmodern criticism repudiate the notion of a relatively fixed, unitary identity, reject traditional gendered identities, and strenuously deny that anatomy is destiny. Postmodern critics created a politics of the psyche by unmasking Western logos (reason), theories of psychic unity, and gender definitions as tyrannies. During the 1960s and 1970s schizophrenia signified for some of these dissidents an antidote or at least a meaningful protest against the most tyrannical and destructive aspects of Western culture. From its source in French surrealism, "paranoia criticism" (which assumed the existence of and tried to subvert a paranoid trend in Western culture) entered the academic mainstream mainly through Jacques Lacan and Michel Foucault.[16] The ideas of the French poststructuralist and postmodern intelligentsia became the political banners of a variety of groups escaping from the margins of male-dominated, scientistic European culture. For a variety of reasons, semiotics became an important vehicle for the transportation of dissident views. All of the dissidents shared a critique of Western values and norms connected with the Enlightenment and Western science. Despite their own emphasis upon discontinuity, however, these dissident views have genealogies of their own. The postmodern intelligentsia continues earlier democratic projects to grant freedom and justice – Fukuyama would add "recognition" – to all.

Postmodern critics continue the project of earlier democratic intelligentsias by extending the culture of criticism and seeking greater inclusion on new terms of groups formerly labeled inferior or abnormal. In order to destroy invidious distinctions and apparently durable norms, postmodernists show, usually by means of semiological critiques, that the things we thought to be permanent and fixed by nature are mere constructions. However, when confronting the issue of identity and identification, world historians deal not just with semiological critiques of a wide array of cultural products, but with ordinary people on the "ground floor" of culture, to use Von Laue's term. What forms of collective identity will emerge as ordinary human beings encounter each other in new ways during the process of globalization?

Eisenstadt examines the social and cultural elements of collective identity and observes that "the construction of collective identities has been going on throughout human history ... in different economic and political-ecological settings, from small city states to great kingdoms."[17] McNeill points out that until quite recently the vast majority of people lived in rural areas. Though connected in various ways to international webs of trade and communication, people for the most part have lived in "vivacious primary communities," usually villages, where the criteria for moral behavior were unambiguous. Like Von Laue, McNeill reflects on the possibility of salutary reformulations of religion, but sees how problematic this may be in the changed circumstances of global life and wonders how people will adapt themselves to the "continual bombardment by messages from outsiders and unbelievers."[18] Mazlish, for whom technology plays a central role, entertains the notion that a dense network of global communication might indeed shape a global identity.[19] Other proponents of globalization present a variety of scenarios for the outcomes of cross- or intercultural contact through the media. Many share the feeling that we are on the verge of something quite unprecedented.

The views represented in this volume make clear that several traditions flourish in world history. The progressive one, descending from the quest for heavenly cities, still seeks to establish the directionality of history. Fukuyama takes his stand on global convergence toward the liberal democracy and market economy predicted by modernization theory. Not even he, however, has the temerity to speak in the prophetic voice and predict a secular form of salvation. Most of the contributors are realists in that they do not believe that they are simply constructing out of earlier texts the structures or systems that they describe and the trajectories that they plot. Adas, Green, Mazlish, McNeill, and Wurgaft examine historiography – the theories, practices, ideologies, schools and styles of thought, periodizations, and definitions that have affected the shaping and reshaping of the field.

These authors, along with Abu-Lughod, Eisenstadt, Sanneh, and Von Laue, explore the structures and processes of world history: the expansion of the human community, its changing ecologies and technologies, the merging of formerly separate groups, the macrostructure and microstructure of political, social, economic, and cultural continuity and change. They examine the central and continuing role of religion in shaping group identities; the trends that dissolved empires and made nation-states the preeminent political form of the twentieth century; and those that are dissolving identities based upon nation, gender, and race to fashion something unprecedented in world history. The diversity of their views and the liveliness of their debates demonstrate the vitality of the field. They plot the course of globalization by shaping into models of world history a mass of data from diverse areas. Their own larger hopes for their fellow human beings sometimes prompt them to speak in the first person, as McNeill does when he concludes:

> The changing shape of world history has been the principle professional concern of my life. I commend it as a worthy and fascinating pursuit, apt for our age, and practically useful inasmuch as a clear and vivid sense of the whole human past can help to soften future conflicts by making clear what we all share.[20]

PART I

Mapping the Field

1

The Changing Shape of World History

William H. McNeill

Histories of the portion of the earth known to the writer are properly classed as world histories inasmuch as they seek to record the whole significant and knowable past. By that standard, therefore, Herodotus and Ssu-ma Chen were world historians as well as founders of their respective historiographical traditions. Among the Greeks, however, Thucydides promptly discarded Herodotus's discursive, all-embracing approach to history, offering instead a pridefully accurate, sharply focused monograph, dealing with twenty-seven years of war between Athens and Sparta.

These alternative models remained normative throughout Greco-Roman antiquity. Livy's vast, patriotic history of Rome approximated Herodotean inclusiveness; and Polybius may have deliberately aspired to combine the logical rigor of Thucydides with the scope of Herodotus. Though impossible to equal, Thucydides's precision was easier to imitate than Herodotus's inclusiveness, and most Greco-Roman historians accordingly inclined towards the monographic, political-military focus that Thucydides so magnificently exemplified.

Jewish sacred scripture elaborated a different historical vision, according to which Almighty God governed all peoples, everywhere, whether they knew it or not. For about a millennium, defeats suffered by successive Jewish states made such a vision of human history implausible to unbelievers; but Christianity, when it emerged to dominance within the Roman empire in the fourth century AD, brought to the fore a modified, expanded, but fundamentally Jewish, and entirely God-centered, view of history. Christians subordinated secular pagan to sacred biblical history, and thereby reversed the balance between Herodotean and Thucydidean formats for history, since, from Jewish and Christian points of view, all history was world history, being part of God's plan for humankind.

The Christian epos – Creation, Incarnation, and Day of Judgment – owed nothing to pagan historiography, but Christian historians, from Eusebius (d. 340) and Orosius (d. 417) onwards, felt compelled to fit bits and pieces of the pagan record into their histories of how God had dealt with humankind. Innumerable medieval chronicles, therefore, begin with Creation, and hurry through familiar landmarks of the biblical and pagan past in order to attach local and recent events – at least perfunctorily – to the central, sacred meaning of human experience on earth. History, detached from God's purposes, was blind, pointless, misleading; and for something like a thousand years, Christians refused to consider such folly, even though their most painstaking recording of recent events left God's purposes stubbornly inscrutable.

In China, no such transformation of prevailing views ever took place. Instead, Ssu-ma Chen's vision of how to write and understand history prevailed from his own time until the collapse of the Manchu dynasty at the beginning of the twentieth century. The central idea was that Heaven chose virtuous hereditary rulers and allowed (or contrived) their overthrow whenever a ruling dynasty became corrupt. Each new dynasty began virtuous and strong only to decay, sooner or later, provoking the transfer of Heaven's mandate to a new ruler, whose virtue was confirmed by his practical success in reducing China and surrounding barbarians to obedience. The power of Ssu-ma Chen's vision is attested by the fact that his dynastic frame for Chinese history still dominates scholarship, even among Westerners, who have never believed that the ruler's personal virtue assured supernatural support.

Muslim, Buddhist, and Hindu outlooks upon history also took shape during the Middle Ages. In general, these learned traditions paid less attention to history than the Christian and Chinese did; but all agreed on the overriding importance of supernatural intervention in human affairs; and by subordinating earthly events to God's will, as Muslims did, or to supernal processes and interventions, as Buddhists and Hindus did, all agreed that world history was the only meaningful kind of history, since supernatural entities governed human affairs along with the rest of the universe according to rules of their own.

Consensus concerning the decisive role of transcendent beings or forces in history was challenged when a discordant, man-centered version of history found voice in Italy soon after 1500. What inspired the new type of history was the palpable convergence of Italian city-state politics with patterns of Greek and Roman antiquity. Study of pagan writers in privileged circles of a few Italian towns revived as this convergence became evident; and by about 1500 such studies had ripened sufficiently to allow Machiavelli (d. 1520) and Guicciardini (d. 1540) to reaffirm the autonomy of human actions by writing local, monographic, and entirely secular histories in the Thucydidean mold.

They derived their inspiration unabashedly from pagan writers, and settled accounts with the biblical framework of universal history simply by leaving God out, not mentioning Him as an actor in history at all.

This was both shocking and unacceptable to most Europeans. Accordingly, a renaissance man like Walter Raleigh (d. 1618) in England, and, almost a century later, the pious and eloquent Bishop Bossuet (d. 1704) in France, reaffirmed the centrality of sacred history and attempted to weave what they knew about the biblical and pagan past into a more perfect whole. Their works remained incomplete and never approached their own time; partly because both were bogged down by a rapidly increasing fund of knowledge about events of the more recent past, and partly because God's will remained obscure (or at least radically disputable) when called on to explain the tangled record of those same events.

Meanwhile, a flood of information about the Americas and other formerly unknown parts of the earth assaulted European consciousness. A few gestures towards fitting the newly discovered peoples into the inherited Christian frame of history were indeed made. In particular, how the inhabitants of America descended from the sons of Noah became a subject of debate. But for the most part, European learning reaffirmed (or at least paid lip service to) Christian truths, explored new fields of knowledge, accumulated more and more information about the past, and about far parts of the earth, and dodged the question of how to fit all the new data together. This remained the case until the eighteenth century when radical efforts to organize empirical knowledge systematically (stimulated partly by Newton's spectacular success in physics and astronomy) began to meet with apparent success in such fields as botany.

In these same centuries, the Chinese, Muslim, and Indian traditions of learning were far more successful in resisting challenge from without, improving upon the Europeans by refusing to pay attention to new and discrepant information. When a few self-styled "Enlightened" thinkers, located mainly in France, began to abandon the inherited Christian framework of knowledge entirely, guardians of inherited truth in Asia were not impressed. Instead, serious efforts to come to grips with what eventually became undeniably superior European knowledge and skills were delayed until almost our own time.

Against this norm, the volatility of European learning in general, and of historiography in particular, should perhaps excite our wonder. At the least, we ought not to scorn the centuries-long lag time needed to accommodate new and discrepant information. We in the historical profession persist in the same behavior today, remaining for the most part content to work (often unconsciously) within a liberal, nineteenth-century interpretation of history whose principles, if overtly affirmed, would embarrass most of us because we no longer believe them.

Vico (d. 1744), Voltaire (d. 1778), Gibbon (d. 1794), and Herder (d. 1803) pioneered the eighteenth-century effort to improve upon the inherited biblical frame of history. Each in his own way desacralized the past, even though both Vico and Herder remained Christians. Like Guicciardini and Machiavelli, they assumed that human will and actions shaped events; unlike their Florentine predecessors they undertook macrohistory, finding large-scale patterns in the past, whether cyclical, as Vico and Herder did, or cumulative and, at least sporadically, progressive, as Gibbon and Voltaire did. Classical history and philosophy played a central role in shaping their outlooks. Only Voltaire in his *Essai sur les Mœurs* (1756) paid much attention to non-Europeans; and his praise for China and his respect for Muslims was largely inspired by his distaste for the Christian church. Hence nothing like a global view of the past emerged from eighteenth-century efforts to correct the Christian interpretation of history; but the autonomy of human action was vigorously affirmed, with or without an ultimate, increasingly distant, Divine control.

This compromise between pagan and Christian heritages carried over into the nineteenth century, when the liberal vision of history took shape. This is what still lurks in the background of contemporary American historiography. The core idea was simple enough: what mattered in history was the sporadic but ineluctable advance of Freedom. This allowed nationalistic historians to erect a magnificently Eurocentric vision of the human past, since Freedom (defined largely in terms of political institutions) was uniquely at home among the states of Europe, both in ancient and in modern times. The rest of the world, accordingly, joined the mainstream of history when discovered, settled, or conquered by Europeans. A somewhat spurious global history was easy to construct along these lines. Still, for the first time America, Australia, Africa, and Asia found an admittedly subordinate but still significant place in world history, and the entire globe became a theater for the advance of human Freedom.

Within the European past, attention focused on times and places where Freedom flourished or faced critical challenge. Classical antiquity, the barbarian invasions, the rise of representative institutions in the Middle Ages, Renaissance and Reformation, the Enlightenment, and all the magnificent advances of the nineteenth century were what deserved to be studied; eras of darkness and despotism could properly be skipped over since they made no contribution to the mainstream of human achievement.

The United States, of course, enjoyed an especially privileged place in this version of history, since the Revolution of 1776 and the Constitution of 1789 were beacons of Freedom's advance; and the expansion of American wealth and power in the nineteenth and twentieth centuries offered an equally obvious example of the rewards Freedom could bring to its faithful and favored practitioners. This, as I say, is still the scheme that underlies most professional study of history in the United States, even though some rebels have turned everything inside out by making the wickedness of European aggression against other peoples the main theme of modern history, while attacking the white male establishment of the United States for its no less wicked exploitation of various subordinated populations, both at home and abroad.

Obviously enough, this liberal, progressive view of world history (as well as the inside-out inversion thereof) was a naive secularization of the Christian epos. Freedom replaced God as the governing, supernal actor; and privileged free peoples played the terrestrial role assigned to faithful Christians in the divine drama of salvation. Insofar as the professional pursuit of history finds its meaning in this scheme (or in its inversion), we clearly remain bounded by the Christian inheritance, however faint it has become in contemporary consciousness.

World War I was hard to accommodate within what I have called the liberal view of history. Freedom to live and die in the trenches was not what nineteenth-century historians expected liberal political institutions to result in. Moreover, the agonizing years of stalemate seemed to many participants to arise from circumstances entirely independent of human will or intention. Spengler and Toynbee were the two most significant historians who responded to this apparent loss of control, and to the strange disembowelment that Freedom suffered in World War I. The sense of being caught up in processes overriding human purposes, and of reenacting in 1914–18 struggles for power like those that had wracked ancient Greece and Rome, persuaded first Spengler and then Toynbee that human history could best be understood as a more or less foreordained rise and fall of separate civilizations, each recapitulating in essentials the career of its predecessors and contemporaries. Quite consciously, they both drew on their classical education to reaffirm a cyclic vision of human affairs proposed by Plato and elaborated by other philosophers of antiquity down to the Stoics, and applied to history by such diverse writers as Polybius and Virgil.

Their impressively learned books won wide attention between 1918, when the first volume of Spengler's *Der Untergang des Abendlandes* was published, and 1936–54, when Toynbee's ten-volume *A Study of History* came out in three separate installments. To many thoughtful persons, their books gave a new and somber meaning to such unexpected and distressing events as World War I, Germany's collapse in 1918, the onset of World War II, and the breakup of the victorious Grand Alliances after both wars.

Today, when these political resonances have faded, a quite different aspect of their work seems more important (at least to me), since, by cycling through the recorded past, Spengler and Toynbee put European and non-European civilizations on the same plane. This was a real change from the myopic concentration on the glories of Europe's past that had prevailed in the nineteenth century, and, at least potentially, distinguishes the historiography of our age from its predecessors.

To be sure, Toynbee was not long satisfied with his initial scheme, and in the later volumes of A *Study of History* (published in 1939 and 1954) explicitly reintroduced God as an actor in history, subordinating the rise and fall of separate civilizations to a progressive revelation of God's will that came to sensitive souls in times when the moral rules of a given civilization were undergoing irremediable breakdown. This way of combining linear and cyclical macrohistory and of introducing God once more into public affairs won few adherents among historians; and after 1957 his reputation suddenly collapsed, as Spengler's had before him.

One empirical (and probably trivial) reason for this swing of public and professional attention was that the separate civilizations that Spengler and Toynbee had declared to be unable to communicate with one another (save for Toynbee at special sensitive moments in their development) did in fact interact with one another whenever contacts occurred. Adaptation to borrowings across civilizational boundaries was especially important in technological, artistic, and military matters, where the charms of novelty and the rewards of innovation were particularly obvious. By contrast, literary learning resisted intrusion from afar, partly because mastering an alien language in which interesting ideas might be set forth was always difficult, but also because to admit that outsiders had something to say that was worth attending to seemed a confession of inadequacy that faithful transmitters of a revered literary canon were not prepared to make. Nonetheless, defenders of literary and religious truth sometimes borrowed ideas from outsiders, with or without acknowledging alien inspiration.

Cultural and technological borrowings were often incidental to economic exchanges, which have the advantage for historians of leaving material traces behind even when literary records are missing. Long-distance trade existed even before the beginning of recorded history, when the river valley civilizations of Mesopotamia and Egypt began to import strategic goods like metal and timber across quite considerable distances from barbarian lands. Intercivilizational trade, too, was very old. Mesopotamian commercial contacts with India dated back to the third millennium BC or before. Indirect and far more tenuous contacts between Mesopotamia and China started a few hundred years later, though caravans only began to move more or less regularly across the oases of central Asia about 100 BC. Nevertheless, with the passage of time, the scale and range of trade exchanges within Eurasia expanded into Africa and then, after 1500, began to embrace all the inhabited earth.

Historians have, a bit hesitantly, begun to react to the increasing evidence of long-distance interactions that cross the boundaries of traditional scholarly specialization, and a number of persons have set out to construct a more adequate world history than Spengler and Toynbee envisaged by highlighting Eurasian and subsequent global interactions. No one writer stands preeminent in this company, which is divided between those who put primary emphasis on economics – often Marxists or quasi-Marxists like Immanuel Wallerstein and André Gunder Frank – and others who think that religious, artistic, and scientific encounters played an autonomous and more or less equal part with economics and technology in defining the course of Eurasian and then of world history. I count myself in this company, but can also point to such figures as Ross Dunn, the first President of the World History Association, and the company of scholars associated with the International Society for Comparative Study of Civilizations, among whom John Hord and David Wilkinson are among the most vigorous. The very existence of these two organizations, each with its own learned journal, attests to the liveliness that world history has attained in American academic circles; and, as a sign of their vigor, both journals are presently fumbling around in search of a more adequate conceptualization of human history as a whole.

To be sure, terminological confusion is as dense as ever. Yet even though there is no perceptible consensus about what the term "civilization" ought to mean, and no agreed word or phrase to describe the "interactive zone" (to use a phrase introduced, I believe, by Ross Dunn) embracing different Eurasian civilizations, I think it correct to assert that recognition of the reality and historical importance of trans-civilizational encounters is on the increase and promises to become the mainstream of future work in world history. We badly need a word or phrase to describe the human reality arising from encounters with strangers who bring locally unfamiliar skills and knowledge to the attention of stay-at-homes. Ross Dunn's "interactive zone" seems clumsy. My own favorite, "ecumene," carries cramping ecclesiastical associations.

Wallerstein's "world system" is perhaps the leading candidate at present, but it is awkward as a description of such relationships before 1500, when separate "world systems" existed in Eurasia, America, and presumably elsewhere as well, although we know very little about historical change initiated by the non-literate peoples' interactions, and can only hope that sophisticated archaeology may someday make some of the facts accessible.

Still, even though we have yet to agree upon what to call it, the fact that civilized and uncivilized peoples communicated across relatively long distances from very early times, and altered their behavior from time to time in response to encounters with attractive or threatening novelties from afar, seems more and more obvious. It follows that world history ought to be constructed around this reality – the largest and most inclusive framework of human experience, and the lineal ancestor of the One World in which we find ourselves so confusingly immersed today.

What I propose, therefore, in the balance of this essay, is to sketch land-marks in the history of the interactive, ecumenical world system of Eurasia, hoping that even a thumbnail sketch may clarify the concept, and promote the emergence of a more coherent, intelligible approach to world history.

When I wrote *The Rise of the West* I set out to improve upon Toynbee by showing how the separate civilizations of Eurasia interacted from the very beginning of their history, borrowing critical skills from one another, and thus precipitating still further change as adjustment between treasured old and borrowed new knowledge and practice became necessary.

My ideas about the importance of cultural borrowing were largely shaped by social anthropology, as developed in the United States in the 1930s. Clark Wissler had studied the diffusion of "culture traits" among the Plains Indians with elegant precision; and Ralph Linton's textbook, *The Tree of Culture*, adduced other persuasive examples of far-reaching social change in Africa and elsewhere as a result of cultural adaptation to some borrowed skill. But the man who influenced me most was Robert Redfield. He constructed a typology of human societies, setting up two ideal types: folk society at one extreme, civilized society at the other.

Folk society was one in which well-established customs met all ordinary circumstances of life, and fitted smoothly together to create an almost com-plete and unquestioned guide to life. Redfield argued that a remote Yucatan village he had studied approached his ideal type of folk society. Nearly iso-lated from outside encounters, the people of the village had reconciled their Spanish Christian and Mayan heritages, blending what had once been con-flicting ways of life into a more or less seamless whole. Conflict and change were reprehensible, checked by the sacralizing power of binding custom.

Civilized society, exemplified by Yucatan's port city of Merida, was at the opposite pole. There Catholicism clashed with residual pagan rites, and con-tinual contacts among strangers meant that customary rules binding everyone to a consistent body of behavior could not arise. Instead, conflicting moral claims provoked variable, unpredictable conduct. Social conflict and change was obvious and pervasive, feared by some and welcomed by others.

Armed with ideas like these, it seemed obvious to me in 1954, when I began to write *The Rise of the West*, that historical change was largely pro-voked by encounters with strangers, followed by efforts to borrow (or some-times to reject or hold at bay) especially attractive novelties. This, in turn, always involved adjustments in other established routines. A would-be world historian therefore ought to be alert to evidences of contacts among separate civilizations, expecting major departures to arise from such encounters whenever some borrowing from (or rejection of) outsiders' practices provoked historically significant social change.

The ultimate spring of human variability, of course, lies in our capacity to invent new ideas, practices, and institutions. But invention also flourished best when contacts with strangers compelled different ways of thinking and doing to compete for attention, so that choice became conscious, and deliberate tinkering with older practices became easy, and indeed often inevitable. In folk society, when custom worked as expected, obstacles to most sorts of social change were all but insuperable. But when clash of customs created confusion, invention flourished. Civilization, as Redfield defined it, was therefore autocatalytic. Once clashing cultural expectations arose at a few crossroads locations, civilized societies were liable to keep on changing, acquiring new skills, expanding their wealth and power, and disturbing other peoples round about. They did so down to our own day, and at an ever-increasing pace as the centuries and millennia of civilized history passed.

Approaching the conceptualization of world history in this fashion, separate civilizations became the main actors in world history – accepting or rejecting new ways come from afar, but in either case, altering older social practices, since successfully to reject an attractive or threatening novelty might require changes at home quite as far-reaching as trying to appropriate it. Over time, civilizations clearly tended to expand onto new ground; and as they expanded, autonomous neighboring societies were engulfed and eventually disappeared. Such geographical expansion meant that in the ancient Near East what had begun as separate civilizations in Mesopotamia and Egypt eventually merged into a new cosmopolitan whole, beginning about 1500 BC; and, I concluded, an analogous cosmopolitanism began to embrace all the civilizations of the earth after about 1850, when the effective autonomy of China and Japan came to an end.

But when I wrote *The Rise of the West* I was sufficiently under Toynbee's spell to note these instances without diverting the focus of my attention from the separate histories of separate civilizations. The idea of a Eurasian (eventually also African and then global) ecumenical whole, embracing all the peoples, civilized and uncivilized, who were interacting with one another, dawned very slowly. Only after I convinced myself, while writing *The Pursuit of Power* (1982), that Chinese commercial expansion energized the sudden upthrust of trade in Latin Christendom after about 1000 AD, did I realize, with Wallerstein and Dunn, that a proper world history ought to focus primarily upon changes in the ecumenical world system, and then proceed to fit developments within separate civilizations, and within smaller entities, like states and nations, into the pattern of that fluctuating whole.

A weakened sense of the autonomy of separate civilizations went along with this alteration of my outlook. In *The Rise of the West*, I had defined civilization as a style of life, to be recognized by skilled and experienced observers in the way an art critic discerns styles of art. But that analogy is not a good one. Works of art are tangible; whereas "life" is too multifarious to be observed in the way art critics can observe and more or less agree about stylistic affinities. In particular, within any civilization, different groups lived in very different ways. What principally held them together was their common subjection to rulers, whose continued dominion was much assisted by the fact that they subscribed to a set of moral rules, embodied in sacred or at least semi-sacred texts. This, it now seems to me, is the proper definition of a "civilization." Rulers who knew how to behave – paying lip service to prescribed canons of conduct and acting with a more or less exactly agreed upon disregard of the letter of those rules – could and did cooperate smoothly enough to keep a lid on turbulent subordinates for centuries on end across scores, then hundreds and, eventually, thousands of miles. Privileged ruling classes thus constituted a sort of iron framework within which a civilization could thrive. But among subordinated groups widely diverse local, occupational, and sectarian ways of life prevailed. All that united them was the fact that each group had some sort of tacit (or, occasionally, explicit) understanding with other groups, and especially with the politically dominant segments of society, so that they could act as they did without suffering too many nasty surprises.

In such a view, civilizations become rather pale, inchoate entities in themselves. Internal diversity looms large and merges almost imperceptibly into the diversity of neighboring peoples who retained varying degrees of local autonomy but still entered into negotiations with civilized rulers and traders, and, perhaps, with missionaries, craftsmen, refugees, and, sometimes, with colonizing settlers as well. No single recognizable style of life can be imputed to such a social landscape. Diversity, conflict, and imprecise boundaries, yes; coherence and uniformity, no.

Even the canon of sacred writings, to which dominant segments of civilized society subscribed, was full of discrepancies. Consider the Bible, Buddhist and Hindu sacred writings, and the Confucian classics! It required judicious commentary to educe a practicable guide to life from such diverse materials; and, of course, initial diversity implied perennial flexibility, inviting commentators to adjust to ever-altering circumstances by appropriate reinterpretation, age after age, while claiming, characteristically, to be restoring the true, original meaning to the sacred texts. This was the primary function of the literate (often priestly) classes; and explains why new, discrepant data were (and still are in many branches of learning) so persistently disregarded.

If civilizations were as internally confused and contradictory as I now believe them to have been, it puts them very much in tune with the confusion and complexity of the Eurasian ecumenical world system. That system was larger in geographic area, of course, and more attenuated in its internal structure, being without any articulated, overriding canon of conduct because it embraced a plurality of civilizations (and interstitial peoples), each with its own literary definition of moral principles and its own political and cultural rulers. But, for all that, the ecumene was not so very different from the diversity to be found within the borders of any of the larger civilizations that by 1500 were participating in the Eurasian and African circle of exchange and interaction.

The reason was that mercantile practice had, in fact, slowly created a workable code of conduct that went a long way towards standardizing encounters across cultural boundaries. Even the arcanum of religion made room for outsiders and unbelievers, since the principal religions of the Eurasian world – Christianity, Confucianism, Buddhism, and Islam – all agreed in exhorting the devout to treat strangers as they would wish to be treated themselves. Thus, despite the fact that no single set of rulers had ever exercised political sovereignty across the whole Eurasian-African ecumene, a bare-bones moral code did arise that went a long way towards reducing the risks of cross-civilizational contact to bearable proportions. Little by little across the centuries, local rulers of every stripe learned that they could benefit mightily by taxing instead of plundering strangers. Subordinate classes also learned to tolerate outsiders – even alien merchants, whom hard-working peasants and artisans regularly regarded as dishonest exploiters who reaped profit unjustly, since what they sold dear was exactly the same as what they had previously bought cheap from honest men, that is, from themselves. All the same, the poor gradually got used to being cheated by outsiders in the marketplace, just as their forerunners at the dawn of civilization had gotten used to surrendering unrequited rent to self-appointed, strong-armed landowners.

As these attitudes became general, so that an enforceable (and remarkably uniform) merchant law arose in the ports and other great urban centers of Eurasia, and was supplemented by an informal body of customs for dealing with strangers that extended into the rural hinterland, the structure of the ecumenical world system approximated very closely to that of the separate civilizations embraced within it. Accordingly, students of world history should make it the object of conscious investigation, for this is what gives cohesion and structure to their subject in quite the same way that governmental acts and policies give cohesion and structure to national histories. Or so I now believe.

What, then, were the major landmarks in the historical evolution of this, the largest and, eventually, world-dominating framework of human experience?

As one would expect, if I am right in claiming that encounters with strangers were the main drive wheel of social change, the earliest complex societies arose on the river flood plains of Mesopotamia, Egypt, and northwest India, adjacent to the land bridge of the Old World, where the largest land masses of the earth connect with one another. Continental alignments and climatic conditions made this region the principal node of land and sea communications within the Old World, and it was presumably for that reason that civilization first broke out there.

Sumerian literary tradition accords with this notion, since it held that the founders of their civilization had come by sea from the south and subdued the "black headed people" who were indigenous to the banks of the lower Tigris–Euphrates. The newcomers eventually learned to irrigate the swamp lands that bordered the rivers, and thanks to regular and assured harvests were then able to erect earth's first cities on an alluvial plain that lacked timber, metals, and other essential raw materials the Sumerians needed. From their inception, therefore, shipping, supplemented by overland caravans, kept the cities of the Mesopotamian plain in touch (directly or indirectly) with distant sources of raw materials and diverse peoples living within a radius of several hundred miles. And, before long, inhabitants of Egypt and of the Indus valley erected civilizations of their own, thanks partly to borrowed skills and ideas acquired through contact with Mesopotamia, and by doing so promptly established their own zones of interaction with peoples round about, just as the Sumerians had done before them.

Initially, water transport was the main link across long distances. When, at an early but unknown date, human beings discovered the use of sails, the coastal waters of the Indian ocean and its adjacent seas became an especially easy medium of transport and communication. Winds blew equably throughout the year, and their direction reversed itself with each monsoon. This made safe return from lengthy voyages exceptionally easy, even for ships that could not sail against the wind. If Sumerian tradition is to be believed, the founders of the world's first civilization emerged from this sea-room, bringing with them superior skills that had been accumulated, we may surmise, before the dawn of recorded history thanks to contacts with strangers provoked by sea travel.

About 4000 BC sailing ships also began to ply the Mediterranean, where comparably benign (though not quite so convenient) sailing conditions prevailed in summertime when the trade winds blew gently and steadily from the northeast. Safe return to home base often required going against the prevailing wind. Rowing was one possibility, and remained important in

Mediterranean navigation until the seventeenth century AD. Taking advantage of short-lived offshore winds created by differential heating of sea and land was another possibility. Ship and sail design that permitted tacking into the wind was a more satisfactory solution, but was not fully attained until the late Middle Ages. Yet ships that moved up-wind with difficulty, and could not sail the stormy seas of winter safely, were quite enough to provoke and sustain the emergence of Minoan, Phoenician-Carthaginian, and Greco-Roman civilizations. Borrowings from Egypt and Syria were critical at the start – and most such contacts were by sea.

Geographically speaking, the South China Sea was about as hospitable to early sailing ships as the Mediterranean. But the possibility of seasonal navigation in southeast Asia and among adjacent offshore islands did not lead to the early development of cities and literate civilizations, perhaps because no developed civilized centers were at hand from which to borrow critical skills and ideas. Similarly, the most congenial sea spaces of all the earth were the vast tradewind zones of the Atlantic and Pacific oceans; but they too were not exploited until large ships that could tack against the wind had been invented, though Polynesian canoes did carry human settlers to remote islands of the Pacific throughout the tradewind zone. The North Atlantic and North Pacific were far more formidable for early sailors since stormy, variable winds were further complicated by the high tides.

Thus climate and wind patterns set definite limits to early shipping, though it is worth noting that small coracles, made of wickerwork and hides, did begin to fish the coastal waters of the North Atlantic in the fourth millennium BC. Fishermen also embarked from the shores of Japan from an unknown but presumably early date. Accidental drift voyages across the breadth of the oceans must have set in as soon as fishing boats started to venture onto these stormy waters. Drift voyages of Eskimo kayaks from Greenland that fetched up in Scotland in the seventeenth century, and Japanese fishermen who came ashore in Oregon in the nineteenth century, offer a well-attested sample of the random, ocean-crossing dispersals suffered by small craft lost at sea.

A few resemblances between Amerindian artifacts and those of east Asia may result from drift voyages; but fishermen did not carry much cultural baggage with them, even when they survived weeks of exposure; and it is unlikely that the real but trivial transoceanic contacts (including Norse settlements in North America) had enduring consequences of any importance before 1492. Instead, a separate ecumenical system arose in the Americas, centered in Mexico and Peru; but in the absence of an extended literary record, we know far less about its development, and, since archaeology is inherently local, connections among separate sites frequently remain obscure.

Eurasian ecumenical history is far more accessible, even though historians have not yet studied its growth and consolidation in detail. Nonetheless, it is clear enough that the initial primacy of sea transport and communication in holding the ecumene together was gradually modified by improvements in transport overland. Human beings, of course, were rovers from the start: that is how they populated the earth. With the development of agriculture, the diffusion of useful crops set in. Slash and burn cultivators, for example, carried wheat from the Near East to China, where it arrived before 2000 BC. Rice spread from somewhere in southeast Asia and became an important crop in both India and China about a thousand years later. Other, less important crops spread as well, altering human life profoundly wherever they began to provide a new source of food for the population.

Before the dawn of literacy, human portage and wandering had been supplemented, at least in some parts of the world, by caravans of pack animals, which made carrying goods much easier. Long-distance exchange became routine in Sumerian times, when donkey caravans brought metals and other precious commodities from as far away as the Carpathian mountains of Rumania and distributed textiles and other manufactured goods in return. Caravan trade thus came to resemble trade by sea, with the difference that carrying valuable goods through inhabited lands required the negotiation of protection rents with every local ruler, whereas ships usually only had to pay tolls at their ports of destination. Since risk of plunder by some local ruffian was far higher than the risk of piracy at sea, costs of caravan transport remained comparatively high, so that only precious goods could bear the cost of long-distance land transport.

Overland contacts took a decisive new turn after about 1700 BC when light, maneuverable chariots were invented somewhere in the Mesopotamian borderlands. A team of horses hitched to such a vehicle could carry driver and bowman across open country faster than a man could run; and, when new, an array of charging chariots proved capable of overwhelming opposing infantry with ease. As a result, charioteers overran the river valley civilizations of the Near East and India before and after 1500 BC. Others penetrated Europe and China, where the earliest archaeologically well-attested Chinese dynasty, the Shang, established itself about 1400 BC with the help of war chariots. As the spread of wheat (and of some pottery styles from Western Asia) shows, swift wheeled transport and the military superiority of charioteers that resulted did not initiate trans-Asian encounters, but the establishment of the Shang dynasty through the exploitation of military techniques that originated in the Mesopotamian borderlands apparently did inaugurate many of the historical forms of Chinese civilization. This is strikingly attested by inscriptions on oracle bones discovered at the Shang capital of Anyang which are directly ancestral to the characters of contemporary Chinese writing.

Communication between China and Western Asia remained sporadic and indirect for many centuries after 1400 BC. Even when Chinese imperial initiative inaugurated more or less regular caravan trade after 100 BC, goods that survived the long journey remained mere curiosities and expensive luxuries. A few fashionable Roman ladies did indeed clothe themselves in semi-transparent silks from China; and the Chinese emperor did succeed in importing large-boned "blood sweating" horses from Iran, only to find that the scrawny steppe ponies, with which Chinese soldiers had already come to terms, were so much hardier and cheaper to keep that the imported breed could not displace them for anything but ceremonial purposes.

Yet the inauguration of more or less regular caravan trade across Asia did connect east and west as never before; and when, after about 300 AD, camels were brought into general use, caravans became capable of crossing previously inhospitable deserts. The effect was to incorporate vast new areas of Eurasia and Africa into an expanded trade and communications network. Tibet, Arabia, and the oases of central Asia, on the one hand, and sub-Saharan West Africa on the other, entered firmly into the ecumenical system, which simultaneously expanded northward by penetrating the whole of the steppes from Manchuria to Hungary, and even filtered across mountain passes and along river courses into the forested fastnesses of northern Europe.

New and highly lethal epidemic diseases and the so-called higher religions were the two most significant novelties that spread through this expanded caravan world from shortly before the Christian era to about 1000 AD. Material exchanges, like the spread of southeast Asian fruits and other crops to the Middle East with the elaboration of oasis agriculture, or the diffusion of Greco-Roman naturalistic sculptural styles to India, China, and even Japan, were trivial by comparison with the epidemiological and religious changes that this transport system precipitated.

This balance between economic/technological and cultural/biological exchanges altered after about 1000 AD when the ecumenical world system began to respond to innovations within China that expanded the role of market behavior by bringing poor peasants and urban working classes within its scope for the first time. What made this possible was cheap and reliable transport within China, resulting from widespread canal construction. Most canalization was initially undertaken to regulate water supplies for the expanding carpet of rice paddies upon which China's food more and more depended. Then with the construction of the Grand Canal in 605, linking the watershed of the Yang-tse with the Yellow River system, accompanied and followed by other engineering works designed to facilitate navigation through the Yang-tse gorges and other critical bottlenecks, the most fertile parts of China came to be linked by easily accessible and easily navigable waterways. Under the distant sovereignty of the emperor, canal boats could carry comparatively bulky cargoes across hundreds of miles with minimal risk of shipwreck or robbery. This, in turn, meant that even small differences in price for commodities of common consumption made it worthwhile for boatmen to carry such goods from where they were cheap to where they were dear.

Then, when, soon after 1000, the Sung government found it more convenient to collect taxes in cash instead of in kind, as had always been done previously, common people, including the poorest peasants, were forced onto the market so as to be able to pay their taxes. This enormously accelerated the spread of market behavior throughout China. Thereupon, to the general surprise of officialdom, whose Confucian training classified traders as deplorable social parasites, the advantages of specialized production, which Adam Smith was later to analyze so persuasively, started to come on stream throughout the varied landscapes of China. Wealth and productivity shot upwards. New skills developed, making China the wonder of the rest of the world, as Marco Polo and other visitors from afar soon realized. Among the new Chinese skills, some proved revolutionary: most notably for Europe, the trinity of gunpowder, printing, and the compass, all of which reached Europe from China between the thirteenth and fifteenth centuries.

China's westward reach was enhanced by the development of ocean-going all-weather ships, capable of tacking against the wind and of surviving most storms. Such ships, based mainly along the south China coast, where inland canal construction was checked by the mountainous interior, allowed enterprising merchants to extend a new (or perhaps only intensified and expanded) trade network across the South China Sea and into the Indian Ocean. There stoutly built Chinese vessels had to compete with the light craft and experienced mercantile population indigenous to those waters. As happened subsequently, when European ships penetrated the Indian Ocean by circumnavigating Africa, local shipping and trading networks proved capable of undercutting the higher costs borne by large, all-weather, stout-built intruders. But all the same, a comparatively massive infusion of Chinese commodities and Chinese demand for spices and other Indian Ocean products gave a fillip to the markets of the southern seas that soon slopped over into the Mediterranean and helped to stimulate the remarkable revival of European trade in the eleventh century and subsequently, with which historians have long been familiar.

Traders' needs, in turn, provoked Europeans to develop all-weather ships that were capable of traversing the stormy, tide-beset seas of the North Atlantic with a reasonable chance of getting back to home ports safely.

Inventions introduced between about 1000 and 1400, such as double plank-ing nailed to a heavy keel-and-rib frame, powerful stern post rudders, decked-over holds, and multiple masts and sails, made this possible. European shipbuilding followed a course of its own, independent of Chinese or any other foreign model, even though European sailors were always ready to bor-row anything that worked in practice, like compass navigation from China and triangular sails from the Indian Ocean.

Their most fateful borrowing and adaptation, however, was the marriage European seamen made between stout-built, oceangoing ships and cannon, developed initially to knock down castle walls on land. Such big guns, once adapted for use on shipboard, provided European ships with an armament far superior to anything previously known. As a result, when European ships began to sail across all the oceans of the earth, just before and after 1500, they were remarkably safe against attack by sea; and could often overwhelm local resistance on shore with wall-destroying broadsides.

The recoil from such guns was so powerful that only heavy ships could sustain it without shaking apart. The Chinese might have matched European ships in this respect, but for reasons of imperial politics, the Chinese govern-ment prohibited the construction of oceangoing ships after 1434, and made private Chinese oceanic enterprise illegal. Operating as pirates systematically handicapped Chinese (and Japanese) sailors thereafter, and deprived them of any chance of arming their vessels with heavy guns like those European traders carried routinely.

The consequences of European oceanic discoveries are well known, as are the consequences of the extraordinary improvements of transport and com-munication that came after 1850, when European, American, and more re-cently also Japanese inventors utilized mechanical and electrical forms of energy for railroads, steamships, telegraph, and then for airplanes, radio, TV, and, most recently, for the transmission of computer data as well. The most obvious effect of these successive transformations of world communications was to expand the reach of the Eurasian ecumene throughout the globe, en-gulfing the previously independent ecumenical system of America, together with less well-known social complexes in Australia and in innumerable smaller islands. The shock was enormous, and the world is still reverberating to the ecological, epidemiological, demographic, cultural, and intellectual consequences of the global unification of the past five hundred years.

Among other things, global communication and transport made world his-tory a palpable reality. Historians, being the faithful guardians of every level of human collective identity, are beginning to adapt to that circumstance, almost half a millennium after it began to affect human life everywhere. That is why this World History Conference was called – a bit belatedly, one might suppose. Yet that is not really the case, since, as I pointed out already, the historical profession still clings to more local (and more sacred) forms of history, and has not yet agreed upon how to approach the human adventure on earth as a whole.

In struggling with this question, it seems appropriate to emphasize two distinct levels of human encounters that took place across the centuries within the communications networks I have just sketched for you. First is biological and ecological: how human beings fared in competition with other forms of life, managing not only to survive but to expand their share of the earth's matter and energy, age after age, and in a great variety of different physical environments. No other species comes near to equaling humanity's dominating role in earth's ecosystem. Major landmarks are obvious enough, starting with initial diffusion of hunters and gatherers from Africa, followed by intensified broad-spectrum gathering leading to agriculture; and then the rise of civilizations with enhanced formidability *vis à vis* other societies due to their military specialists on the one hand, and their adaptation to crowd diseases on the other. The growing importance of the Eurasian ecumenical world system then takes over, diffusing diseases, crops, and technological skill across larger and larger areas, until after 1500 the process became global. Each time a previously isolated population entered into contact with the ecumenical world system, debilitating exposure to unfamiliar diseases, ideas, and techniques ensued, often with disastrous results for the previously isolated peoples and their cultures.

Uniformity never emerged, and there is no reason to suppose it ever will. Differences of climate and other circumstances require different behavior, and being both intelligent and adaptable, human beings act accordingly. Some forms of life have been destroyed by the human career on earth; many more are endangered, as we all know. Others have been carried into new environments and made to flourish as never before. Some disease organisms and weed species still defy human wishes successfully, but domesticated plants and animals have been radically altered and some entirely new species of plants and animals have been invented to nourish us and serve our wants (and wishes) in other ways.

What makes the human career on the face of the earth so extraordinary from a biological/ecological point of view is that in becoming fully human our predecessors introduced cultural evolution as soon as learned behavior began to govern most of their activity. The consequent cultural attainments of humankind, and their variability in time and space, thus constitute the second level of world history. Attention has traditionally and quite properly centered here because what has been learned can change whenever something new and attractive comes to conscious attention. And since consciousness is extremely motile, cultural evolution immediately outstripped organic evolution, introducing a radically new sort of disturbance into earth's ecosystem.

Yet in some respects cultural evolution still conforms to the older patterns of organic evolution. Initial, more or less random, variation and subsequent selection of what works best is enough to set the process in motion. Contacts among bearers of different cultural traditions promoted further change; but as I have argued already, changes were often initiated to defend local peculiarities rather than to accept what was perceived as an alien, and often threatening, novelty. It follows that even the instantaneous communication that prevails today is unlikely to result in any sort of global uniformity. Human groups, even while borrowing from outsiders, cherish a keen sense of their uniqueness. The more they share, the more each group focuses attention on residual differences, since only so can the cohesion and morale of the community sustain itself.

The upshot has always been conflict, rivalry, and chronic collision among human groups, both great and small. Even if world government were to come, such rivalries would not cease, though their expression would have to alter in deference to the overriding power of a bureaucratic world administration. In all probability, human genetic inheritance is attuned to membership in a small, primary community. Only so can life have meaning and purpose. Only so can moral rules be firm and definite enough to simplify choices. But membership in such groups perpetuates the gap between "us" and "them" and invites conflict since the best way to consolidate any group is to have an enemy close at hand.

Until very recently, rural villages constituted the primary communities that shaped and gave direction to most human lives. But with modern communications and the persistent spread of market relations into the countryside, this has begun to change. Multiple and often competing identities, characteristic of cities from ancient times, have begun to open before the astonished and often resentful eyes of the human majority. How to choose between the alternative collective identities, and how to reconcile conflicting obligations that different identities impose, is the perennial moral problem of all human society. In the past, most rural communities worked out more or less unambiguous rules for making such choices, so that moral behavior was usually obvious to all concerned. In urban contexts, friction and uncertainty were far greater; and today, as urbanity expands into the countryside, ambiguity and uncertainty multiply everywhere.

How to reconcile membership in vivacious primary communities with the imperatives of an emerging cosmopolitanism is, perhaps, the most urgent issue of our time. The material advantages of global exchange and economic specialization are enormous. Without such a system, existing human populations could scarcely survive, much less sustain existing standards of living. But how firm adhesion to primary communities can be reconciled with participation in global economic and political processes is yet to be discovered. Religious congregations of fellow believers emerged in antiquity in response to analogous needs; perhaps something similar may happen again. But contemporary communications expose the faithful to a continual bombardment by messages from outsiders and unbelievers. Moreover, if that could somehow be successfully counteracted, rival religious communities might then clash, with results as disastrous as those arising from the twentieth century's clash of rival nations.

I suspect that human affairs are trembling on the verge of far-reaching transformation, analogous to what happened when agriculture emerged out of broad-spectrum gathering, and village communities became the principal framework within which human lives were led. What sort of communities may prove successful in accommodating their members to global communications, worldwide exchanges, and all the other conditions of contemporary (and future) human life remains to be seen. Catastrophe of unprecedented proportions is always possible. We are all aware of potential ecological disasters, due to pollution of land, air, and water. Social breakdown due to deficient or misguided nurture is perhaps no less threatening.

But human ingenuity and inventiveness remain as lively as ever. I suppose that satisfying and sustainable inventions will indeed occur locally and then spread, as other inventions in times past, having proved themselves in practice, also spread through imitation and adaptation, thus adding to the sum of human skills and enlarging the scope of human life, age after age, through emergency after emergency and crisis after crisis, from the beginning of the human career on earth to our time. Risks may be greater than ever before, but possibilities are correspondingly vast.

We live, whether we like it or not, in a golden age when precedents for the future are being laid down. It seems apparent to me that by constructing a perspicacious and accurate world history, historians can play a modest but useful part in facilitating a tolerable future for humanity as a whole and for all its different parts. The changing shape of world history has been the principal professional concern of my life. I commend it to you as a worthy and fascinating pursuit, apt for our age, and practically useful inasmuch as a clear and vivid sense of the whole human past can help to soften future conflicts by making clear what we all share.

2

Crossing Boundaries: Ecumenical, World, and Global History

Bruce Mazlish

As Humpty-Dumpty said, words *can* mean anything we say they mean; but if our use of them is so idiosyncratic as to convey little or no meaning to anyone else, they will fail as means of communication. It is also true that the meaning of words is historically determined, often changing over time. Words are ambiguous, trailing their disorderly and confused history with them; thus, the word *cleave* in English means both to separate, as done by a butcher's knife, and to cling, as in lovers embracing.[1]

Given the historical nature of words, historians must be especially careful in their usage. In this essay, I want to look carefully at the words "ecumenical," "world," and "global," specifically when they are used to modify the noun "history," for in that context these words appear to exist in a rather Humpty-Dumpty-like "world," marked by unusual ambiguity and messiness. It is hopeless to expect that single meanings will, or should, result from our inquiry, but in the process of examining these three adjectives we may hope to achieve greater conceptual clarity than now exists.

I shall be arguing that although the three terms are often used as synonyms, they in fact are distinguishable and embrace significantly different approaches to history. Admittedly, there are important overlaps among the approaches, which helps to disguise the fact that they have evolved in historically different circumstances. It is the differences that I shall be stressing.[2]

ECUMENICAL HISTORY

What I am calling "ecumenical" history has as synonyms "universal" and "world" (rarely, if ever, "global"). It claims to be universal because it assumes that all human activity is under one guiding principle and can be told as one story. Thus, Bossuet wrote his *Discourse on Universal History*, though enormous parts of the globe were unknown to him. The guiding principle, in his case, was Providence, or God.

Such ecumenical histories were originally religious in conception, appealing, for example, to a Jewish or Christian or Islamic God. Ecumenical history, however, could equally be secularized, as in Hegel and his ordering principle of Reason making its way through time. Even more materialized, of course, is Marx and his communism as the "Riddle of History" solved.

All such ecumenical histories bear within them the prophetic strain, and speak of a known ending (in fact, of course, Marx was more sophisticated than suggested above, and embraced four different variants of history).[3] Let us look more closely, however, at the word "ecumenical" itself. It comes from the Greek meaning "inhabited world." A secondary definition, however, is "tending toward worldwide Christian unity." Which meaning is to dominate? The first will take us closer to world history. The second remains firmly in what I am calling ecumenical history.

Nevertheless, confusion is rampant. Thus, Paul Costello in his treatment of a number of "world" historians (his examples are Spengler, Toynbee, Dawson, Sorokin, Mumford, McNeill, and H. G. Wells, quite a mixed bag) tells us that world histories are "almost inevitably an eschatology," while also informing us that world historians are guided in their "mission" by "the Ecumenical ideal." Then he also characterizes his chosen "world" historians as cyclical in their conceptions.[4]

Is it possible that these are contradictory positions? Eschatology conceives of an end, and, as we have noted, is generally associated with a more or less religious vision of final events. Cyclical conceptions are a more pagan interpretation. Thus, as Charles Cochrane points out, such a conception is opposed to the linearity of Christianity.[5]

If we look at recent "world" historians, such as Spengler and Toynbee, we see that they are really ecumenical historians, given to prophecy and final ends, but employing a cyclical scheme to make their points. The other thing to note is that they focus on "civilizations" (though for Spengler these are the end stages of what he calls "cultures") as if these were organisms, given to birth, growth, decline, and death. As such, they are treated as separate from one another, more or less closed entities.[6] Because Spengler and Toynbee treat such entities as equal, however, they do claim (a claim not always fulfilled in practice, as a close look would show) to bring an ecumenical attitude to what had otherwise been mere Eurocentric historiography.

Without indulging in detailed discussion of Spengler and Toynbee, let me underline their lack of sympathy with the modern world. Foremost is their dismissal of the theory of evolution, surely the most fecund scientific idea of the nineteenth century, thenceforth serving as an essential framework for any understanding of human development. For example, Spengler was a follower of Goethe's scientific work (now discredited), and had nothing but scorn for Darwin. The English scientist, he claimed, had sacrificed Goethe's Nature-Theory to the nineteenth-century cult of the useful and the material. Spengler, of course, offers no discussion of the validity of Darwin's work, and clearly has no comprehension of the theory of evolution.

The situation is as bad in regard to physics (though Spengler was trained as a mathematician). Convinced that physics was dissolving in "annihilating doubt," as evinced by probability theory, Spengler claimed that his theory of cycles made it "possible to foresee the date when Western scientific thought shall have reached the limits of its evolution." As Gerald Holton reminds us piquantly, "in one of the handy chronological charts which Spengler put at the end of his book, he allows us to find that date. It is the year 2000."[7] Well, of course, Spengler's millennial prediction may come to pass; but at the moment, it seems safe to say that his effort at world history appears to exist, historically, in a scientific vacuum.

The case is even worse with Toynbee. His understanding of the creative achievements of modern science can be measured by the names he cites. His outstanding spokesman to express the "language of our modern Western Physical Science" is – J. C. Smuts![8] The turn-of-the-century work of Einstein, Gauss, Lobachevsky, and a little later that of Heisenberg and Planck, finds no place in Toynbee's mind. This is hardly surprising since he is committed to the view that science is merely a translation of mythical language; i.e., it's already known in a different form. Surely, we need not expect an historian of civilizations to understand achievements such as those mentioned above in detail, but we might hope for an awareness of them in his attitude toward modern science.

The fact is that what Costello calls the "world" histories (though, in fact, they are "ecumenical") of Spengler, Toynbee, and the like are fundamentally flawed by their lack of any real understanding of or sympathy with modernity and especially modern science and technology, a lack which is either the result of their anti-modernism or leads them to an anti-modernist stance.[9] As a result, I believe, their work is fatally flawed, giving us little or no significant understanding of our modern world and its past. Only their vision of a history putatively shorn of its Christian and Eurocentric elements, and thus "ecumenical," i.e., worldwide, remains as a positive contribution to historiography.[10]

WORLD HISTORY

Let us then move on from ecumenical history, in its various guises, to what may more properly be called world history. In the sketch so far offered, we have mainly considered what can best be called speculative philosophy of history, a kind of metaphysics, and not the ordinary practice of contemporary historians. Now, we must look more closely at the latter, as they seek to establish large patterns and processes in world history. Here, I will be focusing on William McNeill, along with a few others, as our entry point. Before doing so, however, it is well to recognize the diversity of definitions given to world history. Many of them are extremely amorphous, and most of them reflect different schools within world history itself.

The "Invitation to Membership" of the World History Association (WHA) begins by saying, "If you teach the whole history of the whole world in nine short months, you know the challenge of planning and organizing a meaningful course in world history."[11] Although adherents of the WHA often deny it, this does *seem* to say that world history is "the whole history of the whole world," appearing thus to offer no obvious principle of selection.

A more limited definition is given by Jerry Bentley, the editor of *The Journal of World History*, when he remarks that "my impression is that most participants in the discussion [about the definition of world history] took interactions between peoples participating in large-scale historical processes to be one of the principal concerns of world history." Again, an enormous vagueness seems to envelop such a conception of world history: for example, would every historian of the industrial revolution (even if restricted to one country) – surely, a large-scale historical process – also necessarily be a world historian, and if not, why not? Bentley continues, "Thus, world history represents (among other things) a dialogue between the past and the present, in that it seeks to establish a historical context for the integrated and interdependent world of modern times."[12]

The premier figure of modern world history is, of course, William McNeill. He follows, as he himself has told us, directly in the line of Toynbee. It was Toynbee who inspired him with an ecumenical vision, but it is a vision that McNeill translated into more mundane historical practice. Thus, McNeill's *Plagues and Peoples* is intellectual worlds removed from *A Study of History*. However, like Toynbee, McNeill takes civilizations as his framework of analysis. In McNeill's case, however, these are not hermetic units, but open to cultural borrowings. After Toynbee, the anthropologists Ralph Linton and Robert Redfield influenced McNeill. What interests McNeill, therefore, are "trans-civilizational encounters."[13] It is this interest that then shapes his definition of world history as the study of "interaction among peoples of diverse cultures." Long-distance trade, the spread of religions and plagues, these and a multitude of other factors concern McNeill.

This concern is always informed by a biological and ecological awareness, totally missing as we have seen in his inspiration, Toynbee. Without specifically invoking the theory of evolution, McNeill lives and writes in its environment. The results have been brilliant treatments of processes occurring on a worldwide scale, such as the spread of disease or of military power.

McNeill and others have expanded the scope of world history both in its extension in past time and in geographical extent. One encounters, of course, variants of world history. The crucial variable is one's definition of "world." Thus, Fernand Braudel seems to have abandoned the fascination with civilizations and to have concentrated on "world systems," in the sense of worlds constructed by trade and culture. Characteristically, his book, *The Mediterranean*, is subtitled "The Mediterranean World in the Age of Philip II."

Braudel's disciple, Immanuel Wallerstein, has written *The Modern World-System*, in which with much detail he has tried to show how the modern commercial and capitalist world came into existence. In similar accounts, of course, Columbus's voyage occupies a central place, adding a New World to an Old one. Wallerstein's emphasis in the second volume,[14] however, is on the seventeenth-century mercantile competition among the Western European nations. His is history in the grand style, but with its feet on the ground (or perhaps one should say its legs in the sea).

Carrying the world-system approach even further back in time, Janet Abu-Lughod has suggestively argued for an earlier "system of world trade and even 'cultural' exchange."[15] She finds such a system in the period 1250–1350 AD, which she designates as a "crucial turning point in history." Though lacking an international division of labor, her system conceives of wide areas of the world – European, Indian, and Chinese – as linked in far-ranging trade based on key cities. Applying this approach to even earlier periods, she speaks of the Roman Empire as the "first nascent world system."

What all these variants on world history – McNeill, Braudel, Wallerstein, Abu-Lughod – share is a concern with systemic processes and patterns of various sorts among a great variety of historical and natural phenomena linking diverse populations. In contrast to ecumenical histories, they make less pretense at predictions about the future, and do not focus on civilizations going through fixed cycles.[16] In addition, though forced to rely heavily on secondary accounts, they stay close to the scholarship of ordinary historians, and offer purely secular accounts (even of religion).

In short, these world-system accounts are serious attempts at historical treatments of phenomena that arise on a world scale. And it is at this point that the meaning of the term "world" becomes additionally crucial. It is also at this point that the possible transition arises to global history.

GLOBAL HISTORY

As with ecumenical and world history, there is often obfuscation of differences between world and global history. Thus, in a series edited for the American Historical Association (AHA) by Michael Adas, he speaks of a "'new' global or world history" which differs in fundamental ways from its predecessors."[17] That difference, for Adas, leads to a paraphrase of McNeill's version of world history. Adas's series itself is entitled "Essays on Global and Comparative History," and includes not only an account of Abu-Lughod's thirteenth-century World System, but essays on "The Columbian Voyages ..." and "Gender and Islamic History," and such like.

Adas's series offers serious and worthwhile contributions to World History. I shall argue, however, that it misuses the title "Global History," which needs to be defined afresh in its own, proper terms. That such a need exists emerges even from McNeill, who comments, "I suspect that human affairs are trembling on the verge of a far-reaching transformation," which he compares to the importance of the agricultural revolution.[18]

We encounter the same intuition concerning the need for a newly defined Global History in the important article by Michael Geyer and Charles Bright, whose very title, "World History in a Global Age," indicates the tenuous transition taking place. As they say:

> What we have before us as contemporary history grates against the familiar explanatory strategies and analytic categories with which scholars have traditionally worked. . . . This is a crisis, above all, of Western imaginings, but it poses profound challenges for any historian: the world we live in has come into its own as an integrated globe, yet it lacks narration and has no history.

In their terms, "The central challenge of a renewed world history at the end of the twentieth century is to narrate the world's past in an age of globality."[19]

I believe, along with some others, that our "imaginings" must leap from World History to Global History *per se*. In making this jump, a look at the etymology of the words "World" and "Globe" is itself helpful (words are *not* just what I say they mean, but have an historical nature). Thus, the word "World" comes from the Middle English for "human existence"; its central reference is to the earth with its inhabitants and all things upon it. We can, of course, also speak of imaginary worlds, as in the "next world," meaning life after death. We also use the term to designate a class of persons, as in the academic world. Historically, the discovery of the New World is seen by many as marking the advent of World History. More recently, a First, Second, and Third World has been discerned, demarcating different levels of development in different parts of the World.

Such usage ill accords with the term Global (one cannot substitute New Globe for New World in 1492, or Third Globe for Third World today). There is a different valence to the word Global. It comes from the Latin, "globus," whose first definition is "something spherical or rounded," a "heavenly body." Only secondarily does the dictionary then offer the synonym "earth." The word Global thus points us in the direction of space, and can include the notion of standing outside our planet and seeing "Spaceship Earth." This is a new perspective, and as such one of the keys to Global History.

What are the other keys? I want to turn to them now, but before doing so I need to say a bit more about the transition from World to Global History. I can do so best by suggesting that a definition of Global History must come in two parts. The first is that it focuses on the history of globalization; that is, it takes existing processes, encapsulated in what I shall call the factors of globalization, and then studies them as far back in the past as seems necessary and useful. The second is that Global History is simply about processes that are best studied on a global rather than local, national, or regional level. As can readily be seen, the second definition is a continuation of much that is to be encountered in McNeill's variation of World History, with the major difference of starting from our contemporary situation, openly acknowledging its informed global perspective.

The first part of our definition – the history of globalization – is both the heart and the novelty of Global History. It defines our initial field of study. What is involved in globalization, what are the factors at work in our contemporary "world," these are the questions we must attend to.

In an early attempt to deal with these questions, I declared that

> The starting point for global history lies in the following basic facts of our time (although others could be added): our thrust into space, imposing upon us an increasing sense of being in one world – "Spaceship Earth" – as seen from outside the earth's atmosphere; satellites in outer space that link the peoples of the earth in an unprecedented fashion; nuclear threats in the form of either weapons or utility plants, showing how the territorial state can no longer adequately protect its citizens from either military or ecologically related "invasions"; environmental problems that refuse to conform to lines drawn on a map; and multinational corporations that increasingly dominate our economic lives.[20]

Among others that could be added are global consumerism (obviously related to multinationals), human rights, the displacement of an international political system by a global one (the Geyer–Bright article cited earlier is especially strong in this regard), the globalization of culture (especially music, fostered as it is by satellite communications), and so forth.

What is essential to note is the synergy and synchronicity of these various factors. It is their interaction with one another, in ever-increasing extent and force, that is new, although all of them have their origins in a differentiated past. Globalization is the sum of their combined presences. It is a reality that now affects every part of the globe and every person on it, even though in widely differing local contexts. In fact, one could say that much of Global History has necessarily to devote itself to studying the factors of globalization in relation to a "local" reality, which can take many forms.

Among the practitioners of Global History, one can discern, as in Artificial Intelligence studies, adherents of a strong and a weak interpretation. The former are convinced that globalization has been bringing us into a new, global *epoch*, which replaces existing attempts at periodizations such as postmodern or post-industrial. The adherents of a weak interpretation do not want to go so far, and are content to abstain from what they see as a divisionary periodization scheme, and to concentrate on studying the process of globalization without further claims. For those proponents of globalization who see it as introducing a new period, of course, the issue of when the global epoch "begins" is worth attention (as with when modern history begins), with some opting for the 1950s and others for the 1970s (I place myself in the epochal camp, and opt for the later time). This argument necessarily rotates around the question as to when a sufficient amount of synergy and synchronicity arises to justify the launch of a new periodization.

In back of this argument is a conviction that time and space have been compressed in an unprecedented fashion. The roots of this compression reach far into the past. The development of sailing vessels, from sail to steam, as they cut distance and duration, forms one thread in this account. More recently, we would study the invention of the telegraph, the laying of cables, the introduction of the telephone and then of radio communication. We would want to look further at the satellites now circling our globe, and at the computer linkages they make possible. As we know, we can now communicate simultaneously with every other spot on the globe – 1 billion humans watched the first step on the moon on their TV sets – and can go from one end of the globe to the other in less than a day. It should also be noted that that day is now agreed upon, with the adoption of a uniform calendar.[21]

Another thread to follow is mapping. From the fourteenth century on, Ptolemaic maps guided the opening up of a new world, in which half of a previously unknown globe spun into perspective. Yet, in this burst of vision, it is forgotten that large areas of that globe were still "dark," with parts of Africa unmapped successfully until the end of the nineteenth century. The poles still existed in unknown fashion until recent explorations. Only in our time has the globe come to be more or less fully known (including the depths of its seas), and seen as "full." Now we have extended our vision to the globe as seen from outside, one of many spherical bodies in space. Our map of the globe must now take its place as part of the mapping of outer space.

Such brief explorations into some of the elements that enter into the factors of globalization indicate the way in which they are rooted in the past. Global History *is* an historical inquiry. Yet, its starting point is unabashedly close to the present, newly identified by many of us as a global epoch. The accounts of global historians are heavily tinged by the scientific, technological, and economic "happenings" of recent times. Whether or not one approves of these happenings, global history, as the study of "Wie es eigentlich gewesen," must inquire into them.

We can now attempt something of a summary of the differences between World History and Global History (while acknowledging that, as with ecumenical and world, world and global history are also to some extent on a spectrum). One student in a seminar tried to put her finger on the matter by saying, "Is it correct to say that one could be a world historian in the 1950s, but not a global historian?" This, indeed, puts it in a nutshell. Before the factors of globalization developed sufficiently and came together in the synergistic fashion that we have tried to highlight, the global as we are defining it did not exist. It hadn't "happened." It couldn't be studied. By the 1990s, if not the 1950s or 1970s, however, it has happened and it can be studied.

Of course, for globalization to occur was not simply a matter of science, technology, and economics. Political developments were also requisite. First, the competition between the USSR and the USA in space was essential for the creation of our increasingly satellite-dependent world, with its attendant communications revolution. Next, the decline of communism eroded the old political-ideological divisions of the world, and left the way open to a true global society, in which all countries can and must participate, though differentially.

Modernization was basically a Western imposition. Globalization, in contrast, is a global process, where a new "civilization," to borrow the term, is being created (for better or for worse) by numerous participants: for example, without intending any rank ordering, Japan looms as large as America; Indonesia, Malaysia, Australia, all play parts; China and India increasingly emerge on the horizon; and Germany and Russia, not to mention the European Union, are all caught up in the "happening" of globalization.[22]

Needless to say, such a happening is not foreordained: Global History is not Whiggish. Or, more to the point, the shape it will take cannot be predicted. As with most historians, global historians are aware of the contingency and uncertainty of human affairs. They are not practicing ecumenical history.

Nor are they practicing world history in the primitive sense of "The whole history of the whole world." Rather, global historians, or at least historians of globalization, are trying to establish a research agenda of a fairly limited nature. They know that each of the factors of globalization must be inquired into rigorously and in empirical detail. They know that new actors must be studied, as they increasingly occupy the center of the historical stage: non-governmental organizations (NGOs), such as the human rights and environmental groups along with other third-sector organizations; the multinationals as having almost the equivalent importance of nation-states (of the 100 entities possessing the largest GDPs, forty-nine are multinationals); and the UN, in all its aspects, but especially in regard to its nascent military role.

Global History is essentially transnational in its subjects of study. Yet it would be a grave error to neglect its study of the nation as well. National history, in fact, must be reexamined in the light of the impact of the forces of globalization on the nation-state, and vice versa. The reality is that nations are not going to go away. They are still the preferred means of large numbers of people for organizing themselves for certain common ends: protection of territory, property, economic production, and not least of all, a strong group identity. The literature on the subject is vast. In short, Global History, while it seeks to transcend national history, is nevertheless engaged with the nation-state as a major actor on the international and global stage.

Again, we see a significant difference from World History. The main focus of the latter has been and is on civilizations. For Global History, these are not the important actors.[23] It is not civilizations that today send up rockets, or operate TV networks, or organize a global division of labor. Empires, the carriers of civilizations in the past, are no more; they have been replaced by nation-states (over 190 as of the time of writing and increasing in number). Global History recognizes this fact, seeks to give it its due, and then to study the processes that are transcending the nation-state framework. (In the process, incidentally, the centuries-old division between civilized and uncivilized, ourselves and the "other," is eliminated; there are no longer any "barbarians," i.e., inferior peoples, in global history, only momentarily less-developed ones.)

ACROSS THE BOUNDARY

Global history is still a novel, emerging project, into whose many aspects inquiry is required. For example, another key question revolves around the issue of identity. Will it make sense to talk about a developing global identity? We must remember that, to take one instance, before America became the United States, the original settlers had a colonial identity that was only gradually supplemented and perhaps eventually replaced by a national one. Can the same process occur with a global identity (even though it would be unattached to a world government, which for the foreseeable future appears utopian or even dystopian)? After all, people are connected today *in actuality* in a way that was only previously dreamt of in a vague aspiration to "humanity." Will their sense of themselves begin to approximate their true situation? And what of the historians who write about global history? Will *their* identification with their materials have to be closely reexamined, i.e., their unthinking national attachments and perspectives reappraised?

We could go on to say much more about various facets of global history, but, hopefully, enough has been sketched so as to support the assertion that it embodies a new consciousness, a new perspective – heavily involved with the work of science and technology that has allowed us to view our planet from space while also highlighting our earth's evolutionary and ecological nature – that separates it from previous endeavors, for example, in world history. Exactly how this will play itself out in actual empirical research can only be answered by the work of future global historians.

The main *raison d'être* of this essay has been to introduce additional conceptual and definitional clarity into our historiographic discussions. Historians, by tradecraft and tradition, are generally suspicious of theory. In global history, however, conscious theoretical considerations, coming from the social sciences as well as the natural, are essential to more particular inquiries. Frequently, historians are also distrustful of or uninterested in work done in other disciplines. In global history, multi- or interdisciplinarity moves front and center. The very notion of globalization, in fact, was first explored by sociologists, and future work on its history will have to engage economists as well as economic historians, political scientists as well as historians *per se*, and so on.[24]

Words do matter – in this case because they determine how we conceive of the work in which we are engaged. Of course, arbitrary definitions can be attached to the terms "Ecumenical," "World" and "Global" History. And however we define them, ambiguity will cling to these terms, as well as overlaps. Still, if work is to go forward effectively, it is essential that we also be as clear as possible as to the differences.

There is space enough for world history to seek its own definition and to pursue its own endeavors – I am obviously doubtful about ecumenical history – without its taking an "imperial" turn, and seeking to encompass global history in its domain. Only if we achieve greater clarity about the definitions involved, corresponding as they do to the historical reality developing about us, can the two subfields of history, world and global, each proceed with greatest effect. Although world and global exist on a continuum, we must become fully aware that we are crossing a significant boundary when we enter upon the history of globalization, or, more succinctly, global history.

3

Periodizing World History

William A. Green

Periodization is both the product and the begetter of theory. The organizing principles upon which we write history, the priorities we assign to various aspects of human endeavor, and the theories of change we adopt to explain the historical process: all are represented in periodization. Once firmly established, periodization exerts formidable, often subliminal, influence on the refinement and elaboration of theory.

The ancient/medieval/modern formula currently in use had its origins in Italian humanist thinking, but acceptance of this tripartite mode did not become universal until the nineteenth century. Since then, tripartite periodization has gripped Western academe like a straitjacket, determining how we organize departments of history, train graduate students, form professional societies, and publish many of our best professional journals. It pervades our habits of mind; it defines turf; it generates many of the abstractions that sustain professional discourse. It determines how we retain images and how we perceive the beginning, middle, and ending of things. It is insidious, and it is sustained by powerful vested interests as well as by sheer inertia.

Scholars who endeavor to formulate an acceptable periodization for world history confront far fewer practical obstacles than those who would seek to alter period frontiers in European history or in other established regional histories. World historians encounter neither an entrenched scheme of epochal divisions nor the dead weight of inertia. There is still a comparatively small professional literature self-consciously addressed to the global perspective. World history has only recently emerged as a field of concentration in a few Ph.D. programs. Consequently, there is not a large and well-established graduate faculty committed by training and tradition to a particular mode of periodization, nor are there commonly acknowledged chronological parameters – fields of preparation for comprehensive examinations – that have imposed a standard epochal division upon the field.

An important practical consideration in periodizing world history involves audience. Our primary audience is university students (usually first- or second-year undergraduates), and the chief vehicle for transmitting world history is the textbook. For practical pedagogical reasons, we are compelled to seek reasonable symmetry in our periodization, even though there are vast discrepancies in the availability of historical data for different eras and for different regions of the globe.

How we periodize world history will be influenced by our objectives in teaching the subject. World historians attempt to explain how human societies have been transformed from bands of hunters and gatherers to the types of people we are today. Even today, in an age of space exploration, hunters and gatherers survive in remote regions of the world. The organizational problems created by such diversity of human experience have occasioned different strategic approaches to writing world history.

One approach provides an integrated mainstream treatment of world history. Another emphasizes regional diversity. The integrated approach routinely focuses on the most developed and complex societies, their ups, their downs, their interactions with one another, and their troubled encounters with less complex peoples. This approach devotes paramount attention to Eurasia. Sub-Saharan Africa, pre-Columbian America, and Australasia are less heralded and, for long stretches of time, they pass largely unnoticed. Integrated mainstream world history enables historians to employ common engines of change to explain the historical process, thereby facilitating the identification of universal epochal frontiers.

Regional strategy embraces more of the world's peoples for longer periods of time whether those peoples functioned within the evolutionary mainstream or at some distance from centers of civilization. Conceived as a congeries of regional histories, this approach to world history emphasizes intercultural understanding and carries less risk of offending political sensitivities. Those who advocate a region-by-region approach are able to argue that for most of human history, really significant interaction between major world civilizations was limited and, for the most part, inconsequential. Because rates of change differ from one region to another, the regional approach discourages the use of overarching theories of change that would facilitate the adoption of universal epochal frontiers.

The burden of proof in these matters rests with the integrationists. They must demonstrate that, from an early time, the destinies of the world's peoples (or at least some significant portion of the world's peoples) have been linked. It must be shown that engines of change operating globally have been *decisive* in propelling both the rate and the direction of change across diverse and distant cultures. Unless integrationist theory is convincing on this question, a fragmented, region-by-region approach to writing (and to periodizing) world history might be the most expedient approach.

In this regard, America presents the integrationist with a significant problem. Major civilizations thrived in four regions of the eastern hemisphere several thousand years before the rise of an equally complex civilization in America. Lasting interactions between all the continents did not begin until after 1492. There may have been common experiences within each of the hemispheres; but, prior to 1492, history at its grandest level could only be hemispheric. A completely integrated world history is only possible after the hemispheres were in permanent contact. Unless one wishes to deny that pre-Columbian America constitutes a significant component of the human experience, some degree of fragmentation in writing and periodizing global history is inescapable.

Ideally, all periodizations should be rooted in disciplined concepts of continuity and change. Historical epochs should exhibit important long-term continuities, and moments of transition between epochs should involve the dissolution of old continuities and the forging of new ones. We must identify how powerful historical forces interacted to generate particular forms of change at particular velocities. To do this, we need a theory of change. A single general theory may suffice if we are confident that the paramount forces governing change in the social organism have been constant across the millennia. If the paramount forces of change have varied from region to region or from one age to another, no single theory will suffice. In that case, we must adjust our theory to accommodate the changes we perceive in historical circumstances. European history provides an example. A neo-Malthusian demographic model has been adopted by numerous historians to explain developments during Europe's medieval period. The utility of the model declines steeply for the eighteenth and nineteenth centuries when rapid expansion of commerce, technology, and industry raised per-capita productivity, thereby diminishing the menace of repeated positive checks.

We cannot hope to be value free in our formulation of theory. Our theories reflect our priorities. Medieval writers assigned God a directing hand in history. Their epochal divisions were drawn at dramatic moments of divine intervention. Marx disdained concepts of divine intervention, insisting that human action has always been driven by material forces. More than any other thinker, Marx established priorities for the twentieth century. Other writers have developed alternative theories of change (often in response to Marx), but all, or nearly all, have agreed on the central importance of material forces.

Until now, the identification of period frontiers has generally taken two forms. One focuses on a coincidence of forces, the other on a leading sector. The coincidental approach identifies the convergence of numerous important developments at a single moment in history. The c.1500 CE watershed in Western tripartite periodization rests largely on this type of observation. In the decades around 1500 numerous important events converged: the Ptolemaic perception of the universe was challenged, printing and gunpowder achieved importance, Columbus reached America and DaGama sailed to India, Constantinople fell to the Turks, Luther launched the Protestant Reformation, and the monarchies of England, France, and Spain were consolidated. Taken together, these happenings, it has been argued, dissolved old continuities and gave rise to a new epoch in Western history.

The leading-sector approach concentrates on one overwhelming source of change that exercises decisive pulling power on all others. Proponents of the leading sector might argue that the discovery of the New World with its abundant natural resources and its effect upon Old World understandings of the cosmos was an event of such monumental proportions that it drew the whole of Western society from one set of norms to another.

Both concepts identify major happenings. Both demand the application of organic theories of change. Unless we adopt the view that significant historical forces like those operating in the fifteenth century coincide randomly, we are obliged to seek a theory of change that explains why and how such coincidences occur. Similarly, we need an organic theory to explain how a leading sector becomes leading and how it is related to the powerful forces that follow in its wake. Without such a theory we are like a person who wants to bake a cake but lacks a recipe. This person might identify the ingredients of a cake and place them together on the kitchen counter, but until a recipe is in hand that explains what weight to give each ingredient, how and when to fold them together, and at what temperature and for what length of time to bake them, he or she will not have a cake.

Historians stand at the opposite end of a similar process. For historians, the cake of history has already been made. The historian's task is to determine, as best he or she can, the ingredients from which it is composed, their relative weights, and the manner by which they were integrated. To make a cake, one needs a recipe. To divine why and how history has evolved as it has, the historian needs a theory of change. Theory does more than identify the ingredients of historical problems. It explains the process which gives those ingredients meaning.

Explicit theories of change were not used in the establishment of Western tripartite periodization. For its inventors the mere recognition that numerous important events converged in time was considered sufficient. In redefining European periodization, organic theory would be essential. The principal models currently in use among Western scholars – market-driven division-of-labor models, neo-Malthusian demographic models, Marxian or world-systems models – are compatible with tripartite periodization and with its sixth- and sixteenth-century epochal divides. Nevertheless, as I have attempted to show elsewhere, those same models (except perhaps world systems) would commend the eleventh and the eighteenth centuries much more emphatically than the sixteenth century as decisive moments of transition in European history.[1]

Can theories of change assist us in periodizing world history? Yes, if. ... Yes, if before the sixteenth century one (or both) of the hemispheres was functionally interrelated to the extent that some common engine (or engines) of change exerted an integrating and profoundly transforming influence upon leading civilizations and their hinterlands. If so, how did each civilization internalize and accommodate this common engine of change? How did this common engine influence both the rate and the direction of change? Finally, how did it affect the relative position of each of the major civilizations over time?

This is no small undertaking. Identifying shared experiences among the major civilizations is not a problem. Demonstrating that a shared experience was the paramount means by which the hemisphere and each civilization within it was transformed *is* a problem. It is one thing to apply organic models to regional civilizations where we have ongoing, well-documented interaction between major historical actors (groups, institutions, individuals). It is another to apply organic models where our knowledge of the interaction between historical actors (in this case, whole civilizations) is limited and where there are few reliable data on how different civilizations responded to and were affected by common stimuli (for example, trade, disease, invasion). For the early millennia of world history, available empirical evidence is insufficient to lend strong support to any general theory of change. The most we can hope for is reasonable plausibility. Reasonable plausibility is not an insignificant or insufficient goal. It is precisely what is being sought by scholars in other areas of historical enquiry where theory is critically important, such as psychohistory.

Where do world historians stand on periodization? What theoretical orientations have they employed? In the main, modern writers of world history texts have adopted progressive, evolutionary, materialist theories of change. Their theoretical orientation corresponds to that of the leading progressive and evolutionary theorists of the nineteenth century. Both have embraced human history from its origins to the present, trying to locate critical stages in humankind's long transition from hunters and gatherers to modern world citizens. Both have assumed that there are common and universal qualities to human nature and that human nature inevitably generates social and cultural development. Both have considered change to be gradual and constant; both have identified the direction of change as evolving from homogeneous to heterogeneous, from simple to complex; both have believed that, on balance, change has occasioned betterment in the quality of human life (nineteenth-century scholars were boldly confident of this; contemporary world historians make this case more subtly, sometimes even apologetically). Both have asked the same kinds of questions: how do people become civilized?

It is modern scholars' methods, not their concept of the problem, that chiefly distinguishes contemporary world historians from Comte and Spencer. Nineteenth-century evolutionists placed highest priority on ethnographic evidence. Because humans were thought to have a uniform nature and because most change was considered to be immanent to society, all humans were thought to have evolved along a single upward gradient. Each culture studied by anthropologists from the most primitive to the most sophisticated was thought to represent a stage in the progressive evolution of the species. Modern world historians have redirected their emphasis from ethnographic to historical forms of evidence. We are less disposed to uniformitarianism. Yet we persist in assuming that human beings, by their common nature, respond to similar stimuli in similar ways. On this premise, world historians continue to seek the unifying laws and regularities that enable them to weave the histories of disparate civilizations together in coherent, integrated fashion.[2]

As a rule, they differentiate past societies hierarchically on the basis of their technologies and by the degree to which invention and innovation permitted division of labor and social stratification. They perceive diffusion as the principal mechanism by which technological progress was realized. It is a process by which distinct civilizations dispersed their special skills, products, organization, and culture outward into adjacent regions, just as pebbles tossed into still water generate a concentric outward movement of ripples. The diffusion of advanced products and modes of behavior compromised and seduced barbaric peoples on the periphery of civilized regions. Converging cultural ripples emanating from various distinct civilizations produced action and reaction, borrowing, change, and adjustment between civilizations. War was one means of diffusion, but trade was its principal vehicle.

Trade-driven division of labor theory, a modern derivative of the work of Adam Smith, has consistently been used as a guide to explain the rate and direction of change within civilizations. This "commercial" theory aids in delineating interactions between civilized peoples and "barbarians," and it provides insight into the manner in which contacts, great or small, among leading civilizations promoted interregional borrowings and thereby stimulated social transformation across cultural frontiers. Though widely employed, this theory has not, in its classic form, been used to embrace all the peoples of a region or all the civilizations of a hemisphere within a single inte-grated historical process. An elaboration upon it – namely, world-systems theory – attempts to do that.

Commercial theory has provided material groundwork for a periodization based on spiritual and intellectual breakthroughs. Having noted the rapid growth of commerce in the first millennium BCE, Karl Jaspers determined that vigorous material development generated intellectual breakthroughs in four regions of high civilization. Jaspers called this the *axial age*, defining the breakthroughs as transcendental, a search for immortality and salvation. The four breakthroughs were monotheism among Jews, rational philosophy in Greece, Confucianism and Taoism in China, Buddhism and Jainism in India.[3]

Marshall G. S. Hodgson adopted Jaspers's formulation, advocating a peri-odization that divided world history into two unequal compartments: an *agrarian age*, 7000 BCE to about 1800 CE, and a *technical age* since 1800. The late agrarian age was subdivided into three epochs: *preaxial* (3000–800 BCE), *axial* (800–200 BCE), and *postaxial* (200 BCE–1800 CE). Rising prosperity, accelerated by interregional commerce, provided a fertile intellectual climate for these breakthroughs, Hodgson contended. In the amalgam of Judaic monotheism and Greco-Roman philosophy, Christianity took root. From this triad emerged Islam. Apart from these two "secondary-stage revolutions," few profound religious and philosophical revolutions have arisen since the first millennium BCE.[4]

These axial-age "breakthroughs" provoke questions about the relationship between material forces and cultural values. Did one promote the other, either directly or indirectly? Were the four transcendental breakthroughs linked in any discernible way? Do they provide evidence of interregional inte-gration across the hemisphere? Or, were these breakthroughs distinct phe-nomena, connected only to the extent that they emerged in societies that possessed a literary tradition and some measure of material comfort and social stratification?

These questions were addressed by two separate groups of scholars. Both concluded that transcendental breakthroughs were not the product of direct diffusion of ideas from one civilization to another.[5] Chinese civilization was quite insulated; transformations in India were a derivative of local conditions and culture. Both Greeks and Jews were influenced by Mesopotamian and Egyptian cultures, but the different nature of their societies and the distinct character of their breakthroughs precludes the likelihood that they had a linked experience. Two great civilizations of the age did not have transcen-dental breakthroughs: Egypt and Assyria. The scholars who participated in these studies agreed that high material development was a necessary, if not sufficient, requisite for a breakthrough, but the only shared impulse of all axial-age movements was "the strain toward transcendence."[6] Hodgson died in 1968, leaving unfinished a world history that may have adopted the axial age as a pivot of world periodization. Subsequent world historians have not pursued his insight.

In 1978 Geoffrey Barraclough observed that "Marxism is the only coherent theory of the evolution of man in society, and in that sense the only philosophy of history, which exercises a demonstrable influence over the minds of historians today."[7] The appeal of Marxism has declined precipitously in recent years. World-systems theory has usurped its influence. The most noted practitioner of world-systems theory, Immanuel Wallerstein, has used it to achieve a tightly integrated analysis of the Atlantic basin over the last five centuries. World-systems theory, while neo-Marxist in origin, is a complex elaboration upon trade-driven division of labor theory. It is progressive, evolutionary, and materialist. Although Wallerstein himself questions the utility of the model for pre-1460 world history, others strongly advocate its adoption as a means of integrating regional histories of the eastern hemisphere in a single historical process. Janet Abu-Lughod has described a world system centered in the Middle East during the thirteenth century.[8] William McNeill encourages use of the world system as an overarching ecumenical process as early as 1700 BCE.[9] André Gunder Frank and Barry Gills recommend world-systems analysis as the framework for Afro-Eurasian history beginning at least as early as 2700 BCE.[10]

Frank is the most explicit, if most extreme, theoretician for premodern application of the world-systems approach. He discards traditional categories of analysis, challenges standard notions of periodization, and presents a new paradigm for the study of world history. For the last 5000 years – possibly more, writes Frank – a world system has operated across Afro-Eurasia based upon the transfer of economic surplus between regions. Those transfers integrated regional modes of exploitation and accumulation into an overarching, interpenetrating, competitive order. A universal drive for capital accumulation was the primary motor of change across the hemisphere. Each region possessed a hegemonic center connected to a dependent periphery and to a distant hinterland with which it interacted. The consistent outward reach of these regional systems generated increased interregional economic exchange and competition. Shifting technological advantage, among other forces, enabled first one, then another, of the great regional civilizations to exert superhegemony over others.

Frank and Gills offer a simple model to demonstrate how exchanges of surplus linked not just the elites of separate regions, but the whole economic, political, social, and ideological character of their societies. When the elite of B acquired surplus extracted by the elite of A (whatever the mode of extraction may have been), that surplus linked the two societies' "processes of surplus management, their structures of exploitation and oppression by class and gender, and their institutions of the state and the economy."[11] If B subsequently exchanged part of that surplus to C, then not only were B and C systemically linked in the same "over-arching system of accumulation," but so too were A and C. For Frank, modes of accumulation, not modes of production, are central. His readers (particularly the Marxists among them) are implored to abandon notions of feudalism, capitalism, socialism, and the transitions between them as being useless impediments to a correct world vision.[12]

The Afro-Eurasian world system described by Frank and Gills experienced alternating cycles of expanding and contracting accumulation. These cycles, hemispheric in scope, were generally four to five centuries long; each had an *up* A phase (expanding accumulation) followed by a *down* B phase (contracting accumulation), and each of these phases usually occupied about two centuries. The establishment of regional hegemonies occurred during A phases, sometimes producing a system-wide superhegemon. Periods of contraction (weakening and instability) were often punctuated by invasions from the hinterland, as, for example, the Barbarian invasions of the Roman Empire or the Mongol invasions across Asia. The concept of tying B phases to barbarian implosions seems reasonable, and in some times and in some places it is confirmed by evidence. For some scholars, however, accepting the idea of A phases and B phases operating across a whole hemisphere two thousand years BCE requires a leap of faith. In any case, it can be demonstrated that major implosions from the hinterland between 1700 BCE and 1300 CE have not always synchronized tightly with Frank's B phases.

Since Frank believes an integrated world system was in place several millennia before Europeans expanded to the New World, for him the rise of the West was just one of many hegemonic shifts within the world system. He is therefore loath to focus undue weight on 1492 or to commend Wallerstein's association of Europe's discovery and exploitation of America with the breakthrough to capitalism. Whether European capitalism originated with the exploitation of the New World – which Frank questions – is not a decisive issue.

Will world-systems theory provide manageable and coherent periodization for world history? It is too early to know. No one has written a comprehensive world history using world-systems theory as the integrating concept. Skeptics would argue, with good reason, that the overarching theoretical work of scholars like Frank exceeds our current capacity to synthesize critical information from various regional histories. We simply do not know how universal world-systems history will play out, what continuities and discontinuities will command highest attention. Although world-systems theory and related approaches include several distinguished adherents, debate on the matter is just beginning. This is a time for asking questions that will inform the debate.

One can concede the logic of Frank's point that exchanges of surplus between A, B, and C may have linked the three parties in one overarching system of accumulation. What needs answering is how important, in relation to all other forces at work in archaic and ancient societies, such exchanges were. What was the relative value of foreign as opposed to domestic exchange in these societies? What proportion of aggregate annual income was represented by interregional exchange? To what extent were interregional exchanges conducted in strategic supplies, raw materials, or other goods that may have affected the defense capabilities of hegemonic elites, whether those supplies were used to facilitate the maintenance of order at home or to protect territorial frontiers? What evidence do we have that the interregional exchange of surplus altered cultural habits, value systems, and religious orientations in significant ways? It may be remembered that scholars who explored relationships between material development and axial-age transcendental breakthroughs found no consistent correlation between the scale of interregional commercial contacts and the achievement of transcendental religious or intellectual breakthroughs.

We know that people living in different cultures often respond differently to economic stimuli and that people of the same culture respond differently at different times.[13] Max Weber demonstrated in his *Protestant Ethic and the Spirit of Capitalism* (1904–5) how, over time, economic orientations changed significantly within Europe. The strong materialist bias of our time often prompts us to ascribe powerful economic motives to historical actors whose chief incentives were not materialist. This is true of two giant figures of European overseas expansion. The contemporary biographer of Prince Henry the Navigator, Zurara, was explicit on the matter. Although Henry was not immune to material interests, his obsession with discovery was overwhelmingly driven by religious motives.[14] Pauline Moffitt Watts makes a similar point in evaluating the cosmological orientation of Christopher Columbus.[15]

Whatever reservations one might have about the capacity of the center–periphery–hinterland model to provide an integrated explanation of historical development, we are well advised to study world-systems theory for suggestions on the timing of important transitions – the ebb and flow of A and B phases and the rise of particular hegemons or superhegemons. Although Frank identifies A and B phases, his work is not helpful to those who seek a pragmatically manageable periodization. Unless I misconstrue his arguments, Frank sees 5,000 years of world-system history as a comprehensive whole. Even though hegemonic power shifted from one locus to another, there have been no rents in the historical fabric, no wrenching transitions. In the twentieth century, he argues, hegemony has shifted from Europe to America to Japan. To presume that a date like 1492 should represent a global watershed is, for Frank, an unacceptably Eurocentric notion.

William McNeill does not fully endorse world-systems theory, although he finds its aspirations praiseworthy. He sees a Middle Eastern world system developing around 1700 BCE. After 1000 BCE, he would merge Greek, Middle Eastern, and Indian societies into one expansive Middle Eastern "great society." China would join this world system around 100 BCE with the opening of caravan trade to Syria. Lethal diseases spread along the expanded trade routes, producing severe demographic decline in both the Mediterranean and Chinese spheres in the third century CE. The recovery that began in the sixth century was accelerated by the rise of Islam. Superhegemony passed from the Islamic regions to China around 1000 AD and to Europe after 1500.[16] I am not certain how these observations translate into formal periodization, if indeed that is McNeill's intention. One might presume something like the following: segment one, to 1700 BCE; segment two, from 1700 BCE to c.300/600 CE; segment three, c.300/600 to 1500; segment four, since 1500.

McNeill has shown us that epidemic disease has had a powerful impact on world history, notably in the demographic declines of Chinese and Mediterranean civilizations after the second century AD, in the formation of a single hemispheric disease pool by about 1000 AD, in the eruptions of bubonic plague in the sixth and fourteenth centuries, and in the devastation of native Americans after 1492. Still, it is hard to see how one could employ disease as the central driving force in human affairs, although disease must serve as a major factor in any episodic construction of period frontiers.

The issue of disease does provoke some doubt about the extent to which interregional exchange via the world system had integrated the eastern hemisphere before the second century BCE. If the spread of lethal disease across trade routes from the Pacific to the Mediterranean at the end of the second century occasioned significant demographic decline at both ends of the system, why, it must be asked, were these catastrophic effects so long delayed? If an "overarching" and truly "interpenetrating" world system had existed for a millennium or two, is it not probable that these destructive biological effects, occasioned as they were by interregional contacts, would have been experienced earlier?

Beside world-systems theory, there are several avenues of approach that might, in time, provide an overarching theoretical foundation for world history. One, perhaps the most compelling of them all, is ecological. It would involve interpreting human experience in the context of a universal eco-

system in which people have been involved in complex patterns of interdependence with all other forms of life, animal and vegetable.[17] Some scholars
have suggested gender relations as a basis for the organization of world history
courses, if not for the structuring of comprehensive texts. Neither of these
orientations currently commands the attention given to world systems. In
fact, no general theory of change being employed by world historians today is
as fully refined or as well articulated as world-systems theory. It is a powerful
explanatory tool. Numerous problems have to be resolved in the theory;
numerous questions must be answered. The jury remains out.

In the meantime, we must go on writing and teaching world history,
updating texts and reorganizing syllabi. We have to make choices about coverage and about periodization. There is a strong possibility that neither
world-systems theory, nor ecological theory, nor any other theory will provide
a satisfactory framework for all of world history. If, in the end, we are obliged
to accept some degree of fragmentation in our presentation of world history,
should we not go a further step and concede to a decidedly regional approach,
giving roughly equal attention to all regions of the globe? This would gratify
cultural relativists and those who resent the minimal attention usually given
to sub-Saharan Africa and pre-Columbian America. Here, the response
should be a practical and purely sensible one. It makes no more sense endlessly to disassemble our subject than it does to erect unities where they may
not exist. Some people, some places, some institutions, and some belief systems are more enduring, more significant, more universal, and more influential to the whole human experience than others. They demand primary
attention. The balance being struck by most writers of world history seems to
me a correct one. Peoples who functioned at great distance from the mainstream should not be ignored; neither should they serve as major elements in
the presentation of or the periodization of world history.

Although we may lack an overarching and integrating theoretical framework for periodizing world history, we still have the practical need, as authors
and teachers, to separate six millennia of human experience in chronological
compartments having some measure of coherence. For the moment, we are
compelled to exercise arbitrary eclectic judgments on global periodization,
not unlike the writers and teachers whose judgments about European history
gradually produced Western tripartite periodization. This may be regrettable.
It is not disastrous. It involves our seeking a practical solution to an
inescapable pedagogical problem. Most world historians have personal preferences on periodization. Few of these preferences are lodged in systematic
theory, yet many of them are highly similar even though similarities may arise
for different reasons.

I too have a preferred formulation which, I readily admit, is highly eclectic and *not* the product of an overarching and systematic theory of change. It has four parts, and I proffer it humbly. Like Hodgson, I would have a long early sweep, from 3000 BCE to roughly 1000/800 BCE. My second period, 1000/800 BCE to 400/600 CE, would extend through the several regional efflorescences of this era to the demographic crises and the barbarian implosions that disturbed both the East and West, roughly 400/600 AD. The third age, emphasizing exceptional Islamic and Chinese achievement, would taper toward 1492.

To me, 1492 is a commanding moment of global transition for many material and cosmological reasons, none being more compelling than the biological and ecological ones studied by Alfred Crosby. Charges of Eurocentrism do not trouble me. There is no necessary connection between Eurocentrism and the adoption of a world history watershed at 1492. Had the Pacific been less formidable and had the Chinese managed to discover America in 1492, we would be just as likely to advance that date as a major global watershed. In any case, too many contemporary Western scholars are obsessed about Eurocentrism. Eurocentrism takes many forms. It is ironic that some of the most dedicated historical materialists, scholars like André Gunder Frank, are quick to condemn Eurocentrism in others. Barraclough considered such sturdy materialism to be a decidedly Western (one might say, European) orientation to the past. He wondered whether world history written from an Asian perspective would not be substantially less materialist. I do as well.

PART II

Rethinking Structure, Agency, and Ideology

4

The World-System Perspective in the Construction of Economic History

Janet Lippman Abu-Lughod

I INTRODUCTION

In that Empire, the Art of Cartography reached such Perfection that the map of a single Province occupied a whole City and the map of the Empire, a whole Province. In time those Enormous Maps no longer sufficed and the Colleges of Cartographers raised a Map of the Empire that was the size of the Empire and coincided with it exactly ... the Following Generations understood that the expanded Map was Useless, and ... relinquished it to the Inclemencies of the Sun and ... Winters.

Jorge Borges[1]

Historians are often asked to review books whose contents overlap to some extent with works they published earlier. Since the appearance of my *Before European Hegemony*,[2] three such books came to me for review. One, by Jim Blaut, "confirmed" many of my views about Eurocentrism and world systems, although I thought the author was *too* extreme in his critique of conventional scholarship, which he dismissed as pure Western intellectual bias.[3] The other two were more unsettling to my confidence, because they were so sincere and temperate, while viewing "my period" through such very different optics.

The first, by historian Alan Smith, was yet another entry into the debate about why the West "rose" and how Europe transformed the "rest of the world" after 1400.[4] It joined the enormous literature about the European-centered world system, primarily from the sixteenth century onward. His opening three chapters, however, examined the pre-sixteenth-century world-system, asking "why the wider world was unable to sustain the momentum it once generated and [to] maintain the lead over Europe it once enjoyed" (231). Despite Smith's attempts to make his book less dismissive of Eastern accomplishments, he ended with a commonly encountered explanation: that Eastern cultures lost their dynamism because they failed to develop Western-style capitalism, a thesis refuted in my *Before European Hegemony*, which Smith could not respond to because it came out after he completed his text.[5]

This was disconcerting, to say the least. How had we reached such different conclusions? Smith tended to accept the existing "line" of many Western historians on the pre-sixteenth-century period, buttressing his discussion chiefly by references to their secondary sources, whereas I had questioned this received wisdom. Stimulated by doubts and alternative hypotheses, I had therefore examined far more (and somewhat different) secondary sources and had spent much more time examining primary sources, at least those that were available in French, English, and German translations. The end result was a narrative that reconceptualized the period. Who is right? I don't know. But the discrepancies between his account and mine are great. Jim Blaut would have dismissed Smith's book as just another example of Eurocentric "tunnel vision," but I am less sanguine about this "easy way out."

The second book – with a very different optic and one that clearly cannot be dismissed as Eurocentric – was Jerry Bentley's *Old World Encounters*,[6] which I consider a sound and even exciting addition to the growing literature on the premodern world system. Bentley and I share a commitment to examining world history through more than Western eyes[7] and an assumption that any attempt to write global history must treat the parts of the world as interconnected and interactive. And yet, the basic variables we used to trace such interconnectedness and subsystem integration differed drastically.

For the sake of simplicity one can think of the process of globalization as taking place along three related dimensions: the political, the economic, and the cultural, although these are always intertwined.[8] In this explanatory trinity of "causes," Jerry Bentley's *Old World Encounters* comes down squarely in the cultural camp. Paying special attention to ideological, religious, and other cultural forces, Bentley reconceptualizes the global system between roughly 800 and 1500, arguing convincingly and with copious examples that the world's "great" religions played central roles in spreading and channeling not only cultural patterns but trade and political alliances in the premodern world. Using paths of religious conversion and selective migratory movements of traders, jurists, and priests as his most powerful explanatory variables, he reminds us secularists that we cannot afford to ignore religious factors if we are to understand the causes and consequences of the specific geographical expansions that gave shape to global patterns over centuries of fluidity and change.[9]

In contrast, until fairly recently global histories of premodern times were heavily focused on political and military empires, which may account for the error Immanuel Wallerstein makes when he claims (in *The Modern World-System*, volume 1) that before the sixteenth century, there were only world empires – not world economies making up a singular world system in which trade and the division of labor yielded an increasingly globalized economic system. It has been the task of other scholars to support the primacy Wallerstein gave to economic factors, but to argue that such world economies were also found much earlier and in non-European places.[10] Their works demonstrate that at a number of times and places in the premodern period, complex interregional, if not international, trading systems developed whose range far exceeded that of any empire. While acknowledging the significance of military power and cultural affinities, these works tend to make economic variables central.

So – who is right? Or is that the wrong question? If we grant that, as the epigraph reminds us, a map of the world as large as the world would be useless, then some principles of selection and interpretation are necessary to organize the materials. However, this leaves open a number of "right paths." I want to argue in this essay that multiple visions can be enriching, even though fraught with difficulties and confusion.

II METATHEORETICAL DILEMMAS

The more I work in the field of global history, the more convinced I become that definitive answers to historical questions are impossible, and the more intrigued I have become with the process of "making history."[11] And my *crise de conscience* has now begun to spread alarmingly to all of the social sciences as well. My concerns are, of course, not new. In his 1931 review[12] of Werner Sombart's *Die Drei Nationalökonomien* Robert Park, taking a much more philosophical and sanguine position than I can manage, readily acknowledges that:

> Historical knowledge is based on, and limited by, experience and insight; the insight of the man [sic] who writes, but also the insight of the man [sic] who reads. Therefore, as has been frequently pointed out, history has to be constantly rewritten to make it intelligible to each new generation. The social sciences are more or less in the same situation as history.[13]

The issue, then, is not about "making" history, but about "remaking" it.

However, that moves us no closer to a resolution, especially when the passage of time alone does not account for the discrepancies.[14]

I am not taking a radical "postmodernist" position that leaves readers without criteria for discriminating among different accounts of history. Radical hermeneutics has gone too far, in my opinion. While we must all modestly acknowledge the limitations of knowledge, I do believe that some accounts are "more credible" than others, and that while there is no absolute metric against which to measure "truth" in interpretation, there are certainly some guidelines governing methodological integrity and responsibility, and some ways to strengthen reflexivity in a writer.[15] If we did not believe something of this sort, we would have to give up all hope that "progress" is possible in the rewriting of history. I find support for this belief from those very philosophers and epistemologists whose writings have sometimes been cited to buttress discussions of the relativity of all knowledge. Gadamer's immunizing prescription, which I will follow for the rest of this essay, is reflexivity.[16]

But before that, let me begin with the obvious point that all narrative is "constructed" by an author, or to play with Marx's phrase, "men and women make their historical narratives, but not entirely as they choose." This statement is less controversial when applied to the narratives of fiction writers, so we might first present some quotations from practitioners of the art of fiction before proceeding to "historical science."

The first quotation I take from novelist Jeanette Winterson's book, *Oranges Are Not the Only Fruit*.[17]

> Of course that is not the whole story, but that is the way of stories; we make them what we will. It's a way of explaining the universe while leaving the universe unexplained. ... Every one who tells a story tells it differently, just to remind us that everybody sees it differently. ... People like to separate storytelling which is not fact from history which is fact. ... Very often history is a means of denying the past. Denying the past is to refuse to recognise its integrity. To fit it, force it, ... to suck out the spirit until it looks the way you think it should. We are all historians in our small way.

The second quotation comes from Richard Wright's preface to *Native Son*.[18] Wright says that every imaginative novel:

> represents the merging of two extremes; it is an intensely intimate expression ... couched in terms of the most objective and commonly known events ... at once something private and public. ... Confounding the author ... is the dogging knowledge that his imagination is a kind of community medium of exchange: what he has read, felt, seen, thought, and remembered is translated into extensions as impersonal as a worn dollar bill.

Wright's statement is as applicable to history writing as it is to fiction, although social scientists may be more comfortable with the term "vision" than "imagination."

Historical narrative, however, is not the same as fiction. It is far more dependent upon the collective scholarship of others, and requires judgment, "objectivity," scholarly integrity, and a lot of hard work in dusty archives and libraries. But *significant* historical narrative also involves something else which is extremely "personal." It requires, in addition to immersion in what scholars have come to "know," a partial disengagement from and questioning of that collective enterprise. If disengagement did not take place, we would be condemned always to repeat the same plot, in an endless no-exit loop.

Some analysts have focused on the creative role that new "facts" (anomalies) play in forcing us to recast our narratives.[19] But this is not the only, nor even the most important source of change. Although to some it may sound mystical, the real "way out" is synthetic imagination or vision. Certainly, the element of vision is very strong in writers whose global histories precede those of Smith and Bentley – among others, Eric Wolf, Eric Hobsbawm, Lefton Stavrianos, Philip Curtin, Charles Tilly, and, above all, William McNeill. Without vision one cannot write global history, because otherwise one is lost in a morass of details, many of them accidentally preserved, and incompletely codified.

I became more and more convinced of the significance of imagination or vision when trying to write synthetic history in *Before European Hegemony*. After spending five years absorbing an enormous amount of what was in the historical "community medium of exchange" on the thirteenth century, I stopped researching when I found a pattern that made sense to me. Once that private vision took hold, albeit mysteriously generated not only out of all the sources I had read but everything I had thought about over decades, I stopped researching. But personal visions may be inspired by others. For me, the crucial influence was Immanuel Wallerstein's vision conveyed in the first volume of *The Modern World-System*, a book that appeared in 1974. His approach unlocked a perspective I had long sought, one adumbrated in earlier work by Fernand Braudel[20] but brought more clearly into focus in his *Civilization & Capitalism*. Because of this, I am often referred to as a "world-systems" person. I presume that is why I was asked to give a paper on this approach at the World History Conference. But I shall not try to defend Wallerstein's particular vision, *in strictu senso*, because I believe a global perspective is broader and more flexible than the one adopted by Wallerstein. Its chief value lies in its search for explanations beyond the narrow confines of historical specialization in a given time and place. It is a vision that gives depth of perspective in historical (re)construction.

I became increasingly absorbed with the problem of how historians or social scientists arrive at such visions. This in turn led me to explore on what grounds new visions might either be rejected as too imaginary, or at least provisionally accepted as somewhat more credible than their predecessors. In arriving at my own interpretation of the global system in the thirteenth century I tried to exercise scholarly diligence and strove for integrity in the process of reaching it. That I did not always succeed is, of course, a given. One part of diligence was that, in every subarea in which I was trying to reconstruct history, I found many careful historians who had been trying to reach partial conclusions. My dilemma was this. I had to evaluate their partial syntheses even though I actually possessed *less* concrete information on the particulars than they had. Was this legitimate? How much did my judgment enter into this process?

In thinking over how I culled material from secondary sources, the first thing I note is that I came to "trust" certain historians more than others and turned to those "trusted informants" for further guidance and additional bibliography. Perhaps something like a "self-fulfilling prophecy" was at work; such choices gradually foreclosed access to other potentially competing forms of explanation.

How did I reach such judgments about relative trustworthiness? In part, I was impressed with the degree of mastery over known sources which "good" historians seemed to command. Second, however, I was also affected by their comprehensive coverage of what I considered to be important "variables."[21] At the same time, I came to distrust explanations advanced by some locale-centered historians. I felt that out of ignorance they sometimes neglected non-local causes which, it seemed to me, were patently responsible for local events. At other times, again from tunnel vision, they seemed to emphasize the *unique* aspect of a given local occurrence, without recognizing that almost identical processes were taking place simultaneously in other parts of the world.[22]

As a consequence of a process of criticism, trust, acceptance, and rejection, a parallel process of closure inevitably began to occur in my mind. It is this latter process that particularly interests me. And this returns me to Gadamer, who called for reflexivity and self-conscious awareness, not as a way of guaranteeing objectivity (which is neither possible nor, if I read him correctly, desirable),[23] but as an antidote to *hubris*. In what follows I shall try to be faithful to Gadamer's prescription.

It seems to me that writing synthetic history is really not very different from writing any other type of social science analysis, even an "ethnography" in which, presumably, one has greater (and less biased) access to "what is happening" than one has to the accidental residues of the past with which historians must work.[24] I mentioned this to a colleague who appreciated the problem immediately and suggested I look at Kurt Wolff's book, *Surrender and Catch*.[25]

In brief, "surrender" refers to an initial stage of true openness, a certain self-restraint that a researcher needs to exercise to prevent premature interpretation. "Bracketing of prior knowledge" might be an appropriate term here. Those of us who have done sociological fieldwork recognize in this one of its cardinal rules.[26] At the early stages of research one wants, as much as is humanly possible, to "bracket" the cultural-and-idiosyncratic apperception mass that observers carry with them to "make sense" of the world.[27] In the beginning, one also engages in "thought experiments" and the search for "counterfactuals." Paul Deising, in a recent book, emphasizes how important a role counterfactuals play in guarding against false cognition.[28] Since social psychologists have found that "subjects are apparently not aware of their own cognitive processes," the only way to guard against a confirmatory bias is through counterfactuals, where one tries to prove the opposite. In history, the testimony of "the other" constitutes a starting point for the location of counterfactual interpretation.

But although we can accept the theoretical importance of absolute openness, we also know that it is psychologically impossible. In William James's "big booming confusion" of the world, one will always be somewhat selective, if only to keep one's sanity. All that "surrender" requires, then, is a self-conscious effort to avoid premature closure.

However, one cannot suspend closure forever – nor could one ever write anything in its absence. Closure, however involuntary, is what I think Wolff meant by "catch." In ethnography and other social science research, we often use the term "redundancy" to operationalize that moment. We tell our graduate students that they have gone to enough meetings, made enough observations, interviewed a sufficient sample, and so on, when they sense that they are no longer "learning anything new." The same thing happens in historical research.

That makes it sound as though the process were an objective one. Quite the contrary; it is highly subjective. Once we have "caught" – or more accurately, "been caught by" – an explanation that makes sense to us, our receptivity declines precipitously. The "catch" phase is what psychologists would call the apprehension of a gestalt or pattern. Good historical and social science writing is distinguished from dull and uninteresting work exactly by the presence of this pattern recognition (some call it vision) and by the ability of the writer to narrate it in a way that "convinces" readers and influences them to "see" the patterning in the material which, admittedly, has thus been selected to substantiate it.

Where does that gestalt come from? I would suggest that there are three necessary (but not necessarily sufficient) sources of that "catching" of patterns:[29] *eccentricity, ideology, and idiosyncrasy.* I have intentionally selected terms that to most practitioners of science have very negative connotations. They are the antithesis of the presumed ideals of scientific inquiry, namely: objectivity (in the sense of being uninfluenced by the perspective of the observer); value- or at least interest-free (in the sense that predilections or biases of a non-scientific sort do not enter the observations); and inter-subjectivity (in that scientific findings are strengthened when they are reproducible, rather than idiosyncratic).

I want to demonstrate that these three "sins" are not only inevitable but in some ways highly creative. It is they that yield the unique gestalt of a project which then becomes part of the apperception mass of later scholars. Each new gestalt enriches the collective enterprise of constructing narratives. While reflexivity can minimize the distortions that the three "sins" introduce, such "distortions" are part and parcel of creativity. They are "new seeings" that grow out of that strange combination of the personal and the collective that Richard Wright makes the central desideratum of an imaginative novel. In that sense, they are not so much sinful as enabling. How does one strike a balance between these two?

Eccentricity

Eccentricity is the mirror image of ethnocentricity. By ethnocentrism I refer to the natural embeddedness of observers in their own time and place and to the cognitive maps to the world and their discipline according to which they have learned to organize their materials. Gadamer refers to this as the observer's historicity. Language codes are only a part of this, albeit an important part. My way of attempting to deal with this was to try to examine not only documents from my own time and place, but to enlarge the range of the collective dialogue by reading primary documents (albeit in translation!) from as many different places in the thirteenth-century world system as I could, attempting *verstehen* while also treating these texts as evidence not for what happened, but for how what happened was selectively crafted into a narrative that both revealed and concealed. Where possible, I tried to put texts from different perspectives in dialogue with one another: for example, I self-consciously paired accounts of the Crusades as described by Christian and Muslim writers, or descriptions by port officials and by the merchants themselves of what happened to foreign traders in Chinese ports. I was trying to de-center accounts, to view them ex-centrically. A world-system perspective helped me to do this.

Ideology

However, I could not help but select from the non-Western accounts those elements that seemed to me to be significant and meaningful. And I could only judge evidence as significant and meaningful when it fitted into my culture's definitions of evidence[30] – and thus into my culture's "ideology." By ideology, then, I mean deep sets of beliefs about how the world works. Some of my colleagues at the New School call this "theory," whereas Kuhnians tend to call it a paradigm. But it is important to recognize that, even here, there is opportunity for creativity. While certain forms of explanation are eliminated by ethnocentrically determined parameters, every culture's ideological repertoire includes a range and variety of often mutually exclusive positions, from which culture-bound historians and social scientists select.

Certain cynics dismiss what I am calling "inevitable ideology" as mere irrationality. Thus, David Faust[31] seems to suggest that a Kuhnian paradigm serves mainly as a *nonrational aid* to scientific judgment. A paradigm tells us mostly about cognitive processes, rather than about the "real world." Deising, who does not necessarily agree with the radical view that paradigms are merely codified biases or irrational beliefs, cites Faust as arguing that everything is ideology, in the sense I am using the term. Paraphrasing Faust's position Deising says:

> Given the complex and contradictory data available in any scientific field, scientists are likely to nonreason every which way and produce a great variety of incompatible theories almost at random. But a striking paradigm channels their thinking (availability bias) and produces nonrational agreement. The result is a scientific community sharing a single (arbitrary) theory. This is precisely what Lakatos[32] called "mob psychology" in his (mis)interpretation of Kuhn, except that he didn't like the idea; he assumed that scientists are rational. Similarly, Nisbett and Ross[33] observe that the effect of scientific evidence is to polarize opinion, since supporters of each theory interpret the evidence to fit their theory and become convinced that they are right and everyone else wrong.[34]

There is some truth in this. As a political economist I believe that political and economic factors play a central role in shaping world history. Others may proceed from an ideology with a different foundation. I accept the fact that persons with intellectual integrity, but whose deep belief system or ideology is different from mine, will write a narrative that differs from mine, as did Jerry Bentley. We seem not to be able to convince one another, but I am willing to acknowledge that our narratives can enrich one another. My responsibility is only to guard against naively deducing "reality" from my ideology, and that can be accomplished to some extent by reflexivity and an exposure to other competing ideologies.

I also do believe in chaos theories – in nonlinear irregularities that may conceal regularities, and in trajectories where similar starting points can lead to perfectly reasonable, *but different* and therefore not completely predictable outcomes. I also believe in the systemic quality of the world, which means that there is no simple unilinear relationship between "independent" and "dependent" variables. In fact, I believe so strongly in this paradigm that I literally cannot see how a historian can operate with a different set of beliefs about the world.[35] But note that a predilection for approaches and a sensitivity to specific types of evidence do not give me answers, only a terrain for preferential investigation. Once on my terrain, I still must keep my eyes open. But what I see is partially idiosyncratic.

Idiosyncrasy

Idiosyncrasy is the easiest "sin" to define and yet the hardest to defend against. It is the personal – what makes us individuals, what gives to any author his or her "voice," and I would add, almost everything that makes books different from one another. The biography of an author (whether of history or ethnography) does make a difference in the gestalt the author will "catch."[36] It seems not at all accidental to me, then, that many of the major transformations in how we think about the world have come from persons at the margin of a discipline.

Non-historians are more likely to produce novelty than very well-trained ones. Non-specialists may see things quite differently from the "outside." And scientists must often undergo a process of forceful "unseeing" before they can be captured by a new gestalt. When one reads the biographies of the major figures who have contributed to chaos theory, for example, one learns that they have all "withdrawn" and "rejected," as their first steps in exploring new ways of seeing. The discontinuities of their professional careers are striking. It is as if they *need* to bracket what they know in order to know something else. And in this, biography plays a surprisingly major part. Similar characteristics emerge when one examines the lives of individuals who have contributed to artificial intelligence and other new fields of investigation.[37]

In short, eccentricity allows one to escape from the ethnocentricism of accumulated wisdom, ideology gives the necessary focus for any investigation, and idiosyncrasy, rather than something to be extirpated, is the major source of new vision. But from where can this new vision come? From idiosyncrasy, in the sense of the unique process of accumulating within a single mind an atypical accretion of training, information, and experiences, all of which must with considerable struggle be arranged in a coherent pattern. That struggle often takes place below the level of full consciousness. We know only that, out of a massive chaos generated by the interaction between our "material" and ourselves, at some deep level we have a series of visions and experience closure – often quite suddenly after sleep, but only after long periods of steady "data gazing." And we are caught.

III FINAL COMMENT

Therefore, although eccentricity, ideology, and idiosyncrasy have traditionally been viewed as "sins" in conventional epistemology, my argument is that not only are they inevitable, but, if treated with caution and complexity, they can also be enabling. In this essay I have stressed "hermeneutical" issues. But please do not misunderstand me. I do not intend to substitute these elements of creativity for *criteria* of scholarly excellence or even "correctness."

Thus far my discussion has been a bit mystical and disembodied, as if "scholarship" were detached from the "real world" and insulated from the social forces that produce it. It would be misleading to leave the reader with such a partial view. First, under "ideology" I have assumed throughout the more conventional wisdom of a more standard "sociology of knowledge," one that acknowledges that the struggle for truth is a fundamentally political matter.[38] As feminist theorists have recently stressed (coming after a long line of other "dissident" thinkers, of which the most noted is Gramsci), control over the determination of "truth" is the real power in this world. Hegemony in the power to define is what all scholars seek, whether they acknowledge this or not. Thus, after "surrender" and "catch" comes the rhetoric of convincing. But might does not make right, either for orthodoxy or dissent. *La luta continua.*

My most fundamental assumption, however, is that there is a real world out there, even if human frailty prevents its full knowledge and understanding. So long as one recognizes that all knowledge is only tentative, and that closure is only temporarily attained in that ambiguous space between "evidence," with its connection to the real world, and "rhetoric," with its connection to the power structure within which reality is struggled over, we can take courage and continue our work.

I personally have taken heart again, sustained by the wise humility of John Fairbank, one of the great scholars of Chinese history. He advised

> authors ... to look back and give us some record of how their work developed, not because their works are important (they may turn out to be unimportant) but because we need to know more of the process of history writing. Writers of history are not just observers. ... Their view of what "really" happened is

filtered first through spotty and often hit-or-miss screens of available evidence, and second through the prisms of their own interest, selection, and interpretation of the evidence they see. ... Once an author looks back at what he thought he was trying to do, many perspectives emerge. Foremost is that of ignorance. ... Fortunately, no one has to regard it as the last word.[39]

Had I found this quotation before writing a draft of this essay, I could have saved many words and much time. But I consider this conference as part of an ongoing dialogue you historians have been having all along. I am pleased that you should have asked me to join in; perhaps my view as an outsider may offer some words that have not already been spoken before and better.

5

Bringing Ideas and Agency Back In: Representation and the Comparative Approach to World History

Michael Adas

The remarkable revival of world history that has occurred in recent decades has been dominated by approaches stressing macrostructures, aggregate social trends, interregional exchanges, and processes of institutional development. These preoccupations contrast rather sharply with those evident in earlier periods when the writing of global history flourished. As perhaps best exemplified by both Leibniz's and Voltaire's fixation on the Chinese emperor Kangxi as the living embodiment of Plato's philosopher-king,[1] the first sustained episode of world historical writing in the eighteenth century[2] privileged both human agency, in the guise of great men who left their mark on entire epochs of the human experience, and the importance of ideas as causal factors in the development of individual civilizations and as a determinant of cross-cultural interrelationships over time. Both Oswald Spengler and Arnold Toynbee, who were the key figures in the post-World War I revival of history that was global in scope, viewed culture and specifically ideologies as integral elements in the emergence, flowering, and decadence of the cultures/civilizations that centered their organic visions of human societal progression. Spengler's pessimistic, postwar appraisal of the human condition in *Der Untergang des Abendlandes* (Munich, 1918) was grounded in essentialistic, culturally deterministic "soul-images" and a succession of civilizational complexes ("cultures") that were closely tied to world religions, such as Hinduism and Islam, or particular (again essentialized) epistemologies.

By the time he wrote the final volumes of his massive *Study of History* (Oxford, 1933–61), Toynbee had decisively shifted from the environmentalist and social-structural focus of his early writings to a near obsession with the religious efflorescences that he had come to see as the most enduring and significant achievement of civilized development. Toynbee's contemporary, Benedetto Croce, flatly pronounced all of "history the story of the human mind and its ideals."[3]

Like Spengler and Toynbee, Marshall Hodgson and William H. McNeill, who offered models and provided inspiration for the small but steadily growing community of world historians that began to coalesce in the 1960s, treated philosophers and religious movements as fundamental components of the human experience. Religious ideas, institutions, and controversies were, of course, central to Hodgson's monumental, three-volume *Venture of Islam* (Chicago, 1961), which was posthumously fashioned from Hodgson's writings. Though a variant of Spengler's "Faustian soul-image," which privileges science and technology, ultimately proves decisive in McNeill's account of *The Rise of the West* (Chicago, 1963), religious thinkers and systems are treated as major forces driving civilizational development and interaction from the time of the "axial age," which is seen as a pivotal era in global history. But though McNeill and Hodgson had much to do with the resurrection of world history after decades of specialists' assaults had all but banished the work of Spengler and Toynbee from the ambit of the professional historian, their culturally grounded brand of global history was soon eclipsed by approaches that were structuralist in conception and overwhelmingly oriented to questions of political economy. Both Hodgson and McNeill have written fairly extensively on historiographical issues, but neither has tackled the methodology of world history in a rigorous or systematic way. Hodgson's premature death has left us with fragments of that project;[4] McNeill has spent much of his career defending world history from the taunts of its often vociferous professional critics.[5] In addition, in the years since the publication of *The Rise of the West*, McNeill's work has shifted to epidemiological and technological/organizational themes that readily dovetail with the concerns of the world-systems theorists and other social scientists who have adopted structural approaches.

Because the resurgence of world history got under way in the decades when the "new" social history was revolutionizing the historical profession – not only in North and Latin America and Europe but also among the Western-educated intellectuals of postcolonial Africa and Asia – the move away from intellectual concerns is not surprising. As more traditional narrative historians, such as Lawrence Stone, have lamented,[6] the "new" social historians had little interest in ideas or specific actors, particularly if the latter were from the elite classes. They were determined to replace what they caricatured as "great (white) man" history with detailed analyses of the lived experience of the subaltern classes. These trends were, of course, bolstered by historians of the *annales* school (at least in its Braudelian guise that was preeminent in these decades), who were far more interested in the environ-mental and societal underpinnings of world historical development than ideologies, seminal thinkers, or powerful political figures.[7] Thus, in the 1960s and 1970s, when the revival of world history was getting under way, the pro-fession was dominated by research and writing on local history and popular culture, social stratification and class interaction, institutional development and "mass" movements, and demographic trends and shifts in family struc-ture. Works that featured quantification, aggregate analyses, collective and non-elite human agency, and social science theorizing were in; studies that gave contingency, ideology, or individuals their due were suspect.

Excepting the emphasis on local history, the growing number of practi-tioners of world history found the trends exhibited by the "new" social history well suited to the rather formidable obstacles confronting them. Most of the more accessible source materials relating to cross-cultural patterns and exchanges were aggregate and focused on social groups and institutional development. The comparative macroanalysis of broad social, economic, and political trends that came to dominate world history writing and teaching was quite compatible with the work done by area specialists with reference to more confined geographical and social contexts. As a consequence, main-stream world history in its latest reincarnation has been decidedly structural in orientation, devoted heavily to tackling problems and discerning patterns of systemic change in the economic, social, and political realms.

This predilection for structural approaches has been reinforced by the fact that much of the more influential work on world history since the 1970s has been done by sociologists, galvanized by the challenge of adapting rigorous theoretical analysis to the diachronic dimension that has traditionally set his-torical inquiry off from that of other social science disciplines. The impact of sociology on the writing of world history is apparent in what have been the two preeminent approaches in the field over the past three decades or so. The first encompasses a sizable corpus of studies on peasant societies and revolu-tion that was prompted in part by the upheavals in China and the agony of the Vietnam wars. Though some of these were area specific, many were explicitly comparative and aimed at discerning patterns of agrarian develop-ment and protest mobilization with global ramifications.[8] Of these works, Theda Skocpol's *States and Social Revolutions* has had perhaps the greatest and most enduring influence on the writing of the history of protest and revolu-tion with a global dimension. Though informed by previous work (by other sociologists) in dependency theory,[9] Immanuel Wallerstein's version of world systems theory has proved seminal in the development of the second major approach to global history.[10]

Both Skocpol and Wallerstein are sociologists by training, but each has tackled major historical problems, mastered an impressive range and depth of historical source materials, and engaged numerous historians, specializing in a wide variety of geographic areas and time periods, in ongoing and highly productive exchanges and often intensely contested debates. Because I do not intend this essay to be a bibliographic exercise, I want to focus upon key works of Skocpol and Wallerstein to highlight both the considerable advances in our understanding of the processes of global history that their approaches have made possible, and the vital dimensions of that history I believe they have neglected or ignored altogether. Central to this assessment is my conviction that in bringing the state and the world market system back in, Skocpol and Wallerstein, as well as the substantial numbers of historians and allied social scientists who have adopted their approaches and assumptions, have left out a good deal that is critical, and that these lacunae must be filled if we are to achieve fuller understandings of the human experience in its global manifestations.

In many ways Theda Skocpol's *States and Social Revolutions* is a model of comparative historical analysis. She has mastered the relevant theoretical literature and substantial bodies of secondary studies relating to the six major state systems and societies that are the foci of her main case examples. She has chosen these cases carefully, and cogently argued her reasons for employing them. In part because she organizes the study by themes and topics rather than case examples, her comparisons are clear and sustained, her variables consistently and effectively employed, and her theoretical testing and "middle level" findings persuasively argued. Though Skocpol is cautious about the extent to which the patterns of revolution that she discerns can be applied to cases other than the French, Russian, and Chinese examples that she explores in depth (pp. 288–90), the point of her macro-level analysis is to identify factors and conditions with broad applicability that give rise to (or obviate) revolutions in agrarian societies. But as her subsequent work on the Iranian revolution revealed,[11] state crises and agrarian unrest alone could not account for the fall of the shah and the reign of the ayatollahs. A charismatic religious leader and the Shi'i doctrines and chiliastic expectations in which he rooted his revolutionary movement proved central to understanding one of the great mass-based upheavals of modern times.

Skocpol's neglect – and in places her explicit repudiation (pp. 42, 304n, 114, for example) – of the importance of human agency, ideology, and contingency in the revolutionary process not only prompts serious questions regarding her handling of the core case examples in *States and Social Revolutions*, it raises numerous problems that can be traced to her essentially structural approach to historical analysis. Similar problems are also apparent in the pioneering work on peasants and the political process of Barrington Moore, Jr and virtually all of the works dealing with the so-called "great revolutions" written between the 1960s and 1980s.[12] In *States and Social Revolutions* interstate conflicts rage and bureaucratic structures break down with little mention of rulers and state functionaries or their critical misjudgments, which both reflected their political ineptitude and allowed the decline of state structures to spiral out of control at particular historical junctures. New regimes come to power with little or no attention paid to the revolutionary leaders or parties that vied for control, and little mention made of the ideas and ideologies that they repudiated as discredited relics of failed orders or articulated to mobilize mass support for their attempts to create new social and political systems. Skocpol's dismissal of human agency as a causal variable results in a neglect of the pivotal roles of the *sans culottes* in the French Revolution and the urban working classes in the succession of Russian upheavals in 1917, as well as the critical interventions of women at a number of points in both. Skocpol's exclusion of cultural variables leaves no place for Confucian ideals and scholar-gentry values in her analysis of the Manchu failure to repel the imperialist onslaught of the Western powers, or, for that matter, the remarkable success of the Japanese in turning back similar threats.[13]

Skocpol's structural analysis of states in conflict and political and social systems in crisis, tells us a good deal about the causes and consequences of revolutionary upheavals that have done so much to shape the course of modern world history. But systems and processes are never linked to ideologies, movements or political parties, specific events or actual historical actors. We are left then with what Skocpol regards as the "objective, structural conditions" (p. 16) that give rise to revolutions and determine their outcomes, but no sense of the subjective, human input into these processes. Quoting Wendell Phillips approvingly, she argues vehemently for an approach to comparative, cross-cultural and implicitly global history in which "Revolutions are not made; they come" (p. 17).

Although Wallerstein's comparative methodology is a good deal less rigorous and less systematically applied than Skocpol's, he has been much more directly engaged in the writing of world history. In the decades since the appearance of the first of his studies on *The Modern World-System* in 1974, Wallerstein and his disciples have sought to construct a coherent and highly inclusive vision of the rise of a global political economy centered on a capitalist and expansive Western European core area.[14] The impressive range and variety of sources Wallerstein marshals to support his arguments and overall theory in the succession of studies he has published on the rise of the modern world system has both won allies for his prodigious project and forced those who question his findings to engage in serious and sustained debate. Like Skocpol's, Wallerstein's approach is decidedly structural. His central concern is to trace the institutional and societal shifts that led to the spread of the capitalist market system from a succession of core areas in Western Europe, and as a consequence the rise of the West's global dominance from the fifteenth century onwards. Wallerstein's market-exchange version of Marxist reductionism is rather uneasily juxtaposed with an expanding world system organized around modes of production that correspond to differing levels in the global political and economic hierarchy that he elaborates in varying degrees of detail, depending on the region in question: core/wage labor, peasant proprietorship; semi-periphery/tenancy and sharecropping; periphery/"coerced cash-crop," bonded labor and slavery.

Somewhat inexplicably, given Wallerstein's early work on the political economy of African nationalism,[15] his global hierarchy is highly Europecentric. Western Europe is not only (correctly) seen as the core region where the key processes that give rise to the modern world system occur, in the early modern and modern eras its capitalist expansionism is the driving force for human history, or at least the human history that appears to matter. During much of the five centuries in which Wallerstein's capitalist world system dominates global history, rather substantial regions, such as sub-Saharan Africa and South and East Asia, that cannot be readily worked into Wallerstein's schema, are reduced to great black holes, which he and his disciples refer to as areas "external" to that system. Thus, European states or their (in Wallerstein's rendering) anonymous agents are consistently dynamic and proactive; the non-Western societies that are inexorably drawn into the world system are largely passive or at best (and rarely) reactive. Thus, the interchange between the West and the "semi-periphery" and especially the non-Western "periphery" is unidirectional. Impulses flow from Europe to the outside world in ever-expanding circles; non-European areas and societies that Wallerstein brings into the orbit of the capitalist world system at various points in his disquisition are reduced largely to segments of the far-flung systems of extraction that rather mechanically funnel raw materials and profits back to the European core. Interestingly, despite Eric Wolf's determination to view world history from the perspectives of the "peoples without history" who confront this process of European expansionism and the very different approach taken in his early works on these watershed confrontations,[16] his alternative vision of the rise of the modern world system is also centered on the institutions and structures of extraction through which Western Europe came to dominate most of the globe.[17]

Although Wallerstein allows that ideas and values play some role in the capitalization of the world order (see, for example, volume two of *The Modern*

World-System, pp. 65–8), his processual analysis has little to do with intellectual currents, scientific breakthroughs and technological innovations, visionary explorers and expansion-minded monarchs, much less decisive battles or the psychological effects of epidemic disease. When it is treated at all, culture is consistently seen as a dependent variable. But Wallerstein's refusal to take culture, contingency, or human agency seriously means that despite his macroanalytic ambitions, his structural approach to world history ends up being primarily descriptive and decidedly unsatisfying with regard to explanation. In and of themselves, institutions, systems, and processes cannot account for historical change or causality. Rather they comprise the contexts (essential to historical analysis) in which human agents, both as individuals and as members of social collectives, make history. Of course, the contexts themselves have been constructed by other human agents over great spans of time. But neither contexts nor causality in history, whether local or global, can be understood when structures serve as substitutes for human agents.

Ironically, this argument is strikingly supported by the alternative version of world-systems theory set forth in Janet Abu-Lughod's *Before European Hegemony* (Oxford, 1989). Though far less diachronic than Wallerstein's processual analysis that ranges over several centuries, like his the bulk of Abu-Lughod's study is structural and descriptive. Her useful, at times innovative, reconstruction of a world system that existed centuries before the Europe-centered variant that has been the focus of Wallerstein's writings, expands upon a number of well-known accounts of the great Asian trading systems whose origins stretched back into antiquity.[18] But in attempting to explain the breakdown of this system, which spanned much of the "Old World" ecumene, and the consequent emergence of European global hegemony, Abu-Lughod abandons her structural reconstruction of merchant institutions and trade routes, and resorts to contingency and even human agency as key causal variables. Curiously eschewing serious attention to developments in Europe (*Before European Hegemony*, especially pp. 353–4), Abu-Lughod identifies the impact of the bubonic plague pandemic in Asia, the collapse of the Mongol trade routes, and policy decisions at the court of Ming China as critical determinants of these fundamental shifts in global history (pp. 18–20, 358–62).

By contrast, Wallerstein consistently adheres to his structural agenda. He does so even in his detailed analysis of developments in Europe, which, as noted earlier, has prompted numerous non-Western specialists, including Abu-Lughod, to characterize his work as Eurocentric (a point to which I will return below). As a result, Wallerstein's causal explanations are far less clearly drawn and cogent than those of earlier historians. The works of Pierre Chaunu, the great *annalist* scholar of European expansion, provide, for example, a striking contrast to Wallerstein's writings in this regard. Chaunu's seminal studies contain a great deal on institutions, systems, and processes, but they also include extensive discussion of ideas and value systems, pivotal events, and individual agency. His brief but brilliant comparison of the expansive tendencies (or lack thereof) in fourteenth- and fifteenth-century Europe and China remains one of the most compelling arguments to date regarding the causal factors that led to European global hegemony and an example of world history at its most exciting and persuasive.[19]

REPRESENTATION AS A FOCAL POINT FOR CROSS-CULTURAL HISTORY

In both its comparative dimension and its combination of structural and intellectual elements, Chaunu's approach to the history of the expansion of Europe exemplifies the approach to the writing of world history that I should like to argue for in the remainder of this essay. Without jettisoning the organizational and institutional contexts that structural analysts, such as Skocpol and Wallerstein, have employed so extensively, I want to explore approaches to world history in the centuries of European overseas expansion, where my own research and writing has been focused, that give due place to or in fact have been centered upon competing epistemologies, cross-cultural representations of the other, and ideologies of domination and resistance. Though I do not wish to suggest that focusing on these processes provides the only route to viable world history writing, I am convinced that "bringing ideas and agency back in" is essential to tackling effectively several methodological obstacles to the writing of world history that have proved daunting for even its most enthusiastic practitioners. These include (1) connecting the various levels that world history must comprehend, from the workings of the world system to their impact on the lives of subaltern groups and individuals; (2) identifying and analyzing causal factors; (3) contextualizing both European overseas enterprises *and* prior non-Western sites that are drawn into the first genuinely global order and the responses of non-Western peoples to that process; and (4) constructing cross-cultural accounts that meaningfully incorporate human agency and contingency.

Because world history is by definition cross-cultural, the study of the representation of alien others strikes me as an obvious way to integrate the diverse levels and elements that must be pulled together to think, write, and teach about it effectively. Analyzing the attitudes exhibited by peoples confronting alien others, the composite images of the other constructed by both (or all) sides in these interactions, and the ways in which these attitudes and images influence the various parties' exchanges and adjustments to their previous *mentalités* and political or social systems, clearly ought to be central tasks for aspiring world historians. At one level, this analysis involves exploring the meanings and legacies of the essentializing[20] that has invariably been integral to this process. Here Edward Said's exclusive focus on the Europeans' essentializing of "Oriental" peoples and cultures is, I believe, misleading in a number of ways.[21] To begin with, Westerners who have consciously, even proudly, identified themselves as Orientalists have varied widely in approach and degree of sympathy for and depth of understanding of the non-European peoples and cultures that were the objects of their observations and learned treatises.[22] Equally important, their essentializing of the non-Western others was mirrored by Chinese, Arab, or Yoruba essentializing of the European intruders themselves. Because scientific and technological transformations had rendered what Michel Foucault has termed "knowledge/power relations"[23] more immediate and potent for the agents of the expanding West than the peoples they encountered, the consequences of Europeans essentializing non-Western peoples and cultures have been vastly greater than the effects of comparable non-Western responses to the expanding Europeans, or indeed than the impact of the essentializing of any human group to that time.

Thus, it is not surprising that in the postcolonial era, Said and other scholars, particularly those educated in Western languages and disciplines, should focus on the connections between the perceived interests of dominant European social groups and the production of scientific, technical, or ethnographic knowledge. It is also understandable that they have invested much effort in exploring the ways in which that knowledge (on which the practice of essentializing the non-Western others was based) enhanced European power *vis-à-vis* societies and cultures that came to be dominated as a result of Western overseas expansion. But that should not be allowed to obscure the fact that African, Asian, or Polynesian essentializing of the Europeans and European civilization was integral to the construction of the counter-hegemonic ideologies that mobilized and sustained resistance to European expansionism. This essentializing ranged from that produced by pre-contact elites, such as the scholar-gentry of China or the Islamic *ulema*, to the diatribes of Western-educated nationalist leaders, who ultimately wrested political control from the European colonizers.

Identifying which attributes were selected and privileged by observers on *either* side of these cultural divides, and determining why these proved so compelling, are obligatory – if difficult and contentious – tasks for the world historian. These entail close readings of relevant texts and hermeneutic analysis of the lexicon and language forms employed, and suggest the need for collaboration between literary scholars and world historians. But in recent years, the near monopoly of these tasks by scholars of the postmodernist or poststructuralist persuasion has often left the world historian with little more than convoluted and overdetermined reflections on self-referentiality and positionality.[24] Much of this literature, particularly that on colonization, which has proved a popular site for postmodernist scholarship, has been focused on a rather predictable corpus of texts by prominent European authors or spokespersons for the Western-educated elites of the colonized peoples. Little of it has been more than superficially grounded in the actual history of colonialism, much less amenable to linking in meaningful ways with either the workings of the world system or local responses to European hegemony.[25] And despite their intense self-interrogation, postmodernists have very often appropriated the agency of the very subaltern groups whom they seek to rescue from the interpretative clutches of European colonizers or postcolonial administrators. By reconfiguring the intentions of subaltern actors in situations where these have been documented or seeking to "read" the silences so often associated with subaltern victims, postmodernist writers have often imposed their own political and intellectual agendas onto the struggles of "the people without history."[26] Thus, close reading ought not involve – at least for those who aspire to write world history – a plunge into the postmodernist, semiotic quagmire, but rather efforts to contextualize both the ways in which representations are constructed and the language in which they are expressed.[27]

In terms of intellectual history, contextualization of cross-cultural representations may well involve the world historian in an exploration of the competing epistemologies brought together by the many confrontations between the agents of an expansive Europe and overseas peoples and cultures. In the early centuries of expansion, for example, European attitudes towards and ways of conceptualizing the other were predominantly shaped by religious convictions that were in turn informed by supernatural referents and teleological agendas.[28] But in part as a consequence of the great scientific transformations occurring in Europe and a growing power differential between Europe and most overseas societies during these same centuries, European assessments of alien peoples and cultures were increasingly formulated according to the procedures and presuppositions associated with a scientific epistemology that European *savants* celebrated as value-neutral, empirically minded, preeminently rational and universal in its applicability.[29] The thought systems, and the values and ways of doing associated with them, of the peoples locked into encounters with the agents of an expanding Europe were, of course, extremely diverse. But in all cases, these epistemologies had much to do with the ways in which European activities were understood and the Europeans themselves and their civilization were represented. In some situations – most notably in areas that Alfred Crosby has dubbed the neo-

Europes where the indigenous population was sparse and there was extensive settlement by migrants from Europe[30] – non-Western epistemologies, and the peoples who had created them, were simply driven to the physical and social margins of colonized areas.[31] But in areas with dense populations and sophisticated civilizations, indigenous epistemologies persisted long after Europeans had established their ascendancy. They shaped state, elite, and popular responses to European incursions, at times forced major modifications of the Europeans' own procedures and thinking, and ultimately informed the counter-hegemonic ideologies of nationalist leaders throughout the colonized world.[32]

Remaining in the realm of ideas but moving in a different direction, the study of representation is vital to understanding the construction of ideology in the centuries dominated by European global expansion. On the European side, widely divergent images of different African, Asian, Amerindian, and Polynesian cultures fed speculation about the sources and nature of savagery, barbarism, and decadence. Where a given people or society was ranked in the hypothetical hierarchies of human types and conditions that the Europeans were so fond of constructing depended on a combination of contingent, subjective, and structural factors. These included the conditions under which contact occurred, European assessments of the level of material culture and moral probity attained by different societies, European estimates of the extractive potential and labor requirements of different areas, and the widely varying capacity of the peoples encountered to control European intrusions and collaborate in European economic ventures.[33] When combined with the stigmas attached to those who lost their freedom, these highly essentialized representations of different peoples and cultures led to racist ideologies that helped to justify the enslavement of tens of millions of Africans and the indentured servitude of millions of Asians.[34] They also influenced the formulation of variants of the civilizing mission ideology that gave moral purpose to European conquest and colonial rule, and provided rationales for the global division of economic functions in which Europeans provided the capital (both specie and machine) and entrepreneurial/management skills and the rest of humankind supplied cheap labor and abundant land.[35]

As the preceding examples suggest, both representations and the ideologies that were informed by them had significant impact on the policy making and actual undertakings of European conquerors and colonial administrators. They influenced decisions ranging from what sorts of labor systems were to be imposed and which peoples were to be recruited into colonial armies to whether or not a particular kingdom should be attacked or annexed and what subjects and levels of education ought to be made available to colonized peoples. But decisions regarding overseas ventures and colonial policy making were not driven by images and ideas alone. They were formulated in response to accounts (based on widely varying amounts of information or misinformation) of conditions in specific regions and locales; calculations regarding the likely responses of affected peoples; and the degree of leverage that European agents of the expansion process believed that they could exercise in interacting with them. Each of these considerations suggest further levels of contextualization for the world historian. And here the intellectual concerns that I have hitherto privileged can be articulated with the study of the structures, institutions, and global systems that have dominated so much of the recent history of the early modern and modern eras. On the one hand, and perhaps obviously, European representations, epistemes, ideologies, and policies need to be analyzed in relation to the political economy of Europe itself and the workings of the expanding European variant of the global economy. But equally critically, world historians need to contextualize in detail the responses and independent preoccupations of the non-Western peoples and cultures that have inexorably been drawn into a common global system over the past five or six centuries.

CONTEXTUALIZATION AND VARIETIES OF EUROCENTRISM

One of the most fundamental criticisms of Wallerstein's approach to world-systems theory relates to the contrast between the inordinate amount of effort and space that he has devoted to rehashing longstanding debates regarding the origins of capitalism in Europe, and the superficial attention he has given to contextualizing the areas and societies into which the Europeans expand. Strictures against this imbalance have often been associated with broader charges concerning the Europe-centrism of Wallerstein's historical perspective as a whole. In fact, as Janet Abu-Lughod makes clear in the introductory and concluding sections of *Before European Hegemony* (especially pp. 4–9, 12–14, 20, 363–4), one of her motives for reconstructing the world system that existed centuries before the Iberians began to expand overseas was to correct for Wallerstein's Eurocentric explanations for the rise of the modern world system. But I believe that both Abu-Lughod's charge of Eurocentrism and her alternative explanation for the shift to the Western-dominated world system that has been the focus of Wallerstein's research and writing are premised on a distorting conflation of the senses in which the term Eurocentric has been employed. Though Abu-Lughod has made a major contribution through her painstaking efforts to reconstruct much of the pre-expansion world system that preceded the one which began to emerge in the fifteenth century by Wallerstein's reckoning, her attempt to explain the collapse of the first and the subsequent rise of the second with reference to contingent, non-European variables, such as the impact of the plague on Asian civilizations or China's retreat from sea power, is, I believe, misconceived and unconvincing. Contrary to Abu-Lughod's assertions, Wallerstein and numerous scholars before him[36] are correct in assuming that the causes of Europe's transformation from a peripheral zone on the fringes of Islamic civilization to global hegemon must be sought primarily in Europe itself and its interactions with rival civilizations.

In defense of Eurocentrism of this variety, I would further argue the need to stress European exceptionalism if we are to understand the comparative and global dimensions of the process of European overseas expansion.[37] In addition to an analysis of the complex forces that gave rise to capitalism, which have been emphasized by Wallerstein and many of his Europeanist critics, one would need to take into full account contingent factors, ideas, and human agency. As Harry Miskimin has argued,[38] for example, the bubonic plague, which Abu-Lughod sees as a key source of the relative decline of the east Asian segments of the thirteenth–fourteenth-century world system, also devastated much of Europe. But Miskimin shows how the plague affected overseas expansion in a number of critical ways. It spurred advances in ship design to compensate for declining numbers of available oarsmen for traditional Mediterranean vessels, and promoted a surge in consumerism among the survivors of the pandemic, with a concomitant demand for "exotic" imports from Africa and Asia. The expanding market for imports from overseas suggests the importance of including motivation on the part of individuals, such as Henry the Navigator, and social groups, from monarchs and naturalists to missionaries and merchants, in any analysis of the causes and nature of European global expansion. Although these factors, which highlight human agency, were stressed by pioneering scholars, such as Chaunu, Parry, and Lopez, in Wallerstein's structuralist rendering they are reduced to systemic imperatives or by-products of market extensions.

Europe's exceptionalism can also be traced in the impact of its revolution in scientific thinking on expansionism, particularly in terms of advances in instrumentation and of drives to explore and map the seas and continents and collect all manner of specimens in overseas locales.[39] All of this can be set in a global context that reveals Europe's preexpansion marginality, relative to Islamic, Sudanic, Indian, or Chinese civilizations, as a source of technological or crop diffusion, as a center of population concentration or urban growth, and in terms of levels of political organization, of military power, and of its trading relationships with other areas in the vast trading system that spanned the Euroafroasian ecumene. But these very weaknesses again underscore Europe's exceptionalism with regard to its openness to borrowing from other civilizations and its capacity to integrate ideas and artifacts received, particularly from the Islamic empires and South and East Asia.[40]

In Wallerstein's failure to contextualize in any depth the non-European societies that are relegated to his periphery or seen as external to the modern world system, his work is Eurocentric in ways that have proved extremely problematic for many non-Western area specialists, and have limited its value for those historians who have broken from the "Europe plus some non-Western add-ons" variety of world history.[41] As Abu-Lughod has demonstrated so convincingly,[42] Wallerstein's approach takes no account of prior trading networks that spanned civilizations and continents. The areas that he labels "external" and virtually ignores in the early installments of *The Modern World-System* not only contained some of the most populous and advanced of early modern societies, they included major participants in the great trading system that stretched from the Mediterranean down the East African coast to the China Sea. Until well into the eighteenth century,[43] this series of trading networks can be seen as alternatives or even rivals to the European-centered orbits that Wallerstein, with the advantage of hindsight, privileges as *the* world system. Important recent research[44] demonstrates that despite their advantages in the military application of sea power, the Europeans were in most instances marginal players in what Wallerstein, understandably in view of his overall argument, dismisses as external areas. In these alternative zones, as well as in areas that Wallerstein includes in his periphery, Europeans were also highly dependent on African, Asian, and Amerindian comprador merchants, moneylenders, and brokers; coopted nobles and local headmen; and indigenous laborers, servants, artisans, and clerks.[45] European reliance on soldiers and policemen recruited from colonized or indigenous peoples in overseas areas has also been extensively documented.[46] More recent research has shown how dependent even some of the more rarified European overseas enterprises, such as transfers of science and technology and scientific research, were on indigenous savants, guides, research assistants, craftsmen, and artists.[47]

These patterns of dependence drawn from diverse areas of European involvement suggest a number of major correctives to Wallerstein's world-systems model that are based on the work of area specialists who have expended great effort to reconstruct the non-Western contexts in which cross-cultural confrontations and exchanges occurred and European dominance was eventually asserted. To begin with, as Steve Stern has argued,[48] Wallerstein's highly reified categories of semi-periphery and periphery, which account for those portions of the non-European world not designated "external," obscure significant differences between regions within colonized areas, and even within specific locales. Stern has shown, for example, that the labor systems employed by the Spanish colonizers in both the Andes and the Caribbean ranged from tribute systems and slavery to share cropping and free wage contracting. Thus, two zones within one colonial system, clearly belonging to Wallerstein's periphery, contain labor systems that his model locates in core or semi-peripheral areas. Surveying recent works on Asian trade, John Willis tackles in a rather different way the poor fit between Wallerstein's world-systems theory and actual conditions in areas lumped together as peripheral or external with the observation that Wallerstein's "paradigm has no place for developments that have not yet led to the economic peripheralization of an area within the modern capitalist system."[49] Working within the emerging world system in the early centuries of European expansion, Alan Smith seeks both to disaggregate the very notion of *a* periphery through an exploration of the diverse ways in which non-Western agents in a variety of social and economic positions sought to cope with the challenges posed by the spread of merchant capitalism from Western Europe.[50]

On the basis of his Mexican research and monographic studies drawn from other Latin American areas, William Taylor concludes that Wallerstein's superficial handling of non-European contexts and perspectives has led him, among other things, to underestimate seriously the influence of the state – here in the guise of the colonial regime – while focusing almost exclusively on the impact of capitalist, market forces.[51] This inattention to the politics of domination, particularly at the regional and local levels, has also been reflected, according to Taylor, in Wallerstein's neglect of the vertically organized, patron–client webs that were indeed central features of colonial administrations in most areas. Taylor's general estimate of the deficiencies of Wallerstein's pronounced Europe-centrism is worth quoting at some length:

> To describe local social structures, integration, centralization and standardization only in terms of capitalism and external dependencies neglects the role of local modes of thought and practice and local arrangements of power in forming these dependencies. It removes attention from local elites and collective action, leaving the impression that colonial Spanish American economies were directed only towards exports, and that all centers of economic decision making were located outside Latin America.

Wallerstein's failure to give serious attention to contextualizing non-European case examples has led, in turn, Taylor argues, to his underestimation of the importance of the decidedly pre-capitalist tribute systems that provided the main institutions of extraction over much of Africa, Asia, and Latin America.[52] In this regard, it should also be noted that Wallerstein's variant of the world system has no place – excepting, one assumes, his conceptual void of the external areas – for the primarily subsistence systems of "free" peasants that supported perhaps a majority of the world's rural population in the fifteenth century and a substantial portion of humanity well into the nineteenth century in many areas of the globe.[53]

There are thus formidable objections to the privileging of Wallerstein's expansive, Eurocentric, capitalist system at the expense of serious contextualization of the analysis of its effects on the non-Western areas drawn into or persisting alongside its market-exchange network. These suggest that more balanced, nuanced, and inclusive approaches to world history need to be found. These alternative approaches ought to take into account the ways in which the peoples beyond the European "core" resisted, accommodated, appropriated, reconfigured, or simply survived the projects and institutions of the *needy* and aggressive Western nation-states that spread from what had once been the periphery of the "Old World" ecumene. Thus, world historians ought to adopt an interactive and integrative approach to the study of European expansionism, which *can* usefully be seen as the one historical process that binds and gives coherence to the writing and teaching of the world history of the early modern and modern eras. Depending on a variety of factors, ranging from geographical location to demography and level of technological advancement, different areas and societies were drawn into the process of European expansionism in varying degrees at different periods of time. Owing largely to the growing advantages in power and productive capacity that successive Western European societies enjoyed as sites of the scientific and industrial revolutions, since the fifteenth century all human societies and cultures have been forced to cope with political, socioeconomic, and cultural challenges emanating from the West. But to comprehend patterns of resistance or schemes of appropriation arising from the myriad cross-cultural negotiations and exchanges that contacts with agents of an expanding Europe set in motion, the cultural dimensions – epistemologies, representations, and ideologies – and individual and collective agency on the non-Western side of these encounters must be taken into account as fully as those of conquistadors and colonial officials.

Fortunately, we already possess a number of studies of these episodes of cross-cultural interaction and reconfiguration that suggest some of the ways these elements might be worked into the writing of global history. Though I cannot begin to do justice to all of these works, I would like to note several whose authors have employed strategies in the study of cross-cultural encounters that strike me as especially valuable for those attempting to write or teach world history. Thus, I have focused on those works that illustrate approaches that I believe tackle some of the major obstacles identified in recent years by historians and allied social scientists struggling to write methodologically rigorous and compelling world history.

ARTICULATING THE LAYERS OF MODERN GLOBAL HISTORY

As Thomas Holt has pointed out in his recent presidential address to the American Historical Association,[54] perhaps none of the rather daunting problems confronting the historian is as formidable as that of articulating the different levels of historical analysis that need to be addressed. The issues Holt identifies are of particular relevance to world historians, whose work, as I have argued, ought to encompass a variety of levels from the macroanalysis of the workings of global systems to the exploration, insofar as the sources permit, of the everyday, lived experience of individuals in societies drawn into cross-cultural exchanges. To do so, they must infuse the contextual analysis of world systems and structures and aggregate socioeconomic transformations with serious attention to ideas, human agency, and contingency. Here recent elaborations of the possible uses for social historians of Antonio Gramsci's fragmentary (necessarily, given his long imprisonment) concept of hegemony[55] are of special relevance.

As Raymond Williams has argued,[56] Gramsci's significant reworkings of Marxist theory provide the basis for an approach to world history that combines the analysis of systems and structures (base) with that of ideologies and the subjective, lived experience of social groups and individuals (superstructures). Not only did Gramsci insist on historical analysis that viewed each level of equal importance theoretically, he called for an "interactive" approach centered upon the detailed study of the interplay between contextual structures, institutions, and political-economic transformations and the construction of ideologies and social alliances. Gramsci's concept of the "historical bloc" is of particular importance to world historians because it makes it possible for them to move beyond the Europe-centric fixation on class stratification and conflict that has dominated so much of Marxist thinking. The decidedly diachronic thrust of Gramsci's concept of hegemony also underscores the need to be attentive to shifts over time in social alignments and ways of conceptualizing both hegemonic and counter-hegemonic ideologies. As Jackson Lears has shown with reference to examples from United States history,[57] the tension between these competing ideological currents compels the historian to give serious attention to rituals and symbols of legitimacy, which Theda Skocpol once dismissed as analytical dead ends but has more recently seen as critical aspects of revolutionary mobilization.[58] As Skocpol has long urged and Lears sees as a major advance on "orthodox" Marxist thinking, organizing social analysis around Gramsci's concept of hegemony requires that the definition of the state be broadened (from the "orthodox" Marxist view of it as a mere extension of class interests), and its role as an autonomous player in social and cultural struggles clearly taken into account.

Although their authors have not always explicitly employed Gramscian analytical prescriptions, a number of important recent works on the incorporation of diverse non-Western societies into an expanding global system have adopted approaches that combine in colonial settings analysis of the different levels identified by Holt with reference to United States history. These include: the workings of global structures and processes; extensive contextualizations of pre-colonial polities and socioeconomic systems; thorough grounding in indigenous cultures; and detailed attention to epistemologies, cosmologies, symbolic systems, and the colonized peoples' representations of themselves and the European others.

The temporal and spatial range of these studies varies widely, from the more than three centuries and vast Yucatan peninsula covered by Nancy Farriss's monumental study of *Maya Society under Colonial Rule* (Princeton, 1984), to the peasant communities of the region in Tanzania that Steven Feierman calls Shambaai in his innovative account of *Peasant Intellectuals* (Madison, 1990) during the past century, and the widely dispersed Amerindian peoples and territories (Choctaw, Pawnee, and Navaho) that form the core case studies of Richard White's comparative analysis of *The Roots of Dependency* (New York, 1983).

Individual actors appear (usually briefly) at various points in time in Farriss's account of the Mayas under Spanish colonial rule. But her main focus is on collectivities, from the machinations of conquistador elites to detailed discussions of changes in Maya community and family structure during the different stages of Spanish advance and retreat. Like Feierman's study of the peasants of Shambaai, Farriss's history probes into the Maya's views of and interaction with their environment and the links between approaches to that environment and the forces of the supernatural world. Both examine the ways in which environmental/cosmic interaction is connected to social and personal well-being and the powerful challenges that the coming of European colonial rule posed for indigenous belief systems, definitions of community, and psychic and physical health. And both authors devote substantial portions of their highly original accounts on the impact of European expansion in specific locales to examinations of the diverse techniques and organizational modes that the Maya and the people of Shambaai used to accommodate and incorporate, reconfigure or resist, the demands, forces for change, or alien ideas and material artifacts that made up the potent baggage of the European intruders.

In *Roots of Dependency*, Richard White focuses on many of the themes and processes that preoccupy Farriss and Feierman, and he shares their privileging of ideological and epistemic variables as mediators of systemic social and institutional confrontations between European colonizers and indigenous peoples. For this reason, his rather cursory invocation of Wallerstein's world-systems model seems an unnecessary add-on that does little to advance his own theoretical or narrative agendas. But White's three case studies not only convincingly encompass global and regional contexts, his concept of "the middle ground" provides the world historian with a strikingly effective way to envision and analyze cross-cultural interaction, particularly in the early modern, pre-industrial centuries of European expansionism.[59] The middle ground provides a site where global and local forces, political economy, and symbol systems converge. It is a zone where epistemologies and ideologies clash (and sometimes merge), and where representations, and the essentializing they invariably contain, most directly affect policy making, strategies of dominance and survival, and decisions for accommodation or resistance. In White's application of the concept, it is highly diachronic, focused on the ways in which the middle ground is preserved or violated by the peoples and societies in contact over considerable spans of time as well as on its inevitable transformation from a contact zone, where independent societies with rough parity clash and borrow, to an annexed territory or European settler society.

Although the studies of Farris, Feierman, and White provide superb models for the aspiring global historian in terms of the levels of cross-cultural interaction they comprehend and their combination of structural and ideological/epistemic analysis, a number of more narrowly focused studies also provide suggestive approaches. These include the richly textured monographs of Reynaldo Ileto and Vincente Rafael on the ways in which the Filipinos reconfigured the religious doctrines, rituals, and institutional arrangements of the Christian, Spanish colonizers to accommodate indigenous epistemologies and cosmologies and provide impetus for movements of protest and sustained cultural resistance.[60] Even more directly concerned with the linkages between the colonizers' representations of the other and techniques and ideologies of domination, Mick Taussig explores the uses of terror in cross-cultural interaction, while Syed Hussein Alatas shows how European colonizers used representations of undisciplined, indolent, and improvident "natives" to justify often harsh regimes of labor and extraction imposed on subjugated peoples.[61] In influential essays, Terence Ranger and Bernard Cohn have identified the many ways in which European colonizers, "traditional" leaders, and emerging nationalist elites represent themselves and the other and reconfigure, even reinvent, European *and* indigenous customs, rituals, and ideas to stabilize collective identities or enhance legitimacy.[62] These processes have figured prominently in a number of fine, recent studies on colonial social and political relationships and the emergence of regional, subaltern resistance and nationalist elites.[63] Richard Eaton's account of *The Rise*

of Islam and the Bengal Frontier, 1204–1760 (Berkeley, 1993) also provides a
model for the study of cross-cultural interactions that were (partly in this
case) contemporaneous with the centuries of European overseas expansionism, but were centered on other culture complexes (here Muslim and Hindu-
Buddhist-animist) and confrontations, and for which the spread of capitalism
and European colonialism were peripheral.

CROSS-CULTURAL REPRESENTATION AS A GENDERED PHENOMENON

A number of the works cited thus far deal with some of the gender dimensions of cross-cultural representation. But a substantial corpus of more recent
contributions to the history of the age of expansion and colonization are centered on gender issues in a variety of ways that illustrate how the writing of
world history can both incorporate and contribute to our understandings of
these questions. In fact, as Joan Scott and others have observed,[64] a gendered
approach provides critical ways to overcome the problems of levels of analysis that, as we have seen, present daunting challenges to the practitioners of
world history. Not only does gender analysis allow us to come at questions of
social divisions and transformations as well as cross-cultural interactions from
alternative vantage points that are central to these processes, it mandates the
contextualized investigation of social relations, symbolic systems, hegemonic
and counter-hegemonic discourses, and subjective identities. All of these
concerns have been evident in recent studies that have explored the ways in
which feminine and masculine roles and positions became major sites of
cross-cultural contestation in colonial contexts. Some of this work has
focused on European women's representations of themselves, those constructed by European men or colonized peoples, and the ramifications of
these processes in a variety of colonial contexts.[65] But investigations of representations of indigenous women by Europeans – males and females – and
colonized males have allowed historians to begin to give voice to what had
been the most neglected of "the peoples without history."[66] In what is one of
the most detailed and sophisticated of these studies to date, Karen Hansen
brings together the political economy of settler colonization; class, gender,
and racial representations and interaction; and everyday lives and subjective
responses in an account of master–servant relations that covers nearly a
century of cross-cultural contact, intermingling, and confrontation.[67]

In my own work on the impact of Western science and technology on
Asian and African peoples and cultures, I have become increasingly aware of
the centrality of gender considerations in the processes of European expansionism and the cross-cultural interchanges that resulted. Though I alluded
to the significance of gendered perceptions in my study of *Machines as the*

Measure of Men (1989), I did not begin to accord them the attention they deserved or treat them as an integral part of my analysis of the relationships between shifts in material culture and the construction of cross-cultural representations. Consequently, my subsequent research and writing has increasingly focused on questions relating to the impact of gender representations on aspects of the process of Western expansion/colonization and non-Western responses. These range from the ways in which the perceived position of women in overseas cultures shaped European observers' estimates of the level of cultural development as a whole achieved by different non-European peoples to policy ramifications with regard to education and employment, for example, or the widely held European assumption that only males were biologically suited for scientific activities and technical occupations.[68]

My current research on African and Asian responses to the Great War has revealed the centrality of racial and gendered representations in the attributes assigned to the dominant Europeans, which were enshrined in different versions of the civilizing mission ideology. In the colonizers' discourse – including at times the thinking of Western-educated Africans and Asians – discipline, punctuality, industriousness, self-control, rationality, and empiricism, for example – were qualities associated with Western masculinity. Their binary opposites[69] – indiscipline, tardiness, indolence, lack of control, emotionality, and intuitiveness – were seen as inherent to the psyches and personality make-up of racially inferior, colonized peoples *and all women*. The assault on Western assertions that their scientific and technological achievements confirmed these essentialist representations and the consequent assumptions of racial and gender superiority held by Western, male colonizers was a central, perhaps defining, strand in the first genuinely global discourse that was elaborated by Western, Asian, African, and African-American intellectuals in the decades after the war.[70]

ALTERNATIVES TO STRUCTURALISM IN THE WRITING OF WORLD HISTORY

As the foregoing examples should amply illustrate, viable strategies have been devised that comprehend the different levels and dimensions of cross-cultural interaction that need to be included in the writing and teaching of world history. But most of the works discussed here and others that grapple with these complex processes have been confined to specific geographical locales. Consequently, their contributions have often been limited primarily to problems of interest to area specialists and little known to those engaged in the often daunting task of mastering the prodigious literature of relevance to world historians.[71] These tendencies to compartmentalization have, of course, been evident in the discipline of history at least since the time of its professionalization in the late nineteenth century.[72] The obvious need to overcome this fragmentation and area studies isolation suggests yet another dimension that ought to be incorporated into the writing and teaching of world history: the serious and sustained application of the comparative method.

Although they are routinely conflated, world and comparative history ought to be seen as different kinds of enterprises. The first is largely a matter of perspective and range, which has hitherto often involved identifying macro-patterns, more often than not on the basis of seemingly random and patchy selections and applications of illustrative examples and supporting sources. But broad perspectives and stray cross-cultural references should not be confused with systematic comparison, which has developed into a distinct social science methodology largely due to the efforts of sociologists and political scientists rather than historians. Among other things, the serious application of the comparative technique involves rigorous searches of relevant materials for appropriate and manageable case examples, which are then tested for their comparability to other likely case studies. As Theda Skocpol and Margaret Somers have argued so cogently,[73] comparative analysis also requires the identification of independent and dependent variables, and conscious decisions about the logic(s) of comparison to be employed. Care must then be taken to apply these variables consistently in analysis both within and across the case studies selected, and to distill explicitly from this analysis recurring patterns and causal explanations for similar or contrasting outcomes. Of particular importance in historical comparison is the detailed contextualization of the case examples chosen. As we have seen, for the world historian this contextualization involves articulating a variety of levels from global processes to local, even individual, ramifications and responses.

The critical impact that a growing corpus of comparative historical studies have already had on identifying issues, discerning general patterns, and advancing the research agenda for subfields as central to cross-cultural history as slavery, protest and revolution, migration, colonialism, frontiers, gender, the family, and industrialization,[74] amply demonstrates the potential returns of the serious application of the comparative method to the writing and teaching of world history. As such works as Leo Spitzer's *Lives In-Between* (Cambridge, 1988) illustrate, detailed and diachronic comparisons of carefully selected case studies can also allow the historian to combine effectively the workings of world systems and regional social and institutional transformations with the cultural dimensions of the human experience. Spitzer's work is particularly noteworthy for the ways in which by employing prosopography and personal accounts, he shows the world historian how to integrate subjective responses and the everyday, lived experience of individual men and women into generalizing narratives. His grounding of the comparison of regional variations on global patterns of uprooting, migration, and acculturation in family and personal histories affirms an interactive approach to the age of Western expansion built around the ways in which non-Western peoples and societies received, negotiated, reconfigured, and incorporated influences emanating from a capitalist, industrializing European core area.[75]

Spitzer's extensive use of family and personal records suggests a final but fundamental issue regarding the methodology employed in writing and teaching world history that I wish to address: the use of primary sources. I think that it is reasonable to conclude that the dismissive attitude manifested by many professional historians with regard to both comparative analysis and world history has much to do with the failure to use primary sources on the part of many historians and fellow social scientists committed to these approaches. That this neglect of primary evidence is apparent in works (quite appropriately) dedicated to identifying broad, cross-cultural patterns and developing generalizing theories makes them doubly suspect for substantial segments of the profession. From this perspective, those world or comparative historians who rely on secondary sources alone have abandoned the kinds of evidence whose selection, evaluation, and interpolation are seen as defining to the historian's craft and critical to distinguishing it from other social scientific and humanistic endeavors.[76] Eschewing the critical examination of primary documents, world and comparative historians are left to engage in the process of selection at one or (often many) more levels removed the evidence contemporary to the events and processes they are attempting to understand. They are forced to choose between other scholars' interpretations, and may well be inclined to privilege that interpretation or supporting evidence which best fits their own theories or arguments.[77] As Theda Skocpol has conceded, this way of proceeding is particularly troublesome because comparativists (and, one might add, world historians) "have not so far worked out clear consensual rules and procedures for the valid use of secondary sources as evidence."[78]

All of this is not to argue that world historians ought to engage in the sort of exhaustive research in primary sources that defines the monographic approach to historical writing. But Spitzer and White, among numerous others, have demonstrated that the quite extensive use of published and archival documents can be combined to good effect with the secondary sources that have been the mainstay of comparative and world history. Here the importance of the rigorous application of the comparative method is underscored by the need for the cross-cultural or global historian to gain sufficient mastery of the historiography pertaining to relevant areas and time periods to determine the availability and relative utility of the primary sources for each of the potential case examples on which her or his analysis is to be based. The skillful deployment of selected primary sources allows the cross-cultural historian to test his or her secondary data and interpretations, and in tandem with comparative analysis to come up with original approaches to familiar materials and problems.

The relatively higher accessibility and quantity of elite-authored primary materials raises further obstacles. But at both levels, analysis centered on the construction and impact of representation ought to have great appeal for cross-cultural historians. As I have attempted to show, the study of representation not only allows one to bring ideas, ideology, and human agency back into the writing of world history, it provides a narrative and analytical orientation that is conducive to the effective articulation of the multiple levels – from world-systems processes to local/subjective responses – that ought to be integrated into a methodologically sound study of history with comparative or global perspectives. Systematic comparative analysis of these multiple dimensions of the history of representation facilitates the sort of "middle-level generalizing" that makes for the best sort of world history. Integrating broad patterns with culturally based narratives should also produce books and lectures on world history that are more compelling to a broad audience than the impersonal and aggregate-oriented structural approaches that have thus far dominated the post-World War II rebirth of the field.

6

World Histories and the Construction of Collective Identities

S. N. Eisenstadt

I INTRODUCTION

In this essay I define world history or world histories as developments of relatively intensive intersocietal or intercivilizational contacts and interrelations. I will analyze the impact of world history on the construction of the collective identities of societies experiencing such contacts and interactions. A basic assumption of this analysis is that no society (with the possible but doubtful exception of some, in the former anthropological parlance, "tribal" groups) has ever existed in isolation. Societies probably always interacted, even if the scope and intent of their contacts varied greatly in different cases. I also assume that the boundaries of the broader frameworks for interaction as well as of any single "society" have also been continually changing.

The construction of the boundaries of social systems, collectivities, and organizations entails delineation of their relations with their respective environment or environments. However it is wrong to assume that there is a natural environment of any society or of any pattern of social interaction. It is meaningless to refer to the "natural" environment "out there." Rather, each pattern of social interaction, each "society" constructs its own environment continuously. Of course, in the construction of an environment, any society must have access to some material resources.

Each ecological setting provides a range of possibilities with respect to such resources, and social agents choose among them. Once such choices have been made, they set the limits or the boundaries of the system and generate its particular sensitivity to environmental changes. These systemic sensitivities are created not by material resources as such, nor by technology as such, but by different social actors shaping and reshaping the environment with different technologies. The construction of a great variety of environments in different ecological settings has been a distinctive feature of world history.

Moreover, changes in various components of international systems impinge on different social actors and groups within societies, and such interaction activates various potentialities of change, of protest and conflict. It is the recognition of, on the one hand, the ubiquity of such broader frameworks, and on the other, of their volatility and changeability that lies behind the analysis presented here and behind the term "world history" as it is used here.

In sharper focus this analysis assumes[1] that populations which live within the confines of what has been designated as a "society" or a macro-societal order are not usually organized into one "system," but rather into several structures, including political systems, economic formations, different ascriptive collectivities, and civilizational frameworks. It is only very rarely that members of such a population are confined to any single "society," even if one such "society" seems to be the salient macro-order for them; usually they live in multiple settings or contexts. Such collectivities, social systems, or civilizational frameworks are continuously constructed in interactions, often struggles, in which ideological, "material," and power elements are ceaselessly interwoven. These processes are structured, articulated, and maintained by different social actors and supporters, above all by different coalitions of elites, counter-elites, and groups of influentials interacting with the broader sectors of the society. Each "system" with its flexible and continually changing boundaries is sustained by different coalitions. The different structures – the "systems" or collectivities – evince different patterns of organization, continuity, and change. Differential change occurs in various areas of social life, further articulating the fine structure of the systems.

II THE CONSTRUCTION OF COLLECTIVE IDENTITY

Within this general analytical framework I would like to address here a problem which has been hitherto relatively neglected in the scholarly literature – namely, the process of constitution or construction of collective identities that has been taking place in different groups and societies under the impact of such interrelations. This analysis of the constitution of collective identities is based on several assumptions which differ from those of both classical sociological analysis and contemporary analyses of ethnicity or nationalism.[2]

Many of the recent theories of nationalism and ethnicity veer between viewing ethnicity (and possibly also nationalism) as either natural and primordial, or as "imagined" communities which developed in modern times in response to the expansion of capitalism, industrialism, and imperialism. Contrary to these assumptions, I assume that collective identities are socially constructed, and that their construction has always been a basic dimension of the constitution of societies or of social order. This approach eschews the implicit assumptions of most classical sociological and anthropological accounts, in which the construction of collective identity is either naturally given or historically ephemeral and secondary to power or economic relations. Rather, I assume that collective identities are constituted by the social construction of boundaries, and of trust and solidarity among the members of the collectivity. A central aspect of such construction is an accepted definition of "similarity" among its members, as against the strangeness, the differences distinguishing the other or others. Such a distinction poses the problem of crossing the boundaries: How can a stranger become a member? How can a member become an outsider or a stranger? Religious conversion and excommunication represent obvious illustrations of the crossing of boundaries.

The construction of collective identities is influenced or shaped, as is that of most arenas of social activity, by distinct codes or schemata. Through them ontological or cosmological premises and conceptions of social order prevalent in any society influence the definition of the major arenas of social interaction and the structures of preferences.[3] The major codes for the construction of collective identity are those of *primordiality*, *civility*, and *sacredness* (sacrality) or transcendence.[4]

The primordial code[5] focuses on such components as gender and generation, kinship, territory, language, race, and the like for constructing and reinforcing the boundary between inside and outside. This boundary, though constructed, is perceived as naturally given. The second, civic code, is constructed on the basis of familiarity with implicit and explicit rules of conduct, traditions, and social routines that define and demarcate the boundary of the collectivity.[6] These rules are regarded as the core of the collective identity of the community.[7] The third code – the sacral or transcendent – links the constituted boundary between "us and them" not to natural conditions, but to a particular relation of the collective subject to the realm of the sacred and the sublime, be it defined as God or Reason, Progress or Rationality.[8] Such codes can be found in various preliterate and above all "archaic" societies – usually embedded or interwoven in the two other types of codes – but the purest illustrations of such collective codes are the axial-age religions which will be discussed in section III.[9]

These three codes are of course ideal types. Moreover, within each there may develop many variations. Thus, to give only two illustrations, within the general framework of primordial orientation there may develop different emphases on territory, culture, language, or other components of primordiality. Similarly, the differences between non-axial and axial religious ontological conceptions, and to follow Weber's nomenclature, between this-worldly and other-worldly orientations, have been abundantly analyzed.[10] The construction of collective identities entails in any concrete situation different combinations of the basic codes outlined above, and of different contents of such codes, which also vary in their importance in such situations.

The construction and reproduction of collective identity or consciousness is attained through a combination of the promulgation and institutionalization of models of social and cultural order with various attempts to control the production and flow of resources. Such models of cultural and social orders – the Geertzian models "of and for society"[11] – represent and promulgate the unassailable assumptions about the nature of reality and a social reality prevalent in a society, the core symbols of a society, the evaluation of different arenas of human activity, and the place of different symbolic ("cultural") activities as they bear on the basic predicaments and uncertainties of human experience.

Thus the construction of collective identity is closely related to the basic cosmological and ontological conceptions that are prevalent in any society. Through interaction between the carriers of these visions and those of different solidary collectivities the boundaries of different collectivities are formed and the criteria of membership within them constituted.

It is through the promulgation, institutionalization, and interpretation of such models that, in D. M. Schneider's terms, the construction of "identity" and membership in different collectivities is combined with the range of "code" available to those participating in such collectivities,[12] thus setting up Durkheim's pre-contractual elements of social life, the bases of mechanical solidarity.[13]

The models of social and cultural orders are most fully articulated in rituals and ceremonies. Induction of the members in the collectivity assumes special importance and occurs in various rites of initiation and collective rituals. Such processes define the "similarities" of members of a collectivity and its boundaries. However, the promulgation of the models is always connected with contestation of power, control of resources, and struggles over discursive hegemony.[14] Thus the construction of collective identity is never, in any society, homogeneous or undifferentiated. It always entails multiple, often competing constructions and interpretations.

All of this is closely related to the division of labor, to social differentiation, to control over resources, and to the regulation and legitimization of power. The construction of solidarity entails consequences for the conception of authority and its accountability; for the allocation of resources, above all for the structuring of the entitlements of the members of the collectivity as against the outsiders.

The construction of collective identities has been going on throughout human history in all human societies, in different economic and political-ecological settings, from small city-states to great kingdoms. Contrarily, some of the recent studies on nationalism and ethnicity implicitly assume that the primordial component of collective identity has been continually reconstituted in different historical contexts and above all under the impact of inter-civilizational contacts. In the processes of construction of collective identities various "international" forces or intersocietal interactions were clearly of great importance. They become much more prominent historically with the disintegration of relatively narrow tribal or territorial units, in connection with the crystallization of Great Archaic Empires – Ancient Egypt, Assyria, or the Meso-American ones – and later axial-age civilizations.

These processes of disintegration and reconstruction were in all cases connected with advances in agricultural and transport technology, with growing mutual impingement of heterogeneous economic (nomadic, sedentary, etc.) and ethnic populations, with some degree of international political-ecological volatility in general, and with processes of immigration and/or conquest in particular. All these cases of growing internal structural differentiation involved the concomitant crystallization of new broader collectivities, and new patterns of collective identity.[15]

It is even possible to identify different patterns of such breakdowns of relatively narrow collectivities and of the concomitant recrystallization of broader ones in the processes of emergence of the early states. The details of such differences are of course quite rich, but it is possible to distinguish between two broad types which can be identified already in the transition from tribal to so-called early states.[16] The importance of such different patterns or modes becomes even more salient in comparing the processes connected with the emergence of the Archaic Empires with those which gave rise to the axial-age civilizations.

These types of recrystallization can be distinguished according to the degree to which there develops a congruence – or lack of congruence – between social differentiation in terms of social division of labor on the one hand, and the performance of elite functions and of the positions of control connected with them on the other. Each type of recrystallization gives rise to different types of institutional patterns: of collectivities, of collective identities, of centers, of center–periphery relations, of social hierarchies.

Within congruent societies (good illustrations of which among tribal early states are, for instance, the Asante in Africa), new broader cultural-political frameworks were based on the reformulation of the preexisting – kin and territorial – criteria and symbols of collective identity. Such reformulation took place above all through extension of kin units into a combination of kin–territorial entities, based on more diversified and more encompassing subunits continually designated in revised primordial kin and/or territorial terms.

A broadly similar pattern of reconstruction of collectivities and of institutional complexes developed also in many of the Archaic Empires, of which ancient Egypt is probably the best illustration, in city-states such as those of ancient Phoenicia, or in various more decentralized tribal federations – all of which exhibited many so-called "patrimonial" features.[17] In such more "developed" congruent societies the crystallization of more complex institutional structures and collective identities was usually connected with the reconstruction and widening of the kinship and/or territorial elements and ascriptive symbols in the construction of collective identities and conceptions, with the growing importance of broader territorial units as opposed to purely local and/or kinship ones. These designations were closely connected with the prevalence of cultural models and conceptions ordaining relatively low levels of tension between the transcendental and mundane orders, but in which there developed an extension and diversification of the basic cosmological conceptions. This line of development brought with it an increasing specialization of elites. They were embedded in various, sometimes very complex and wide-ranging, ascriptive units characterized by a close correspondence between structural differentiation and differentiation of elite functions.

In contrast, a second line of development can be identified. It was characterized by growing discrepancies between structural differentiation and differentiation of elite functions. It also fostered the development of autonomous elites, who pioneered more radical developments or breakthroughs in cultural orientations, especially in promoting the radical conception of the tension between the mundane and transcendental orders. Such development can be identified in early nonliterate states – among, for instance, some of the Yoruba states, in Ife and Oyo or the Manding in Africa, and above all it was characteristic of the development of the axial-age civilizations.

III Axial-Age Civilizations

By axial-age civilizations (in Karl Jasper's nomenclature)[18] we mean those civilizations that crystallized during the centuries from 500 BCE to the first century CE, within which new types of ontological visions, of conceptions of a basic tension between the transcendental and mundane orders, emerged and were institutionalized in many parts of the world – in ancient Israel, later in Second-Commonwealth Judaism and Christianity; Ancient Greece; Zoroastrian Iran; early Imperial China; areas affected by Hinduism and Buddhism; and, beyond the axial age proper, Islam.

Axial-age civilizations brought about some of the greatest revolutionary breakthroughs in human history. Revolutionary ontological visions, which first developed among small groups of autonomous, relatively unattached "intellectuals" (a new social element at the time), particularly among the carriers of models of cultural and social order, were ultimately transformed into the basic "hegemonic" premises of their respective civilizations. In institutionalized forms they became the predominant orientations of both the ruling as well as of many secondary elites, fully embodied in the centers or subcenters of their respective societies. At the same time, institutionalization gave rise to numerous heterodoxies and secondary interpretations of the hegemonic one.

Elites in all of these civilizations attempted to reconstruct the mundane world-human personality and the sociopolitical and economic order according to the appropriate transcendental vision, the principles of the higher ontological or ethical order. There developed a strong tendency to define certain collectivities and institutional arenas as the most appropriate ones for resolving the tensions created by the separation of transcendental and mundane. Arenas of "salvation" created new types of collectivities or endowed seemingly natural and primordial groups with special meaning in terms of the tensions and their resolution. The most important transformation of this sort was the construction of "cultural," "religious," or civilizational – as distinct from ethnic or political – collectivities.

There were also strong tendencies to construct a societal center or centers to serve as the major autonomous and symbolically distinct embodiments of the resolution of this tension of respective ontological visions; as the major loci of the charismatic dimension of human existence. The center's symbolic distinctiveness from the periphery received a relatively strong emphasis; yet at the same time the center tended to permeate the periphery and restructure it according to its own autonomous visions, conceptions, and rules. Sometimes this tendency was accompanied by a parallel impingement by the periphery on the center. In these civilizations, the processes of center formation and reconstruction of collectivities were connected to the construction of Great Traditions as autonomous and distinct symbolic frameworks, and to the concomitant transformation of the relations between the Great and Little Traditions.[19] Hence we see attempts by the carriers of the Great Traditions to permeate the periphery and move the Little Traditions into the orbit of the

Great ones; as well as attempts by the carriers of the Little Traditions to profane the Great ones, to dissociate themselves from them, and, paradoxically
enough, to generate in addition a distinct ideology of the Little Traditions
and the periphery.

It should be stressed that in the axial civilizations the development and
institutionalization of the perception of basic tension between the transcendental and the mundane order was closely connected with the emergence of
a new social element, of a new type of elite, carriers of models of cultural and
social order. These were often autonomous intellectuals, such as the ancient
Israelite prophets and priests and later on the Jewish sages, the Greek
philosophers and sophists, the Chinese literati, the Hindu Brahmins, the
Buddhist Sangha, and the Islamic Ulema. Initial small nuclei of such groups
of cultural elites or of intellectuals developed the new ontologies, the new
transcendental visions and conceptions, and were of crucial importance in
the construction of the new "civilizational" collectivities and the concomitant patterns of collective identity.

With the institutionalization of axial civilizations, a new type of intersocietal and intercivilizational world history emerged. Within all these civilizations there developed, in close connection with the tendencies to reconstruct
the world, a certain propensity to expansion, in which ideological, religious
impulses were combined with political and to some extent economic ones. To
be sure, political and economic interconnection have existed between different societies throughout human history. Some conceptions of a universal or
world kingdom emerged in many post-axial civilizations, like that of Genghis
Khan, and many cultural interconnections developed between them, but
only with the institutionalization of axial civilizations did a more distinctive
ideological and reflexive mode of expansion develop. This mode of expansion
also gave rise to some awareness of creating possible "world histories" encompassing many different societies. The impact of "world histories" on the constitution of collective consciousness and identities of the different societies
became more clearly visible.

In close connection with the axial civilizations' tendency to expansion
there developed new "civilizational" – "religious" – collectivities, distinct
from political and from "primordial" ones, yet continually impinging on
them, interacting with them, continuously challenging them, and provoking
continual reconstruction of their respective collective identities. Such
processes were effected by the continual interaction between the new
autonomous cultural elites and the various carriers of solidarity and political
elites of the different continually reconstructed "local" and political
communities.

IV HISTORICAL CASE STUDIES

The Second Temple Jews

During the axial age there emerged a multiplicity of different, divergent, yet continuously mutually impinging world civilizations, each attempting to reconstruct the world in its own mode, according to its basic premises, and very often aggressively confronting the others. Axial civilizations varied with respect to the ways in which the relations between the universalistic "axial" orientation and the "local" and political groups and "subcultures" were reconstituted within different societies encompassed by them. All of this affected collective identities.

To give one example, the Jewish collective identity that emerged during the period of the Second Temple differed, even though developing from, the more ancient Israelite one. This new collective Jewish identity, to follow Shaye J. D. Cohen, had a dual character. It was both a nationality and a way of life crystallized as a product of the Maccabean period. Only then, according to Cohen, was "ethnic" or "national" self-definition supplemented by a "cultural" or "religious" one. This development also made possible the important "Hellenistic" phenomenon of "conversion" to Judaism. Cohen further claims that the Hellenistic world not only served as a foil against which the Jews redefined themselves, but also provided the very conceptions that underlay the new Jewish self-definition.[20]

The Jewish response to Hellenism was only one among the different communities in the Near East. However great the variations among them – be they Egyptian, Greek, or Phoenician communities – the impact of Hellenism, and later of the combination of Hellenistic and Roman civilizations, became a central focus of the reconstitution of their respective collective consciousness or identity. The Jewish case presents the unique combination of an "ethnic" identity with a cultural and religious one with universalistic claims – claims which were later on taken up and transformed in Christianity.[21] The other Near Eastern societies on the whole accepted Hellenistic or Roman hegemonic claims to be the only or major bearers of universalistic civilizations and reconstructed their collective identities either by incorporating some of these claims into their own self-definition or by rejecting them.[22] The different responses were shaped by the confrontation and combination of the basic cosmological and ontological conceptions and the premises of social order of the universalistic civilizations with those of the various continually changing "autochthonous" political and local collectivities.

The Japanese through the Tokugawa Period

Japan provides a most instructive illustration of the importance of autochthonous forces, first in its encounter with two axial civilizations, Confucian and Buddhist, and later with the Western world's ideological, military, political, and economic system.[23]

Early in Japanese history there developed a very distinct type of collective consciousness or identity – a political and ethnic identity or collective consciousness, couched in sacral-primordial terms.[24] Unlike Europe's – or China's, Korea's, or Vietnam's – Japan's collective consciousness did not develop within the framework of a universalistic civilization with strong transcendental orientations. Japan, to be sure, was greatly influenced by its encounter with Chinese Confucianism and Buddhist civilization. However, in contrast to what happened in the realm of the axial civilizations, Japan resolved its confrontation with universalistic ideologies by apparently denying them rather than attempting to relate them to its primordial symbols.

This collective consciousness was constructed around the idea of a sacred liturgical community and the uniqueness of the Japanese collectivity or nation. This conception of a divine nation, or to follow Werblowski's felicitous expression – of sacred particularity – did not, however, entail its being uniquely "chosen" in terms of a transcendental and universalistic mission. It did not entail the conception of responsibility to God to pursue such a mission.

Japan's conception of sacred particularity usually held its own when confronted with successive waves of universalistic ideologies (Buddhist, Confucian, then liberal, constitutional, progressivist, or Marxist), all of which seemingly called for a redefinition of the symbols of collective identity. With the exception of small groups of intellectuals, redefinition in a universalist direction did not take hold in the Japanese collective consciousness. Instead the premises of these religions or ideologies were reconstructed in Japan and combined with sacral, primordial, and natural terms.

Reformulations of the Japanese collective identity entailed very intensive orientations to "others" – China, Asia, the West – and an awareness of other encompassing civilizations claiming some universal validity. But they did not entail the participation of the Japanese collectivity in such civilizations and its reconstruction according to these universalistic premises. The reformulations did not generate the perception of Japan becoming a part, whether central or peripheral, of such a universalistic system. In extreme form they asserted that the Japanese collectivity embodied the pristine values enunciated by the other civilizations and wrongfully appropriated by them. This yielded a very strong tendency – which played an important role in Japanese society from the Meiji up to the contemporary period – to define the Japanese collectivity in terms of "incomparability" very often couched in racial, genetic terms, or in terms of some special spirituality. Such definitions of the Japanese collectivity made it impossible to become Japanese by conversion. The Buddhist sects or Confucian schools – the most natural channels of conversion – could not perform this function in Japan.

The ability of Japanese elites to promulgate and "reproduce" such extreme denial of the universalistic components of the axial-age civilizations which were continually impinging on them was closely related to some of their basic characteristics, the most important of which from the point of view of our analysis is that Japanese elites were not strong and autonomous. The common characteristic of these elites and their major coalitions was their embedment in groups and settings (contexts) that were mainly defined in primordial, ascriptive, sacral, and often hierarchical terms, and much less in terms of specialized functions or of universalistic criteria of social attributes.[25]

True, many cultural actors – priests, monks, scholars, and the like – participated in such coalitions. But with very few exceptions, their participation was based on primordial and social attributes and on criteria of achievement and social obligations issuing from the different particular contexts shaping these coalitions, and not on any autonomous criteria rooted in or related to the arenas in which they were active. These arenas – cultural, religious, or literary – were themselves ultimately defined in primordial-sacral terms, notwithstanding the fact that many specialized activities developed within them.

In contrast to Japan, in axial civilizations continual changes took place in the composition and structure of different autonomous cultural elites, some of which were the bearers of the universalistic visions. This gave rise to continual confrontations of hegemonic elites and various bearers of heterodoxies and sectarian visions, and between such elites and the carriers of the solidarity of different local groups as well as of political collectivities.[26] The continual changes in composition of autonomous cultural elites and in their relations with other such elites gave rise to very important changes in the constitution of identities of the different societies encompassed by different axial civilizations. One of the most important changes, from an ecumenical conception of the civilizational collectivity to more territorially centered ones, widely took place in many of these societies around the sixteenth to eighteenth centuries.

Medieval and Early Modern Europe

One such important shift which was to be of crucial importance for the development of modern world history took place in European civilization, from around the sixteenth century on. The shift can be best understood against the background of European medieval and modern history. Central to that history was the continuous construction and reconstruction of chiefdoms, municipalities, feudal fiefs, cities as well as of tribal or trans-tribal, regional, proto-national, and national communities. Indeed, one of the most distinctive characteristics of European historical experience has been the continual constitution of multiple, often competing communities, each with claims to be the best representative of Europe's broader civilizational framework.[27] The multiple centers and subcenters, as well as the different collectivities which developed in Europe, tended to become arranged in a complicated but never unified or rigid hierarchy. Although no center was clearly supreme, many of them aspired not only to political but also to ideological predominance and hegemony.

Europe's major collectivities and central institutions constituted themselves in a variety of ways, all of which entailed different combinations of the usual terms and codes of collective identity: primordial attachments and traditions, and transcendental as well as traditional civic criteria. The continuous European restructuring of centers and collectivities revolved around the oscillation and tension between the sacred, primordial, and civil dimensions. While, for instance, many collectivities were defined and legitimated mainly in primordial terms, they also attempted to arrogate sacred and civil symbols of legitimation.

Closely related was the structure of center–periphery relations that developed in Western and Central Europe. In common with Imperial societies, such as those of China or the Byzantine Empire, Western and Central European societies were usually characterized by a relatively strong commitment among the elites of these societies – in the centers and periphery alike – to common "ideals" or goals; the center permeated the periphery in order to mobilize support for its policies, and the periphery impinged on the center in order to influence the shaping of its contours. Many of these European centers aimed at universal expansion which would encompass other centers and communities, and such expansion was often legitimated in universal terms, very often religious and ideological ones, giving rise to wars of religion or to ideological wars. But in contrast to purely Imperial regimes (like those of China or the Byzantine Empire), in Europe a multiplicity of centers and collectivities persisted. The interaction of the periphery and of various subcenters was much stronger.

The potential for such center–periphery interaction was rooted in Europe's structural and cultural pluralism. Europe experienced continuously increasing levels of structural differentiation. Parallel to this it developed a multiplicity of cultural orientations: the Judeo-Christian, the Greek, and the various tribal ones; and a closely related multiplicity and complexity of ways to resolve the tensions between the transcendental and mundane orders, through either worldly (political and economic) or other-worldly activities. It was out of these orientations that the multiple components of construction of collective identity in Europe developed.

Europe from at least the late Middle Ages was characterized by a relatively high degree of symbolic and ideological articulation of the political struggle and of movements of protest; by a high degree of coalescence of changes in different institutional arenas; by a very close relationship between such changes and the restructuring of political centers and regimes.

V THE MODERN NATION-STATE

Europe

We can find in this European background the dynamics that produced from the sixteenth century on a number of outcomes that were crucial in shaping the modern world. The most important outcome of the European processes was the formation of the absolutist states which later were transformed in the wake of the Great Revolutions into modern constitutional, later democratic states – often into nation-states; the development of new state–society relations, most notably in the emergence of a civil society; the concomitant transformation of political processes; and last but certainly not least the development of capitalist, later industrial-capitalist, types of political economy.

As in preceding historical periods, the different concrete types of collective identity or consciousness that developed in Europe combined primordial, civil, and cultural-religious components or orientations and continually oscillated around these components, but there developed some far-reaching changes in the contents of these components and in their concrete constellations – leading to the crystallization of the nation-state as an ideal and as a reality alike.

Among the most important such changes was the development of the very strong emphasis on territorial boundaries as the principal loci of the institutionalization of collective identity; of new, mainly secular definitions of each of the components of collective identity; of the importance of the civil and procedural components thereof; and of a continual tension among the different components. Closely related was the strong tendency to impose ideological formulations on these components of collective identities, and the concomitant tendency of the newly constructed collectivities and centers to acquire charismatic authority.

The emphasis on the territorial components of collective identity entailed the development of a very strong connection between the construction of states and that of the major, "encompassing" collectivities – a connection which later became epitomized in the construction of the nation-state. The crystallization of the idea of nation-state entailed the congruence between the cultural and political identities of the territorial population; the promulgation, by the center, of strong symbolic and affective commitments to the center, and of a close relationship between the centers and the more primordial dimensions of human existence and of social life.

The interweaving of the construction of states with that of new types of collective consciousness and boundaries was, as Lipset and Rokkan[28] have shown, a result of the resolution of the religious cleavages which arose in Europe during the Reformation and Counter-Reformation. Such resolution entailed the reconstruction and redefinition of components of collective identity in different patterns of primordial, civil, and cultural orientations – giving rise to different types of nation-states.[29]

Japan

One would imagine that the emphasis on territoriality in Tokugawa Japan should have led to the natural adoption of the European "nation-state" model. Yet in fact the situation was rather more complicated.[30] The general analytical considerations which we have identified in the expansion of axial civilizations and their impact on the construction of collective identities apply, albeit in concretely different ways, to the construction of varieties of modern collective consciousness and variations of the universal model of the nation-state. The preceding analysis indicates some of the distinctive characteristics of Japanese collective identity, its impact on the development of modern Japanese collective consciousness, and on the conception of the Japanese nation-state.

The collective identity and its institutional implications promulgated by the Meiji made Japan appear to be the most pristine nation-state. Yet the construction of the collective identity of the Meiji state was not based on a continual confrontation with a universal civilization of which it considered itself to be a part.

Unlike Europe, where the construction of national ideologies usually entailed strong tensions with universalistic religious orientations, no such tensions developed in principle in the ideology of *kokutai*. At most this ideology emphasized that the Japanese nation, by virtue of its primordial and sacral qualities, epitomized to a much higher degree than any other civilizations those very virtues which were extolled by these other civilizations, the Chinese one earlier on, and the Western one in the modern era.

A very interesting illustration of the persistence of the "primordial" conceptions of the Japanese collectivity in modern times can be found in the attitude of some very distinguished Japanese leftist intellectuals in the twentieth
century to Marxism. In common with many Chinese intellectuals of such dis-
position, these Japanese intellectuals, such as Kotuku or Kawakawi Hajime,
attempted to de-emphasize the "materialistic" dimensions of Marxism and
infuse them with "spiritual" values, with values of spiritualistic regeneration.
But while most of the Chinese intellectuals tended to emphasize the transcendental and universalistic themes of "classical" Confucianism, the
Japanese ones emphasized the specifically Japanese spiritual essence.[31]

Very interesting and significant in this context are the ways in which
modern Japanese historians, following the major tenets of modern Western
historiography, attempted to place Japan within the context of world history.
As Stefan Tanaka has recently shown in his incisive analysis, most of these
historians, who naturally refused to accept the Western characterization of
the "Orient," first redefined it as autonomous, equal to the West. Yet faced
with the problem of their own relation to China and its disintegration, most
of them ended by taking Japan out of the "Orient," making its history distinct,
separate, and unique, and often portraying Japan as the bearer of the pristine
values which other civilizations – Western or Chinese – claimed as their
own.[32]

VI New-World Civilizations

Distinct patterns of modern collective identities developed not only in Japan,
India, China, and Southeast Asia, but within Western civilization itself. Of
central importance for our analysis is that such distinct patterns developed in
the Americas – in the North American colonies and ultimately in the US and
in Latin America.

In both the United States and Latin America we can trace the crystallization of new civilizations, and not just, as Louis Hartz has claimed, of "fragments" of Europe. It is indeed quite possible that this is the first – and also the
last to date – case of the crystallization of new civilizations since that of the
great "axial" civilizations.[33] De Tocqueville, of course, clearly saw this: it was
indeed the central theme of his analysis of *Democracy in America*.[34] Latin
America did not have a de Tocqueville, but Alexander von Humboldt[35] in
the nineteenth century, and such literary figures and scholars as Octavio Paz,
Richard Morse, Howard Wiarda, Roberto de Matta, and others in the twentieth century,[36] have indicated in their work how new civilizations crystallized in Latin America.

The modern American civilizations emerged through the radical transformation of Europe's civilizational premises and institutional patterns. All of this crystallized with the emergence of modern societies and polities after the Reformation. The absolutist pattern that emerged in Counter-Reformation Spain and Portugal and the more constitutional patterns appearing in England and the Netherlands were both built on prior historical bases.[37]

In Protestant Europe such patterns formed through at least the partial incorporation of heterodox teachings and groups into the center, producing a relatively strong emphasis on equality in religious and political arenas. In Counter-Reformation Catholic Europe, above all in Spain and Portugal, the new regimes crushed heterodox sectarian groups and based themselves on a growing monopolization of the promulgation of the basic cultural premises by Church and state, along with closely related strong emphases on hierarchy.[38] Thus the central axes around which these two patterns crystallized in Europe were those of hierarchy–equality, of relatively pluralistic "ex-parte" as against homogeneous "ex-toto" conceptions of the social order, and correspondingly different institutional structures.[39]

These European tendencies were intensified and radically transformed during the "Europeanization" of the Americas, giving rise to new civilizational formations. The differences between the two Americas went far beyond the variations to be found in European societies. The working out of symbolic and institutional tensions between equality and hierarchy, between free and controlled access to the center, was at the heart of such radical transformation.

The crystallization of the new institutional formations and patterns of collective identities in the Americas was effected, as was true of the axial civilizations analyzed above, by the interaction between the basic orientations of the major social actors: the settlers; the settling agencies; the politico-ecological conditions of settlement; and the mode of encounter with the native population.

The combination of these factors and continuous feedback governing the transformation of the structure of the major social institutions and elites – especially their cultural autonomy – explain why the US and Latin American countries became not just "fragments of Europe," as did to some extent Canada, Australia, or some Caribbean countries, but indeed new civilizations which differed greatly from their European origins.

In the North American colonies, and later in the United States, this process was carried out by dispersed autonomous groups, many of them Protestant sects, with the Anglican Church and the British government playing a less important role. By contrast, in Latin America after the first wave of conquistadores the transplantation of European premises and social-cultural orientations was, on the whole, effected under the centralized authority of the Crown. The latter monopolized access to the major resources of the colonies – land and manpower – and in principle denied the settlers any great degree of self-government.

In North America in an unprecedented way settlers were the bearers of religious and cultural orientations which emphasized equality and direct and unmediated access to the sacred. These orientations gradually evolved into the premises of North American (later United States) civilization.[40] Ultimately there emerged among English-speaking settlers in North America two major institutional patterns, the US and the Canadian ones, the former as a distinct civilization, the latter initially, at least in the intent of its rulers, as a "fragment of Europe."

Latin Americans emphasized metaphysical hierarchy to a much greater extent even than Counter-Reformation Spain, with weaker emphasis on the autonomy of the economic and technological spheres.[41] In many ways it was in Latin America that the Thomist hierarchical conceptions become fully institutionalized far beyond practices in Spain or Portugal, not only in the curricula of universities, but also in the overall conception of the social order and in the political realm.[42] In contrast to European societies, in which even the Counter-Reformation was not able to do away with egalitarian components in the political arena, there developed in different Latin American countries a totalization of the hierarchical principle. This change was the reverse of those that took place in North America.

Latin America

Within Latin American civilization there could be found a great variety of institutional patterns, whose differences became much more pronounced after the wars of independence and throughout the nineteenth century, but all of them shared certain basic premises which survived a number of changes.

The first such change was the crystallization of patrimonial states characterized by very great overall administrative centralization. But given the wide geographic spread of the Empires and a lack of autonomous access of the active cohorts of the population to the centers of power and of resources, there developed within this centralized patrimonial state a paradoxically high degree of *de facto* local autonomy.[43] Concomitantly, major European political institutions, namely the representative ones, were replaced by a combination of royal *audiencias* and various local arrangements.[44] A highly legalistic culture resulted, in which the legally defined institutions were embedded in the hierarchical patrimonial structure and conceptions. Legally constituted cultural and educational institutions such as the universities were brought under royal control in the Spanish Empire to a much greater extent than in Spain itself to become among the most important promoters of absolutist doctrines. Later, after the wars of independence and the promulgation of constitutions, based on formal equality, there did develop, as we shall see later, a special relationship between the hierarchical and the egalitarian principles.

Although originally the Spanish (and Portuguese) Empires aspired to establish a unified homogeneous Hispanic (or Portuguese) collective identity focused on the motherland, in fact, in Latin America, a much more diversified situation developed.[45] From relatively early on there developed multiple components of collective consciousness and identity – the overall Spanish, the overall Catholic, different local Creole, and "native" ones.

At the same time, the strong hierarchical statist orientation was not, significantly enough, connected with the development of a parallel commitment to the political realm as a major focus of collective consciousness.

Hence, side by side with the formal hierarchical principles, there developed multiple continuously changing social spaces structured according to different principles and identities, with relatively shifting boundaries and with the possibility of the incorporation of many of these identities into the central arena.

Such possibility was due to the fact that this mode of construction of collective identity entailed a wide-ranging inclusiveness which has made it possible, as Merquior has indicated, not only to incorporate wide sectors of the Indian population in the overall Catholic and local identities, but also enabled them to develop, after the traumatic experiences of the conquest, at least in some Latin American countries like Mexico, Brazil, and to a smaller extent Bolivia and Colombia, a rather special type of cultural resurgence and even reintegration into the center.[46]

The United States

By contrast with that of Latin America, the pattern of collective identity that crystallized in the United States was eventually defined in inclusive ideological universalistic, non-primordial, and non-historical terms. It entailed the delineation of very sharp boundaries of the collectivity, informed by the basic premises of the American civil religion. This collective identity grew in part out of the transformation of the "messianic" and millennial strands of the early American sociopolitical endeavor.

A crucial aspect of the new American civilization was the construction of a mold based on a political ideology strongly rooted in the Puritan religious conceptions, in a Lockean political orientation, and in the Enlightenment. The Puritan conceptions entailed a strong emphasis on the special covenant between God and the chosen people, a covenant oriented to the creation of a deeply religious polity as it took shape in the late nineteenth century.[47]

The polity of the United States was characterized by the following: a strongly egalitarian, achievement-oriented individualism; republican liberties, with the almost total denial of the symbolic validity of hierarchy; disestablishment of official religion beginning at the federal level; basically anti-statist premises; and a quasi-sanctification of the economic sphere. Religious sentiment and religious values imparted a strong "messianic" and millennial dimension to the early American sociopolitical endeavor, made both solidarity and individualism central components of collective identity, and together with the anti-statist orientation gave rise to a distinct new civil religion.[48]

Primordial orientations or hierarchical principles could be permitted in secondary informal locations, but not as components of the central premises and symbols of the society. Thus, the US civil religion could not easily accommodate the "Native" Americans, with their overwhelming primordial identity, completely unrelated to the new ideological framework, and claiming a totality of its own. Hence Native Americans were virtually excluded from the new collectivity. While seemingly recognized as distinct nations, in reality they were at least until recently relegated, in a highly repressive way, to marginalized positions in the American collectivity.

At the same time a distinct attitude developed toward those – especially ethnic – immigrant groups which were willing to accept the basic terms of the American collective identity, and the basic premises of American civilization.

Given the weakness of primordial components in the construction of American collective identity, there was scope for tolerance, much greater than in Europe, not only of religious diversity, but also of groups which defined their secondary place in terms of primordial components. Such tolerance, of course, was predicated on the acceptance of the basic ideological-political premises of American civilization. But the boundaries of the social spaces of such groups were clearly delineated as secondary, even if such boundaries changed in different periods.[49]

The US then had the potential to accept, even if haltingly and intermittently, religious, political, and ethnic diversity – with the crucial initial exception of Native and African-Americans – as long as members of the different groups accepted the American political creed. African-Americans, impaled between their total strangeness in racial terms and their principled partial incorporation after the Civil War into the framework of the American collective, constituted here a rather special problem – "the American Dilemma." It is, of course, no accident that the most severe conflict in

American history – the Civil War – occurred around the problem of full inclusion of African-Americans. On the other hand, European immigrants faced no legal barriers to gaining full citizenship rights. For instance, despite discrimination against Jews, the question of Jewish emancipation – so central in modern Jewish experience in Europe – never arose. Generally, in the United States most ethnic groups, including African-Americans, aimed at carving out more extensive living spaces within the broad American framework for their ethnic traditions and symbols, and for the legitimation or the affirmation of their ethnic activities and organizations in the public arena. Many of the struggles of these groups, especially of the African-Americans, focused on full legal equality within the American framework; and they were greatly supported, as in the civil rights movements in the 1960s, by many sectors of the European-American majority population.

Most of these groups did not challenge the basic symbols and non-primordial institutional civil framework of the United States – although, needless to say, their very success changed the general ambience of this framework. Only the more extreme elements, for instance various groups at the height of the protest movement of the 1960s and 1970s, wanted to subvert that framework. Most ethnic struggles, such as that of the Jews against anti-Semitism, were undertaken in the name of general American values, of the basic premises of the American civilization. Significantly enough, when Martin Luther King was "canonized" by having a special day devoted to his memory, such canonization was made in the basic framework of the American civil religion. Moreover, King's movement was legitimized in terms of his contribution to the promulgation of, and struggle for, the general premises of civil equality of the United States. On the other hand, limited separatist movements developed among African-Americans and to a smaller extent among Hispanics. Most recently, the separatist tendency expresses itself in efforts to define an African-American or a Hispanic-American culture, which could be distinct from the Western European culture predominant in the United States. Colleges and universities and some entertainment media have become the major arenas in which these tendencies are promulgated and in which attempts at their institutionalization have developed. It remains to be seen how great an impact these movements will have compared to Martin Luther King's.

VII Summary

In the preceding discussion we have illustrated how interactions or interrelations between societies and civilizations, and the conceptualizing of such interrelations – above all those which have developed in axial and in modern civilizations – have shaped the construction of collective identity or consciousness. We have shown first of all that such patterns of collective identity are continually constructed from some basic yet continually changing building blocks, codes, or components; second, such codes are continually reconstructed in any society or group through the activities of different social actors; third, that the processes of construction of the components of collective identity have been greatly influenced by the interrelations between different civilizations or societies; and fourth, that confrontation between different actors in such interrelations is a crucial factor in the formation and transformation of the collective identity of their respective societies, including the nature of the primordial components of such identities.

7

Time, Space, and Prescriptive Marginality in Muslim Africa: Symbolic Action and Structural Change

Lamin Sanneh

Writing on the theme of conversion, the Harvard historian of religion, Arthur Darby Nock, spoke in one place of the singular absence of change in non-Western religious and cultural traditions where the most significant thing is the clock striking three and people then waiting for it to strike four.[1] Similarly, in a lyrical passage in a snatch of traditional African music that this writer was able to record on a field trip, the local bard was heard to praise his kinship patron as a broken-down clock, predictable and constant in his largesse, with the refreshing absence of that hard-to-get attitude so notorious among niggardly patrons. This particular patron was always "on time" with his obligations, not departing from the fixed rules of patronly honor. The bard called him "Mr Six O'Clock."[2] Nock meant to criticize what he saw as the inertia of tradition, its false smugness that denies or masks the truth and power of change, while the African bard with musical exhibition as flattery and advertisement of the fact extolled his patron's sense of constancy.

Historian and bard notwithstanding, time and theme may combine to foment radical change, and ritual plays an important role in the thematization of space and duration. By staging specific ritual action people conceive the justification for change, and demonstrate the power to effect it. Two elements may be involved: first, the transformation of the mundane succession of time as repetitive chronology into purposeful, prescriptive anticipation, and, second, the elevation of disjointed episodes and patterns to the level of normative symbols. In the one case we pick up the historical strand of time stripped of its mechanical repetitiveness,[3] so that time ceases to be a passive succession of events and becomes active herald and harbinger of a prescriptive order. This change is achieved through a ritual-prescribed consciousness set in symbolic action marked by stages of separation, transition, and incorporation. The second element arises from being able to extrapolate from a unique set of circumstances some large, all-embracing standard and fashioning symbols capable of forging an integrated web of meaning, value, and behavior. In this way a conceptual, interpretive link is established between the past and the imperative for structural change.

The trained historian need lay no more claim to the central pillars of symbolic anthropology than is needed to develop and promote this issue of symbolic action in human society. The present essay, concerned with critical religious thought and its relation to issues of identity, agency, and structural change, draws on the works of Victor Turner and Arnold van Gennep, supplemented with material from Ibn Khaldún, to probe the normative springs of historical understanding and explanation by focusing on one known feature of social organization, that of mobile groups in active interface with resident populations. It turns out that we can, with profit, apply the analytic material of Turner, van Gennep, and Ibn Khaldún to the role religion plays in the kind of prescriptive action that is a motor of historical change. We restrict our comments mainly, but not exclusively, to aspects of the history of Islam in Africa.

We should identify two major categories for analysis. One is marginality – understood here as historical enclavement – a process that implants minority groups and communities in mainstream societies without weakening or threatening their identity or that of their hosts. The other is mobility or itinerancy of the *tournée pastorale* variety, and how, when it becomes laden with rituals of marginality, itinerancy commences a process of change and renewal, and thus fits into the category of liminality, or threshold. We shall take that up in our concluding comments.

Marginality so used parallels the central place *communitas* occupies in the work of Turner,[4] and helps us to understand the process of religious transmission and establishment of Islamic communities in Africa and elsewhere. The popular use of marginality to describe the socially deprived and economically marginal is different from those of Turner and van Gennep, who stress the positive side of marginal social groups and individuals. And the most cursory review of the historical literature would confirm that "minority" Muslim groups and individuals in Africa and elsewhere were enterprising, commanding considerable organizational skills, and sometimes considerable economic leverage *vis-à-vis* indigenous political hierarchies, especially where in time their numbers included prosperous commercial patrons. Conceived symbolically, marginality is important in the stages antecedent to the pursuit of power. The action of setting oneself apart, or being set apart, for the purpose of preparing to assume power belongs crucially with the marginal status. We should again stress that this positive conception of marginality is different from the popular one where marginal groups are disadvantaged, typically against their will or without much choice on their part. Such groups would be at the bottom of the heap, easy prey for exploitation. This negative marginality is largely an imposed or unwilled condition, lacking the intentionality and initiative of agents. No light of illumination wells up from such a condition, no keen insight or penetrating discovery concerning human character and identity flows from it. Negative marginality, with its hints of force and compulsion, and of suppressed identity, is inferiority. It may serve the purpose and end of real historical agents, but its power arises from external direction, not from inward conviction. As one example below illustrates, this category of marginality includes slaves.

There is, however, the second type of marginality, suggested by van Gennep and Turner, people borne on the tide of mobility and arriving as outsiders or strangers in a new community. In Africa, for instance, stranger communities have played a pivotal role in religious and social change, and in the general demographic reshaping of towns. Such stranger communities fit into long-established categories: the Hausa *zango*, the Fulani *sabongari*, the Tokulor/Fula *ardoën* and *jokriyendem*, the Manding *luntankunda*, or even the Wolof *gan*, including the *nawetan*, to take a few West African examples of what is essentially enclavement. Such newcomers are normally exempt from the rules and requirement of kin obligation, and in return, occupy a position of political neutrality, often symbolized by rituals of transition, for that is what they are, a transitory people on their way from somewhere to somewhere else, a people between and betwixt.

In this group of marginals we find some of the most enterprising and dynamic individuals, people whose horizons have been broadened by time and exposure, whose skins wear the deep hue of the "tanning of travel." They bring awareness of an enlarged macrocosm to their host community, transfusing resident populations with new ideas in the give of foreign expertise and the take of local hospitality. The stranger Muslims negotiate with the host community through community landlords, the *lamdos*, who hold court at fixed times in the social and economic calendar. The *lamdo* is not an independent agent but a mediator and facilitator, conveying messages and running important errands. His (sometimes her) job is to deflect face-to-face encounters between the two groups, to limit relations to the circuitous third person, and to preserve spatial separation between the two groups. His task as *lamdo* will ensure ritual observance of spatial separation, thus lessening the risk of friction between strangers and residents. The *lamdo* is the linchpin of the network, holding together the different needs of boundary-free transient groups and boundary-hinged sedentary populations. His role establishes spatial separation as an aspect of social organization, in fact as an attribute of *territorial passage*.[5] Thus shielded without being discriminated against, such marginal groups or individuals are obviously not at the bottom of the heap in any meaningful sense. Instead their marginality is of the type acquired from being outsiders, outside the kin structure, outside the political system, and sometimes even outside centers of economic power. Their significance lies in their capacity to incubate power, to foment and guide hopes and aspirations for a better and different future, to reconstruct society accordingly, and then to signify the auspicious moment when the chosen few would witness change come to pass. The element of prophetic anticipation that persists in many rituals of transition is in fact a proleptic device to exchange numerical inferiority for moral advantage and to anticipate a future moral rebirth. Enclavement is propitious soil in which to plant the seeds of change judiciously. Time and prayer do the rest.

There is, of course, a risk in marginality of this type. The stakes are great enough to warrant the risk of defiant seclusion, but it may at times be a bad gamble trying to sell falafel in taco country, trying, as it were, to force on local populations habits borrowed from elsewhere. Local rulers may offer hospitality to attract or reward Muslim support, but may then smell the scent of approaching challenge and decide on expulsion in a preventive action to forestall change. Or, marginality may miscalculate the mood for change.

This matter of bringing unsuspecting or reluctant communities to the brink of change was described by John Locke as a hypothetical scenario, and the stages he identified for it conform pretty well to many historical cases in pre-colonial Africa. Let us imagine, Locke argues, destitute Christian missionaries arriving in a so-called pagan country and inserting themselves into the society by taking advantage of the kindness and hospitality of their hosts. The new religion then takes root in the country and spreads gradually. While Christians remain a minority they publicly espouse peace, friendship, faith, and justice for all. But at length they grow powerful and achieve substantial victory with the magistrate of the country converting and becoming a Christian. This fact emboldens the Christians to break all previous accords with the pagans on whom they turn, requiring them to repudiate their ancient religion and customs on pain of being dispossessed and reduced to servitude. Locke derives from this situation a critical moral point, namely, that such an outcome would be merely "the pretense of religion, and of the care of souls," and would be "a cloak to covetousness, rapine, and ambition."[6] However, more relevant to our subject is that for Locke Christian victory accrues to those marginal people able to take the initiative, using time to good effect.

That constructed tableau has an uncanny similarity to the condition of countless communities in Muslim Africa. In one well-known eighteenth-century instance, the Sarki, or king, of one West African pagan state, Gobir, woke up one day to find his Muslim guests had grown in number and confidence, had turned implacably militant and were threatening his kingdom. They were in no mood for conciliation and concession. He had been too sanguine, and rued the day, he said, when he gave friendly sanctuary to Muslims. He later complained to his fellow kings "that he had neglected a small fire in his country until it had spread beyond his power to control. Having failed to extinguish it it had now burnt him. Let each beware," he lamented, "lest a like calamity befall his town also."[7] Thus in numerous places in Africa stranger Muslim communities perceived to represent unacceptable competition have been curbed and given Hobson's choice of taking leave. Their departure, whether actual or symbolic, has usually opened a liminal frontier, with the refugees spreading through new territories and disseminating reform ideas. Instances of such expulsion, however, are rare, for a Muslim enclave often brings new opportunities and is accordingly welcomed.

This appears to be the situation at a certain critical juncture in the history of the medieval West African kingdom of Mali, as described by a contemporary Arab geographer, al-Bakrí. Here is a part of his account, written in 1067/68 AD:

> On the opposite bank of the Níl is another great kingdom, stretching a distance of more than eight days' marching, the king of which has the title of Daw. The inhabitants of this region use arrows when fighting. Beyond this country lies another called Malal, the king of which is known as al-musulmání. He is thus called because his country became afflicted with drought one year following another; the inhabitants prayed for rain, sacrificing cattle till they had exterminated almost all of them, but the drought and the misery only increased. The king had as his guest a Muslim who used to read the Koran and was acquainted with the Sunna. To this man the king complained of the calamities that assailed him and his people. The man said: "O King, if you believed in God (who is exalted) and testified that He is One, and testified as to the prophetic mission of Muhammad (God bless him and give him peace) and if you accepted all the religious laws of Islam, I would pray for your deliverance from your plight and that God's mercy would envelop all the people of your country and that your enemies and adversaries might envy you on that account." Thus he continued to press the king until the latter accepted Islam and became a sincere Muslim. The man made him recite from the Koran some easy passages and taught him religious obligations and practices which no one

may be excused from knowing. Then the Muslim made him wait till the eve of the following Friday, when he ordered him to purify himself by a complete ablution, and clothed him in a cotton garment which he had. The two of them came out towards a mound of earth, and there the Muslim stood praying while the king, standing at his right side, imitated him. Thus they prayed for a part of the night, the Muslim reciting invocations and the king saying "Amen". The dawn had just started to break when God caused abundant rain to descend upon them. So the king ordered the idols to be broken and expelled the sorcerers from his country. He and his descendants after him as well as his nobles were sincerely attracted to Islam, while the common people of his kingdom remained polytheists.[8]

Al-Bakrí's account of what amounts to structural change is framed by ritual. The visiting Muslim cleric bides his time with giving gentle advice inviting the king to embrace Islam, and then, after a disastrous drought pretty much brought the state to its knees, with crop failure, scarcity of water, and the depletion of the cattle stock through futile sacrifice, the cleric repeats the offer he had previously made to the king to adopt Islam. With the circumstances now more propitious for an alternative faith system to strike root in the kingdom, the seeds sown from the first contacts are activated. The ruler, not surprisingly, is predisposed to respond. The drama of the royal conversion then moves to center stage with a rain-making ritual, called *salát al-istisqá*, normally performed on a Thursday night till dawn the following Friday. To that act of conversion is linked the regeneration of the kingdom, so that the coming of Islam to the seat of power is tied in the public perception with the onset of material abundance and, thus, with the structural security of the state. This is not imposed conversion: it is a strategic move by the ruler to co-opt Islam as a rain-making religion, and thus as analogue to the old ideas. It is, in fact, strategic marginality, with change from the top. The fact that the general populace did not, or would not, turn to Islam, or rise in revolt against their renegade king, indicates that the old embankments had not crumbled entirely. First the drought-hit landscape is revived before the faith produces streams in full spate. On the other hand, were Islam to fail in warding off future drought, it would in turn be sucked into the grim cycle of decline and fall.

THE MECCA PILGRIMAGE: HOMECOMING IN A STRANGE LAND

There is a third category of marginality different from the preceding two, and this concerns what we might call prescriptive marginality, the marginality of agency and action. It involves people who out of a strong conviction decide to place themselves outside mainstream structures in order better to challenge and reform them. It often happens that such people draw a following (from the first and second class of marginals, ideally) and withdraw into an exclusive community where they undertake a series of ritual actions for incubating power as a prelude to bursting upon the world. In Muslim Africa the most typical expression of such incubation of marginality is the *hijrah*, the formal withdrawal of a reform-minded group of Muslims in preparation for militant *jihád* and vigilant *tajdíd* ("reform"), although the Mecca pilgrimage precedes it in regularity and practice.

While for ideological marginality *hijrah* might be its quintessential expression, in the *hajj* pilgrimage to Mecca Muslims are immersed in a heightened ritual experience that overlaps significantly with *hijrah* as a form of symbolic social action. As it is, the pilgrimage is essentially a vocation by a minority of Muslims, and in its rituals it acts to shake up habits of mundane routine, like other aspects of religious practice, such as the quotidian Friday congregational worship, or the exacting five-daily prayers. In the annual rite at Mecca, however, the pilgrim has separated and is in ritual transition for an extended period of time. He or she usually follows a regime of intense devotions and that strengthens the sense of liminal power, boosting it with an awakened sense of virtuous *communitas*, which is sustained for the duration of the *hajj*. One account of the *hajj* says in this respect that "it is a great place of assembly where people from all lands foregather, in numbers that God alone knows. When they stand there and their voices rise in prayer and supplication to Almighty God, you would think that the Day of Judgment had come and that all mankind had come together as one. We pray to Almighty God to treat us with His universal kindness at the time of this great gathering."[9] In his own rather individual, poignant way, Malcolm X had come to a similar experience from the *hajj*, noting the importance of prayer there. "In Elijah Muhammad's Nation of Islam we hadn't prayed in Arabic. ... At that time, I had learned those prayers phonetically. But I hadn't used them since. [Now in Mecca] I may not have been mumbling the right thing, but I was mumbling. ... In my ignorant, crippled condition in the Holy Land, I had been lucky to have met patient friends."[10] He testified of his life-changing experience in Mecca, saying, "In my thirty-nine years on this earth, the Holy City of Mecca had been the first time I had ever stood before the Creator of All and felt like a complete human being. ... My thinking had been opened up in Mecca."[11] And so, too, his identity, an American social activist promoting a race-based agenda, was transformed into that of an agent of a world faith based on the fellowship of all believers. It all goes to show the power of the *hajj* for symbolic social actions.

Which, then, prompts the thought that the experience of Malcom X can be generalized for the mass of Meccan pilgrims, because so potent is the ritual effect engendered by the observance that what is suffered by way of hardship, personal privation, or indignity, inconvenience, handicap, or even injustice, merely improves the appetite for commitment. So could a writer observe that:

> The greed of those who direct the pilgrim at the various shrines and the frauds practised so brazenly on them by the people of the Holy City, may call for indignant criticism even from the most devout Moslem. But these lamentable social defects in most cases only serve as a foil to the stimulating effects of crowd psychology as realized at Mecca. The individual pilgrim is awestruck by the mass movement exemplified in the pilgrimage of so many fellow-believers. When he returns to his distant home, no feature of his experience is dilated on with more enthusiasm as he narrates the events of the pilgrimage to his friends. Thus countless individuals are drawn within the mystic spell of a profound class consciousness which is essentially religious.[12]

It is a recurrent subject in the literature on the *hajj* that the rite is a rebirth, a special homecoming of fulfillment, affirmation, a potent sense of regeneration, transformation, and equality among believers. The twelfth-century Muslim Spanish pilgrim, Ibn Jubayr, who undertook the *hajj* in 1183 AD, described his personal experience in 1185. For believers, he affirms, Mecca is holy ground, the place of equal and ample access where they obtain divine merit. Pulsating with the energy and pleas of the devout penitent, the city is a miracle of God's gracious bounty, the target of His mercy and blessings. He continues:

> A manifest miracle is that this Safe City [Mecca], which lies in a valley bed that is a bow-shot or less in width, can contain this vast host; a host such that, were it brought into the greatest of cities, could not be contained. This venerated city, in what concerns it of manifest miracles, namely its expansion for multitudes beyond count, is described only by the true analogy of the ulema [learned doctors of divinity], that its enlargement for newcomers is that of a uterus for the fetus. So it is with 'Arafat and the other great shrines in this sacred land. May God with His grace and bounty increase its sanctity, and in it grant to us His mercy.[13]

The stages of the pilgrimage journey itself are marked by rigorous observance of ritual, including the five daily prayers, the *salát*, augmented now with concentrated forms of supererogatory devotions at Mina, Mount 'Arafat, Muzdalifah, at Safa, Merwa and the Ka'ba, and at the well of Zemzem. The believer "who goes to the pilgrimage, circumambulates the Ka'ba with Turks and Indians, runs between Safa and Merwa with Afghans and Chinese, drinks at the well of Zemzem with Moors and Zanzibaris, makes his sacrifice in the valley of Mina with Javanese and Syrians, listens to the sermon at 'Arafat among Egyptians and Sudanese, and [...] goes back to his little village home enthused with knowledge that he is part of this great brotherhood of Islam, with what seems to him its unconquerable power and unsurpassable glory."[14]

HIJRAH AND IDEOLOGICAL AGENCY

Hijrah, however, attains its most ideologically rarefied, concentrated form of threshold experience when undertaken as a prelude to *jihád.* It becomes the interlude between a discredited and controversial establishment status quo and its displacement in the process of qualitative change.[15]

Ideological marginality demands qualitative change in the pattern of historical development rather than surrender to a timeless, ahistorical ideal. Such marginality looks upon "isolation" as a tactical move, the lucid interval between what is passing and what succeeds it. William James, the American philosopher, once cited Professor Starbuck as asserting that in dramatic conversion, theology intervenes in what would otherwise be a normal rite of passage to intensify and foreshorten the duration of adolescent crisis.[16] James may here be implying that theology strives to incorporate into an absolute and timeless frame what is at heart only a transitional phase, a curtain raiser rather than the spectacle itself. If so then the danger for history is remarkably similar. When historians concentrate on origin and result to render events unique and particular, when they erect boundaries of source and influence to shut off wider connections and more subtle affinities, when, in that case, periodization locks the clock on times, places, and figures so as to deny the manifold uses of history, they are in danger of making a relic of the past.[17] For this reason the apostles of liminality theory have done history yeoman service by taking space and duration and constituting them into a principle of transition and change, what van Gennep calls "changes in condition which are the pivot for social organization and mobilization." That places change right at the core of historical understanding.

In building on the foundation Victor Turner laid with liminal theory, we may identify the position of ideological marginality in three stages of liminal experience. The first is spontaneous or existential *communitas,* where marginal elements are marshaled and organized by the ideal of egalitarian virtue. The second is normative *communitas,* where social norms and mores are thematized for collective appropriation in rites of passage, rites that make no distinctions of status, person, kin, or group (birth, puberty, marriage, and death affect all of us by virtue of our humanity, not by virtue of any achieved result). Finally, we have ideological *communitas* whose members adhere to a regime of utopian idealism, energized with streaks of activist fervor, and set to wrest control of events.[18]

ISLAM IN AFRICA: LIMINALITY AND HISTORICAL CHANGE

It is that ideological dimension that is brought to a sharp point in a passage that has come to be viewed as the manifesto of the Muslim African reform tradition. In that passage the fifteenth-century scholar and firebrand, 'Abd al-Karím al-Maghílí al-Tilimsání (d. 1506), who was visiting the West African Muslim state of Songhay, wrote in 1492 to the king, Askiya al-Hájj Muhammad Ture, to the effect that the Muslim world in their day was at the verge of a critical threshold, and that men like themselves should aid the hastening of that radical dispensation. Al-Maghílí put it in pithy words thus:

> Thus it is related that at the beginning of every century God sends (people) a scholar who regenerates their religion for them. There is no doubt that the conduct of this scholar in every century in enjoining what is right and forbidding what is wrong, and setting aright (the) people's affairs, establishing justice among them and supporting truth against falsehood and the oppressed against the oppressor, will be in contrast to the conduct of scholars of his age. For this reason he will be an odd man out among them on account of his being the only man of such pure conduct and on account of the small number of men like him. Then it will be plain and clear that he is one of the reformers (*al-muslihín*) and that who so opposes him and acts hostilely towards so as to turn people away from him is but one of the miscreants, because of the saying of the Prophet, may God bless him and grant him peace: "Islam started as an odd man out (*gharíb*) and thus will it end up, so God bless the odd men out." Someone said, "And who are they, O Messenger of God?" He said, "Those who set matters aright in evil times." That is one of the clearest signs of the people of the Reminder (*ahl al-dhikr*) through whom God regenerates for people their religion.[19]

There is no doubt that al-Maghílí's own marginal, liminal position, that is to say, his "separation from native land, friends and familiar things," as Suhrawardí describes it, increased his receptivity to the text on reform, and he was thus set to draw Songhay tightly into that ideological net. Three elements combine in al-Maghílí to thrust Muslims into the millenarian age: the prescriptive courage of a scholarly minority, the centennial hope induced by the religious calendar (a hundred-year rite of passage, if you will), and, with the backing of the Songhay state, a resolute will to recast the larger society in the image of the righteous few. These three elements conform nearly exactly to Turner's existential *communitas*, normative *communitas*, and ideological *communitas*, and, what is more, they stamp duration with the program of revolutionary social change.

Al-Maghílí's own existential situation had, therefore, opened him to the insight that the religious vocation at its most authentic, or at any rate at its most rousing, is really a historic minority mandate, a minority that adumbrates the larger world in order to supersede it decisively with its own fresh moral sanctions. (He would have dismissed the idea of a "moral majority," for example, as an oxymoron.)

The reform movements in African Islam, stretching from the fifteenth to the early decades of the twentieth century, have spawned a tradition of moral enclavement where cumulative pressure matures and finally bursts into prominence in historical movements. In such movements Muslims are led by those able and willing to repudiate prevailing customs and attitudes and place the trustworthy few at the head of affairs.

The *hijrah* community is the moral enclave par excellence. The reformers undertake *hijrah* to indicate in a formal way their break with the status quo. While in *hijrah* they observe with unusual intensity the obligatory rituals of purification, prayer, fasting, and dietary regulations. They study the code and the manuals and follow with punctilious faithfulness the letter and spirit of the law. With fastidious care and detail, they water the seeds of rebellion, keeping mainstream structures and institutions in view and within range. So they come up for air by maintaining links with their world, attracting newcomers and sending out sympathizers to keep up the pressure. The *hijrah* community in principle transcends the restrictions and inequalities of life, allowing free and equal access to goods and services, inculcating a common ethical code among its members, and a shared feeling of privileged moral exclusiveness vis-à-vis the unjust and oppressive structures of the world. It is, to cite Turner, "the units of space and time in which behavior and symbolism are momentarily enfranchised from the norms and values that govern the public lives of incumbents of structural positions."[20] What is conceived and nurtured in this special atmosphere has attached to it the seal of virtue, and will on that basis demand unquestioned surrender and obedience.

The heightened attention to ritual observance in the *hijrah* community, for example, helps to promote and elevate ordinary *salát* into an incubatory, exalted rite. The washing or ablution that is done before the prayers becomes a ritual act of separation, of withdrawing from mundane routine and preoccupations; the entry into the mosque an act of transition; the prayer motions a symbol of participation and incorporation into the ranks of the elect. All of this would intensify the feeling of chosenness, of liminal exceptionalism, and thus open the way for impending judgment and action.

The recognized leaders of such *hijrah* communities have often used the *salát* observance to develop a particularly acute form of ritual withdrawal, called *salát al-istikhárah*. It is ritual exclusion for a period of, say, forty days, during which time the cleric seeks guidance from God about the specific course of action he should or should not take. All contact with the outside world is broken off, and at the conclusion of the forty days the cleric is rewarded with a mandate for action, normally in the form of a dream or vision. What comes out of *istikhárah* is deemed safe from the contamination and corruption of this world, since it emerges from the womb of consecrated time and is thus immune to temporal compromise or defect. In the phrase of the masters, the *istikhárah* vessel drips with what is in it.[21] *Istikhárah*, thus, concentrates at one sensitive point the ritual, individual, and social dimensions of revolutionary gestation. It produces the motive power for embarking on change of a specific kind and at a specific time, and bringing to term the fully developed idea of change. In the conditions of ritual seclusion it prescribes the rubric for personal and social transformation. It uses the gaps between the structures to construct a fresh order that discredits the old and thus dramatizes prescriptive objections to the status quo.

Salát al-istikhárah has an abbreviated parallel in *khalwah*, another form of ritual seclusion and preparation undertaken for about a week or so by secular clerics. In spite of the generally recognized risks associated with it, *khalwah* is on frequent demand by ordinary Muslims. A cleric would typically undertake it for a fee at the request of a client with various desiderata: healing, safe travel, marriage, a job, advancement, or a prophylactic. *Khalwah*, however, is a risky procedure, fraught with dangers for the over-eager therapist. It may bring ill-prepared clerics to spiritual grief by reducing them to mere gibberish, unable to give words to their thoughts. Yet *khalwah* does represent in society a recognition that symbolic retreat may be endowed with rare social power, and, even where it goes wrong, *khalwah* may appeal as a last resort against apathy and disenchantment. Those who resort to it demonstrate a dissatisfaction with things and conditions as they are, whether or not they succeed by, or from it. *Khalwah* is their hope of thrusting aside the inhibitions and constraints of the status quo and improving their station in life.

The North Nigerian Fulani reformer, 'Uthmán dan Fodio (1754–1817), illustrates very well what effects *istikhárah* and similar spiritual exercises might produce on those consecrated clerics who undertake them, and what that does in normatizing space and duration. These special rites can have an exceptionally clarifying effect on the mandate for change and the resolve to bring it to pass. Dan Fodio described a vision that occurred to him in 1794. It is a vision wrought in ritual gravitas, crystallizing in the sublime proofs of liminal, exalted chosenness. From it he received his marching orders to embark on revolution, an idea he had long cultivated independent of heavenly visitation, but now with the added weight of divine ratification. In his meticulous account, he begins by stating his age precisely in years, months and even days, wishing us to see symbolic meaning in that threefold division of time.

> When I reached forty years, five months and some days, God drew me to him, and I found the Lord of djinns and men, our Lord Muhammad – may God bless him and give him peace. With him were the Companions, and the prophets, and the saints. Then they welcomed me, and sat me down in their midst. Then the Saviour of djinns and men, our Lord 'Abd al-Qadir al-Jilani, brought a green robe embroidered with the words, "There is no god but God; Muhammad is the Messenger of God" – May God bless him and give him peace – and a turban embroidered with the words, "He is God, the One." He handed them to the Messenger of God – may God bless him and give him peace – and the Messenger of God clasped them to his bosom for a time; then he handed them to Abu Bakr al-Siddiq, and he handed them to 'Umar al-Faruq, and he handed them to 'Uthman Dhu 'l-Nurain, and he handed them to 'Ali – may God ennoble his face – and then to Yusuf – upon whom be peace – and Yusuf gave them back to my Lord 'Abd al-Qadir al-Jilani; and they appointed him to act on their behalf, and said, "Dress him and enturban him, and name him with a name that shall be attributed exclusively to him." He sat me down, and clothed me and enturbaned me. Then he addressed me as "Imam of the saints" and commanded me to do what is approved of and forbade me to do what is disapproved of; and he girded me with the Sword of Truth, to unsheath it against the enemies of God. Then they commanded me with what they commanded me; and at the same time gave me leave to make this litany that is written upon my ribs widely known, and promised me that whoever adhered to it, God would intercede for every one of his disciples.[22]

It was a point of no return. In the approaching apocalyptic time, he felt, the old enemy structures would be brought down, and to hasten it he made the decision to adopt the path of militancy towards the compromising Muslims and the corrupt political leadership that had built its career on short-term cynical expediency. Together these colluding lukewarm Muslims had allowed fleet of foot political compromisers to stroll unchallenged around the commandments of God. Three years later, in 1797, we find the Shehu firmly set on that militant course and making active preparations to arm his followers, directing them to prepare for *jihád*. He commanded that preparing for *jihád* as he directed them was a *sunnah*, a prescribed norm of the Prophet himself. During months of feverish activity, the Shehu used the prayer ritual to bolster the ardor of his disciples. His brother, 'Abdalláh dan Fodio, records that the Shehu "began to pray to God that He should show him the sovereignty of Islam in this country of the Sudan, and he set this to verse in his vernacular ode, *al-Qâdiriyya* ['The Qadirite Ode'], and I put it into Arabic in verses."[23] The Shehu coupled this militant resolve with a decision to emigrate from where he was living in Gobir to Gudu. It was a symbolic act of giving public birth to his movement as well as an act of political defiance: Gobir had been hostile to him and his disciples, and repudiating it would taint it with the stigma of infidelity and enmity towards God. This is the *territorial passage*, in addition to ritual duration, that van Gennep described as crucial to the liminal breakthrough.[24] The Shehu insisted on the *territorial passage*, the *hijrah*, as a prerequisite of sound faith, especially where it entailed severe personal deprivation:

> O brethren, it is incumbent upon you to emigrate from the lands of unbelief to the lands of Islam that you may attain Paradise and be companions of your ancestor Abraham, and your Prophet Muhammad, on account of the Prophet's saying, "Whoever flees with his religion from one land to another, be it [merely the distance of] the span of a hand, will attain to Paradise and be the companion of Abraham and His Prophet Muhammad."[25]

This denunciation of worldly structures is very different from the ascetic norm of world or carnal renunciation. The Shehu and his followers intended no flight from world conquest, merely a tactical move to prepare the better for it. Mystical discipline would for them remove the rust of corruption from truth, and assist the faithful in having their motives refined and polished to prescriptive ends. Consequently, historical analysis should also concern itself, not just with origin and result, but with process and choice. Liminality inscribes action with an agenda and a purpose, so that the Shehu's religious training and his teaching function could culminate in a mandate for change and agency where formerly he only had choice forced on him.

The obvious question, now, is whether revolutionary incubation in its social mode can miss its moment, and if so, what the consequences might be. In other words, can people at an advanced, self-conscious stage of ritual and spatial separation become locked in a state of permanent seclusion, and, as it were, allow the clock to run out on themselves? Is the anchorite enclave viable as a permanent state? We know that many groups have made a virtue of permanent enclavement, and in so doing have stagnated, exchanging dynamic agency for static ideals. The historical record is littered with the desiccated remains of such utopian fossils but, under the right historical conditions, they are quite combustible.[26]

One example, drawn from African Islam, might suffice. In the nineteenth century there arose in Futa Jallon a mass popular movement, called the Hubbubé, whose members repudiated constituted authority and created in the countryside, outside the centers of power, a moral enclave called Boketo. They were led by Abal Juhe, the son and heir of the movement's charismatic founder, Mamadou Juhe, who charged that the inheritors of the utopian ideals of Karamokho Alfa, the Muslim reformer of 1727, had allowed standards to slip for the sake of personal gain. More specifically, the slave question had got out of hand when the Fulbe *mawubé*, the political elite, tried to squeeze increased revenue out of an already impoverished slave peasantry, and then resorted to plunder to increase the size of slave holdings. The over-burdened slave populations became increasingly restive, waiting for a leader to gather the embers of discontent into one burst of fire. They found this leader in Mamadou Juhe, a daring and cunning figure who knew well how to turn the scattered discontent of the countryside into more organized and coherent channels. He used Islam to articulate the grievances of his motley followers on whom he imposed his strong personality. The disenchanted, the overtaxed, the impoverished, the rootless and other flotsam and jetsam poured out from the nooks and crannies and crevices of society to hail the messianic dispensation, an avalanche that shook the countryside. One scholar described the miscellaneous social composition of the Hubbubé, caught up in the fervor of throwing off their chains, and scarcely by a vision of what to build.

> The Hubbu movement mobilized and attracted to the periphery of Futa Jallon the oppressed, the jungle Fulbe, that is, Fulbe of inferior status and extraction who were liable to taxation and to forced labor without mitigation, descendants of pastoral Fulbe recently converted to Islam, certain unassimilated Jallonke, and thousands of slaves concentrated in the *rima'ibé* ("slave camps").[27]

Dr Edward Blyden (1832–1912), the most influential Black intellectual of his day, visited Futa Jallon in 1872 and left an eyewitness account of what he found of the rump of the Hubbubé movement.

> The Hoobos (he writes) are renegade Fulbe in revolt against the king of Timbo. Twenty years ago, on account of the exactions imposed by the Almamy Umaru, they rose in revolt and with their families removed themselves to come and settle the grazing lands between Futa Jallon and Solima country. They are called Hoobos or Hubus because following their departure from their homes they were chanting in chorus a verse from the Coran [sic] in which the word Hubu appeared twice. It says this: "Nihibu ('Nuhibbu') Rusul (Rasúl) Allah Huban ('Hubban') Wahidan", which means those who love the Envoy of God ("without compromise").[28]

Former slaves constituted a major component of the ranks of the Hubbubé, showing how the marginality of inferiority and economic deprivation can be exploited to boost the fortunes of prescriptive marginality and serve the historical end of real agents, as we noted above.

Boketo thus conformed to the classic features of *hijrah*, of revolutionary incubation, that is. When Abal took over the leadership of the movement he intensified his father's reform program. He abolished slavery in the movement and issued a call to all slaves elsewhere to repudiate the bonds of servitude and come to Boketo, the privileged enclave of egalitarian virtue. There the Hubbubé infused from a heady dose of millennial chosenness, turning that intoxicating fervor against the country's discredited *mawubé*. They scoffed at conventional rules, flouted norms of established conduct, and took to loot and general lawlessness. Virtue had turned wild and impetuous.

The Hubbubé became the scourge of the countryside, a ragged band of disoriented malcontents who disdained lawful enterprise and tried to live from plunder and violent sequestration. Cut off from other centers of renewal and without an agenda to launch a sequel, the Hubbubé became sitting targets, or else aimless refugees. Blyden describes their painful demise in these words:

> The Hooboos, those renegade Foulahs, who for thirty years have been a terror to caravans passing through the districts which they infested, have been scattered by the military energy of Samudu ("Samori"), Mandingo chieftain from the Konia country, due east of Liberia. Abal, the chief of the Hooboos, has been captured and banished to a distant region.[29]

In fact Samori's forces dealt brutally with Abal Juhe, his *disjecta membra* being put on public display as a show of triumph. Nevertheless, the fate of the Hubbubé is by no means characteristic of what happens with millenarian movements with spent force. Many of them are spared the fire or the sickle and are left to lie dormant until their vital substance can be absorbed by their successors. Thus have certain key elements of traditional African rites survived and become incorporated into viable forms of local Muslim practice.

Not to give *hijrah* a bad name, at the opposite end of the spectrum from Boketo was the remarkable series of revival centers organized under other religious leaders whose teaching marshaled numerous populations and put them on track to genuine social change. These revival centers came under the direction of the Shádhiliyáh,[30] a Súfí taríqah that first made its appearance in Futa Jallon in the eighteenth century. The *'ulamá*, the scholars, of the Shádhiliyáh cultivated a form of religious exercise called the *diароré*, a litany of ecstatic devotions developed in relative seclusion in village congregations called *missidi*. The *diароré* attracted disaffected peasants, manumitted slaves and economic insolvents, and put them through the furnace of spiritual purification. They emerged a transformed religious elite, exchanging the rags of wretched stigma for the heavenly mantle, and consecrated to the virtuous life from their guides having invested them with a role in a moral cause. The French authorities, fearing that the *diaroré* rites might engulf the colonial machinery of native subjugation, decided to isolate the movement's impact center at Diawia and thus suffocate the satellite communities before they had a chance to become militant and ungovernable.[31] That way, Islam ceased to be "the odd man out," its village votaries swept into the strangling net of colonial subjugation.

Muslim *'ulamá* are only too aware of the harm permanent seclusion, or even settled life in towns, might do to the cause of reform and renewal, and in one case, that of the Jakhanke Muslim clerics, it has been shown how a viable program of internal renewal, *tajdíd*, spanning the centuries, might be established through regular itinerancy, especially in the rural countryside.[32] The ambulatory cleric, as in Chaucer's *Canterbury Tales*, becomes in the Muslim reform tradition the mark and bearer of new horizons.

IBN KHALDÚN ON MARGINALITY AND REFORM

In his *al-Muqaddima*, Ibn Khaldún takes this analysis further and argues that urban conditions are injurious to the cultivation of courage and the life of moral reform. He stresses the blunting effect of the urban environment on the critical powers of religion, saying religion is a noble calling whose ends are opposed to those of commerce and urban living. The person who takes up religion is in effect in a liminal situation, standing in critical judgment over the one immersed in commercial and urban life:

> (B)ecause the things (religious officials) have to offer are so noble, they feel superior to the people and are proud of themselves. Therefore, they are not obsequious to persons of rank, in order to obtain something to improve their sustenance. In fact, they would not have time for that. They are occupied with those noble things they have to offer and which tax both the mind and the body. Indeed the noble character of the things they have to offer does not permit them to prostitute themselves openly(.) They would not do such a thing. As a consequence, they do not, as a rule, become very wealthy.[33]

As opposed to the single-minded and prescriptive tone of the religious vocation, Ibn Khaldún points to the slippery ways of commerce:

> We have already stated that traders must buy and sell and seek profits. This necessitates flattery, and evasiveness, litigation and disputation, all of which

are characteristic of this profession. And these qualities lead to a decrease and weakening in virtue and manliness.[34]

This occupational classification has a corresponding justification in environmental factors. Town life, Ibn Khaldún avers, is suited to the pursuit of commerce in the same way that the countryside is adapted to the special concerns of reform. With great skill and the force of an original mind, Ibn Khaldún describes the social conditions pertaining to the urban–rural matrix and the historical consequences of events there:

> *Countrymen are morally superior to townsmen.* This is because the soul is, by its nature, prepared to receive any impressions of good or evil that may be stamped upon it. ... Now the townsmen are so immersed in luxury, pleasure-seeking and worldliness, and so accustomed to indulge in their desires, that their souls are smeared with vice and stray far from the path of virtue. Countrymen, though also worldly-minded, are forced to confine themselves to bare necessities; they do not seek to indulge their desire for luxury and pleasures. Their habits and actions are relatively simple, hence they are less subject than townsmen to reproach on the grounds of vice and evil-doing.[35]

Thus it is, according to Ibn Khaldún, that we may treat virtue and the moral life as specifically religious concerns and seek their best expression in rural simplicity or in desert austerity. We should also perceive the contrast to this in the forces of corruption and decadence engendered by life in the urban environment. In Ibn Khaldún's view, then, the reform potential of religion develops better in one set of circumstances than in another, and those reform priorities are essential to religious integrity. It is, of course, a wholly different matter what Ibn Khaldún thinks might create one set of circumstances rather than another, but on the issue of fundamental reform motivation, he makes a convincing case that religion is the key, and rural or desert conditions its most hospitable crucible.

This dichotomy is also important, in Ibn Khaldún's view, for understanding the nature of militancy, for that, too, is a consequence of rural or desert conditions. He says that townspeople are in the habit of relinquishing the task of self-defense to their rulers and a professional military class. In the course of time they lapse into habitual lethargy,

> accustomed, like women and children, to look to others for protection; and with time this habit of dependence becomes a second nature. Countrymen and nomads, on the other hand, live a more isolated life, far from large towns and garrisons, undefended by walls or defenses. Hence they look for protection to themselves alone, not trusting others. Always armed and watchful ... they are

ever on the lookout for any sign of danger ... being full of confidence in their own courage and power. For courage has become one of their deepest qualities and audacity a second nature to them, emerging whenever occasion calls.[36]

Ibn Khaldún thus sees towns as notoriously inept at supporting the habit of change and reform, with the people "so immersed in luxury, pleasure-seeking and worldliness, and so accustomed to indulge their desires, that their souls are smeared with vice and stray far from the path of virtue."[37] By contrast, rural or desert conditions "confine people to bare necessities." Consequently such people "are less subject than townsmen to reproach on the grounds of vice and evil-doing." Since change and reform involve upheaval and require a willingness to suffer personal and material privation and acceptance of the risk of working for a future which one might not live to see, they are not naturally appealing to urban social elites, religious and political. That then leaves rural or nomadic conditions in Ibn Khaldún's reckoning as ideal fuel for radical reform, with itinerant clerics, mostly of slender means, tending the flame.

Certainly in the great reform movements in African Islam we see a remarkable connection between village centers, nomadic groups, and the reform initiative. Those that Ibn Khaldún describes as "souls smeared with vice" were called by African Muslim reformers "the venal mallams," *'ulamá al-sú'i*: the court-appointed chaplains who pass their time with lukewarm, indolent rulers, inciting where they should restrain, confounding where they ought to admonish, and obstructing where they should guide. They forgot an eminent tradition which says that "The best of the worldly rulers are those who visit the *'ulamá*, and the worst of the *'ulamá* are those who visit worldly rulers."

THE ALMORAVIDS, THE ALMOHADS, AND REFORM

The theme of the religious critique of worldly affairs has deep historical roots in the rise and spread of Islam, in North Africa and beyond, with desert conditions packing a powerful reform charge into movements of religious and social renewal. Thus it happened that in 1035 AD Berber chieftains from the Western Sahara, representing a strategic intertribal coalition from that part of the Maghrib, left on a pilgrimage to the holy city of Qayrawán, a Málikí orthodox stronghold in Tunisia, founded in 675 by Arab *jihádists* from Egypt. What they discovered of the discrepancy between the correct practice of Islam there and their own corrupted version of the faith shocked them, and so they asked for a missionary to their people. When 'Abd Alláh ibn Yásín turned up demanding radical reform, including strict observance of canonical rites and the suppression of unlimited polygamy, he met with sharp opposition. He undertook a *hijrah* with a band of his stalwarts to a *ribát*, an isolated desert oasis on an island in the Lower Senegal River – on the frontier, that is, between *dár al-Islam* and *dár al-harb*, the sphere of belief and unbelief, where he and his recruits were "confined to the bare necessities of existence," as Ibn Khaldún would put it. There Ibn Yásín set out to incubate his revolutionary teachings, attracting numerous sympathizers. On everyone who joined the community he imposed uncompromising terms of the code. Discipline was rigid, authority unyielding, and sanctions unmitigated. A hundred lashes were administered as indemnity for past sin, five for lateness at prayer and for omitting one *rak'a* or genuflection at prayer, execution for murder, and excommunication for other infringements. He would declare: "You have committed in your youth many reprehensible acts, so it is necessary that you should be subjected to the punishment stipulated by law in order that you may be purified from your transgressions."[38] He imposed on his recruits the duty to perform the prayers fourfold to make up for lost time, a ritual rule that helped heighten the sense of their being on the threshold of messianic favor. By these means Ibn Yásín forged an aggressive faith appropriate to the Berber martial spirit, making holy war the indispensable prerequisite of religious commitment, and aggression the penance for heresy.

In 1056 he and his followers burst upon the scene in North Africa, known as the *al-murábitún*, hence Almoravid. They were appealed to by the disaffected scholars and leaders to come to their country and purge it of all abominations, injustice, and tyranny. These scholars complained to the Almoravid leaders of the humiliation and oppression to which teachers of knowledge and religion were subjected by the Berber chieftains of southern Morocco. The Almoravids would use Málikí law as solvent to refine religious practice and to substitute a normative reform code for Berber intra-clan rivalry. Piety could thus serve the purposes of expedience. The booty he obtained from his *jiháds* he made into a pious endowment, *bayt al-mál*, dividing it into fifths and apportioning it among the faithful. He reformed personal conduct and put in place institutional structures of government to secure and advance the revolution. Ibn Yásín was killed in action in 1059, to be succeeded by Yúsúf ibn Táshifín who led the assault on Morocco in 1061. The following year he founded Marrakesh, and in 1069 Fez fell to him. He marauded on the frontiers of Algeria and established an outpost in Lesser Kabylia. The Almoravids carried through a puritan revolution, abolishing illegal taxes, banning alcohol and destroying musical instruments. Mindful of the problem of balancing the interests of temporal power with those of the revealed code, the Almoravids established a dual leadership structure, with temporal affairs looked after by the *amír* and spiritual matters by the *faqíh* who in practice had superiority over the *amír*. An anecdote recounted how Yahyá b. ʿUmar as *amír* submitted himself to flogging under Ibn Yásín, the spiritual founder, before he was informed of his trangression. The temporal *amírs* were in fact men of piety and virtue, further blurring the putative distinction between the temporal and the spiritual.

This army of desert locusts was now poised to strike northwards into Spain, for centuries under the sway of the Umayyads whose longevity encouraged the kind of hedonist indolence that induces millenarian spasms in the self-righteous. Here is one characterization of Umayyad Spain in its twilight:

> The brilliance of a refined way of life, a disposition for enjoyment which lightheartedly exceeded all the bounds set by religious law, a finely wrought delicacy of behaviour which lent an appearance of frivolity to the outbreak of passions often all too brutal, a stylish extravagance that became less easy to justify with every year that passed when independence was only to be maintained by tribute and recruitment of mercenaries, this frenzy of sensibility drew its bitter charm from the awareness of the approaching end. The poet-king Muʿtamid of Seville (1069–1090) captured the spirit of his age in one line: "Fling yourself into life as onto a quarry, it lasts no more than a day."[39]

On top of this moral decay the Almoravids descended in a heap to set up a reign of truth and a kingdom of virtue. The Umayyad rule in Spain was brought to an end, and ʿAbbásid rule, established in Baghdád since 750 AD, recognized. For the first time since the eighth century, the title of the ʿAbbásid caliph was printed on the *dinár* coins, and the caliph's name inserted in the Friday *khutbah*, sermon. Such was Ibn Yásín's pious reputation that he became a subject of numerous miracles, proofs of his sanctity, intelligence, nobility of spirit and erudition, but a sign, too, that charisma was becoming his monopoly and that of his community and descendants. As the eleventh-century writer, al-Bakrí, testified, "on his tomb stands today a mausoleum, which is frequented, and a hospice (*rábita*) always full of people. Even now a group of them [Almoravids] would choose to lead them in prayer only a man who prayed behind ʿAbd Alláh, even though a more meritorious and more pious person, who had never prayed under the guidance of ʿAbd Alláh, was among them."[40] Al-Bakrí, with Spanish Umayyad sympathies, intends a slight of Ibn Yásín, charging his followers with extremism which flouts the law stipulating that the prayers be led by those more qualified. A legacy was being made out of a heresy. Equally importantly, outsiders and outcasts who were essential in the movement's early success became themselves unwelcoming of strangers and outsiders, indicating that the revolution was turning on itself. Critics looked to the source for the cause of the problem.

Accordingly, Ibn Yásín himself was accused of ordering the flogging of a merchant who recited an otherwise legitimate phrase, only to have the punishment rescinded when someone from Qayrawán recited the phrase as words from the Qur'án. Excess had acquired a pious name.

This stern doctrine suited, perhaps, to a desert *hijrah* in a *ribát* and effective in attracting social outcasts and exploiting their penchant for messianic consolation, would prove too extreme and impractical for the settled but jaded, insecure society of Andalusian Spain, and the Almoravids earned resentment there for their excessive zeal. The rule of the *'ulamá*, endorsed by the greatest scholars of Islam, including al-Ghazálí (d. 1111), collided with the petty jealousies of the various princes for whom membership in the *ummah* as a universal fellowship was too remote an idea to hold any obvious prospects of resolving local disagreements fed by structural fatigue or of self-advancement. Furthermore, the Almoravids adopted a policy of the forcible deportation of non-Muslims. Many Christians were thus removed to Morocco after 1125, a measure sanctioned by Averroës's grandfather, thus denying the empire of the services of some of its ablest citizens. A similar removal of Jews to Fatimid and Ayyubid Egypt, including Maimonides of Córdoba (d. 1204), had also taken place and served further to rob the state of its human and intellectual talent.

In the course of time the candle that Ibn Yásín lit would eventually fall into the hands of another reformer, Ibn Tumart (d. 1133), a Masmúda Berber, whose own zealous advocacy would fan the flame of reform into a fiercely burning torch. The role of reform leader in taking history forcefully and directing it into pre-established channels is thus nowhere better illustrated than in the career of Ibn Tumart, who stunned his fellow Berbers by requiring them in one short symbolic step to make up for centuries of religious neglect.

Ibn Tumart had at first preached against the corruptions of government, journeying from town to town exhorting the believers to repudiate wine drinking, musical instruments, to adhere to rules on gender segregation, strive for rectitude and prepare for the judgment of the Last Day. Yet he came to deem peaceful change as ineffectual, so he retired to the High Atlas where he built himself a retreat mosque in the remote mountains to prepare for armed struggle. By the time he emerged from retreat, he had decided on political revolution in the name of faith to defeat his opponents whose anthropomorphism made them *mushrikún*, polytheists, and *káfirún*, infidels. He proclaimed himself *mahdí* in 1121 AD and swept the country with his militant message. He coupled his anathematizing of the Almoravids with a stern call for a Calvinist interpretation of theology. Between the pure and perfect nature of God and a fallen, corrupt humanity he saw an unprincipled, undisciplined government. Into that moral gap Ibn Tumart inserted his own power. His goal was to clasp society to the unalloyed monotheist creed, with the one God of doctrine reflected in the one community of standardized faith and practice. This emphasis on divine unity accounts for his movement's name, *al-muwah-hidún*, "unitarians," adapted to Almohads. His *mahdist* claims range with the familiar sound of bedouin tribal valor. He announced:

> The following is the promise of God which He made known to the Mahdí, the true promise which He does not change. His obeyer is pure, more pure than any before or to come, as it has been seen in no one nor will be again; there is none like him among men, none that can set up against him or contradict him ... to none can he remain unknown, none can neglect his command. If any comes against him as an enemy he is heading headlong into destruction and has no hope of salvation. He cannot be approached save by what he approves; all things issue from his command. All happens according to his will, but this is also the will of his Lord (God). To recognize him is an essential religious duty, obedience and devotion to him is an essential religious duty, and to follow him and be guided by him. ... The bidding of the Mahdí is the bidding of God, only he who knows him not ascribes it to himself.[41]

Ibn Tumart convulsed Berber society as the Almoravids never did, and created a precedent for historical radicalism in North Africa, as the nineteenth-century Sanúsíyah movement proved.[42] His mahdist program abolished the centuries of interpretation and commentary and brought the original sources of Scripture and *Hadíth* directly to his contemporaries. His style is reminiscent of that of Colonel Qadháfí of Libya and his 1969 revolution in which overnight he replaced the whole class of masters of the commentary with his own decree establishing direct access to the Scriptures. At any rate, *mahdí* Ibn Tumart assumed the mantle of infallibility, thus transforming his orders into authoritative oracles and justification for whatever he commanded. Of Berber stock, Ibn Tumart transformed Islam into an aggressive Berber national cause, with his own *mahdist* status elevating him to the position of Prophet of Islam. He made *jihád* incumbent on the community. In a way that shows the irony of theological abstraction blending easily with political triumphalism, Ibn Tumart's insistence that God cannot be conceived or described by human figures, for such is the exalted nature of the divine being, is combined with his unprecedented move to translate the Qur'án into the Berber language, including the prescribed call to prayers. He demanded that his officials all know Berber, and his own theological writings be circulated in Berber as well as Arabic. This translation activity leavened the Berber lump with a sense of exalted national pride, offering the Berbers on the social margins a basis for ethnic identity *vis-à-vis* their Arab masters at the center. This dual legacy persisted in Berber North Africa and beyond into Spain and elsewhere, where medieval learning and scholarship bore its imprint: the radical reform of the theological and philosophical syllabus to suppress originality and innovation allied to unregulated crude syncretism permitted for the rank and file. This was the age of Averroës and Avempace, an age in which flourished that species of rationalism that preached one truth for the elite and another for the masses. It was the age, too, of Ibn Jubayr, whose famous pilgrimage to Mecca in 1185 we have described.

ISLAM IN INDIA: THE DEOBAND MOVEMENT

The nineteenth-century Deoband movement in British India, with its striking impact on Muslim society, is another good example of how change may be ushered in from the interstices of society, from the gaps outside the political center, where a minority religious group uses its enclave position to put in place a program of reform and renewal. By their use of the Muslim ritual code, both in its provision for personal conduct and for public life, the Deobandis instituted far-reaching changes for their age. As reform-minded Muslims, they adopted measures to place Muslim Indians under conditions of prescriptive marginality and ritual normativeness, so that Muslims could use their exclusion from political power as an opportunity for establishing faith and practice as a normative domain.

The Deoband experience was thus a movement of the periphery, of the margins of space and time where behavior and expectations were momentarily enfranchised from the rules and values governing the public lives of incumbents of structural positions, as Turner would say (see pp. 127–8 above). Deoband itself was a mixed Muslim town in British-administered India about ninety miles northeast of Delhi, where its reputation, steeped in pious legend, favorably overshadowed its mixed heritage. Tradition spoke of the "odor of learning" emanating from its soil, and a revered member of the town's *'ulamá*, Maulana Rafi'ud Dín, reported of having dreamed of seeing the Ka'ba sited in Deoband's garden, and of the Prophet Muhammad, no less, giving milk to students there. All of which guaranteed the founding of a reform school there, so that when the time came to establish the *madrasah* in question, it was credulously reported that the founders all received simultaneous inspired directives to that end.[43] The *'ulamá* of the school turned down British grants-in-aid because such assistance "carried the taint of its non-Muslim source."[44] The founders made a point of the school's prescriptive marginality, saying material security would drain the reserves of faith and enterprise. They continued:

As long as the *madrasah* has no fixed sources of income, it will, God willing, operate as desired. And if it gain any fixed income, like *jagir* holdings, factories, trading interests, or pledges from nobles, then the *madrasah* will lose the fear and hope that inspire submission to God and will lose His hidden help. Disputes will begin among the workers. In matters of income and buildings ... let there be a sort of deprivation.[45]

Deoband became an oasis of virtue, a kept city of the British, true, but only by force of circumstance, for, where it counted, it was a city still sealed with the Prophet's *barakah*. Those who gave to the *madrasah* not expecting to receive any fame or reward, but did it *per l'amore di Dio*, became a source of blessing for the school, their sincerity the school's source of stability. Students developed close bonds with their teachers, a relationship more akin to the Sufi *murshid–muríd*, *shaykh-tálib*, guide–seeker model than to that of the instructor–student variety. Graduates of the school were invested with a *dastar*, a turban, as a symbol of academic "brilliance and exemplary personal qualities."[46]

The Deoband *madrasah* spawned similar reform schools in India, not just knowledge-enhancing, but character-transforming, creating a network linked by family bonds, personal ties, ideological orientation, and doctrinal loyalty, all of it held together by common marks of recognition, approval, and identity. A whole cadre of *muftís* and *shuyúkh*, equipped with knowledge and exalted by *barakah*, efficacious virtue, was created by this fraternal Deoband system, and these religious scholars, priding themselves on their *sharífian* status as outsiders,[47] and on their life of itinerancy, controlled the vital channel that separated British India from the Islamic domain. They inspired the faithful with the breath of divine felicity, and with the pen and the tongue energizing the network. They dispensed authoritative legal opinions, furnished clear ideas on doubtful points of law and practice, devised tightly knit rules to constrain and shackle where compromise threatened, or to inspire and lead where opportunity beckoned. Over 269,000 authoritative legal opinions, or *fatwas*, had been issued and collected in a compendium in the century since Deoband's founding, the enormous output an indication that Deoband was setting out to outflank and outrival the work of British courts in India with their heretical species of Anglo-Muhammadan law.[48] Thus in the *'ulamá*'s quest for correct belief and practice in a largely non-Muslim society, their adherence to the canon was tantamount to a political agenda. Their well-publicized reputation for receiving dreams and visions showed them as privy to an infallible source of knowledge. They were able to understand the true state of worldly affairs and to conjure the future, in contrast to the guesses and approximations of mere mortals. Their secret knowledge was their public capital, their exclusion from government their divine warrant. Yet that public capital was also their secret weapon, and the divine warrant their political mandate. What the Deobandis did was to inherit the mantle of the reforming Moghul ruler, Aurangzeb, and to use it to attract Muslim Indians. Religious identity carried for these reformers the obligation of choice and agency focused on belief and ritual, *'aqá'id* and *'ibádát*. Their task as they saw it "was to revive lapsed practices such as undertaking the hajj and permitting widows to remarry ... and to prevent optional practices being made obligatory, for example, the reading of certain passages in supererogatory prayers or the distribution of sweets upon the completion of the reading of the Qur'án. On this foundation the reformers built, point upon point, to convey to their followers the conviction that they conformed to the *sunnat*"[49] of the Prophet's teachings.

Such rigorous teachings on belief and conduct had the desired effect of emphasizing the moral superiority of Muslims *vis-à-vis* Hindus and the British. The power that accrued to these *'ulamá* they used to effect reform and spiritual renewal, propagating the view that "their standard of correct belief and practice defined them as a group not only separate from but morally superior to the British." The latter had established laws in India that were contrary to the *Sharí'ah*, as a member of the *'ulamá* charged.[50] The idea of open Deobandi confrontation with the British, as, for example, in a military uprising, was never feasible, as the bitter lesson of the 1857 Indian Mutiny and its robust sequel in British military reprisals demonstrated. But moral retreat at the behest of revealed truth can be an effective public weapon which the enemy cannot match. Grounded in divine truth and applied in temporal life, the religious law

> was thus understood to be the equivalent of British culture in its ability to generate a coherent and inclusive system, and superior to that culture in divine sanction and scope. ... [Thus, the] Deobandis, much like Gandhi later, believed that if individual lives were properly ordered, the community's life would be transformed as well. In this belief in ultimate social change, we see an echo of the Deobandi style of indirect influence through the exertion of bodily and spiritual powers rather than through direct confrontation.[51]

Such is the force of liminality that individuals bathed in its transforming light will transform society, in this instance through the steady radiance of peaceful reform rather than through one blazing explosion. Much of the credit for religious and social revitalization among Muslim Indians can be credited to the Deobandis, and this revitalization was diffused throughout the wider community whose understanding was accordingly clarified and deepened.

The Deobandi *'ulamá*, gathered at one key point under "the fear and hope that inspire submission to God and [hope in] His hidden help" and "with a sort of deprivation," sustained an enduring reform impulse in prescriptive marginality. This they accomplished by virtue of their identity as a commissioned guild, by their learning, their independence of British infidel authority, their unwavering view of colonial India as in symbolic breach of orthodox stipulations, and their affinity with all classes of Muslims, particularly the masses whom they roused to a sense of duty. Nineteenth-century Muslim Indian life was influenced by them in a more telling way than many of the Moghul rulers could boast of.

MARGINALITY, RITUAL, AND THE LIMITS OF LIMINALITY: AN ASSESSMENT

As suggested earlier, van Gennep's rule that the rite of passage is accompanied by a corresponding territorial change as a form of social organization is borne out by the distinctions drawn by Ibn Khaldún and African Muslim reformers. Taking van Gennep's insights further, Turner constructed a systematic analytic structure with his observations on liminality and *communitas*, introducing the principle of "the ritual enactment of norms and space" as a criterion of liminal action. It is, perhaps, a weakness of his analysis that although this relativization indicates a reversal of norms, such as bringing the chief down to the level of the commoner, the sacred or exalted to the position of the ordinary and commonplace, and vice versa, it does not imply "anti-structure" in the sense of absence of authority and social organization.[52] Liminal action as such need not result in *communitas*, that is to say, it need not depend on the absence of "social structure," since "social structure" can persist even in denial and rejection. However, *communitas*, in terms of the millenarian virtues of equality and fellowship, already incorporates elements of the liminal threshold. In either case organization and structure are central, and so, on the face of it, is openness and the welcoming of newcomers. The *jihád* community as *communitas* of the *záwiya* kind, for example, typically includes the members of the founder's family in its leadership structure, and their descendants as well as those of the founding members reinforce kinship bonds. Turner anticipates this criticism, and says such *jihád* communities share "the fate of all spontaneous *communitas* in history [and] undergo what most people see as a 'decline and fall' into structure and law. In religious movements of the *communitas* type," Turner argues, "it is not only the charisma of the leaders that is 'routinized' but also the *communitas* of their first disciples and followers."[53] If this is saying that revolutionary religious movements do not conform to much in the threefold distinction of *communitas*, then that is little different from saying that *communitas* as anti-structure is too restrictive a concept to be serviceable. Turner pairs *communitas* with anti-structure, perpetuating with that identification the unhelpful restriction of structure to a this-worldly pragmatism.[54]

As it is, this conceptualization does not fit Islam in the cases examined here. Muslim reform is no less this-worldly for its angels and dreams and visions, no less pragmatic for its high-minded theology, no less structural for its mystical fervor or its austerity and range. Perhaps, as Turner himself hints, we can rescue his scheme with Martin Buber's notion of community, where there is social interaction "*with* one another of a multitude of persons," a community that "experiences everywhere a turning to, a dynamic facing of, the others, a flowing from *I* to *Thou*."[55] What, however, is left of *communitas* as anti-structure by this stage can be embraced in successful liminality.

Whatever the case, applied in that qualified way to Muslim African societies, Turner's theories, especially when appropriately supplemented with Ibn Khaldún's formulations, can deepen our grasp of the handicaps inherent in mainline urban Muslim practice and make us realize its weakened reform potential. Even if they are in the majority, such Muslims would still lack the qualitative potential for change, in effect behaving like a minority. That is not, as Turner was inclined to see it, because they are enmeshed in social structure, but because urban pressure consumes creative energy and inhibits prescriptive radicalism. Urban Muslims thus may show outward piety but they have lost the inward truth. (The hypocrite, says 'Uthmán dan Fodio, the Fulani reformer, is etymologically a desert animal that goes through one hole and comes out of another. Compromising Muslims, he charges, are like that.) If enclavement eventually occurs in such urban corridors, then the liminal seed of change and transformation will be sown, with time and prayer to water it. As an unnamed poet expressed it, "He who is in this world, though city-pent, is a traveler, and his journey goes on, though he knows it not."[56]

CONCLUSION

In conclusion, we may return to the distinctions about different kinds of marginality, and look again at the symbolic power of the rite of itinerancy, of travel and mobility that is set to religious or moral purpose. The *hajj*, for example, is this type of mobility, and, set as such in the religious calendar, it allows for the regular periodic renewal and re-enactment of the rite for individuals and communities, for pilgrims and their originating societies. At home, among kin, relatives and friends, and prone to half-heartedness and lapses, the Muslim lives an ordinary, workaday life, his or her identity a

routine natural fact without much intellectual significance. However, as a pilgrim involved in journey and transition, as a recruit in *hijrah* or an adept in a
záwiya, he or she is in the realm of the sacred, out of the ordinary and into
the extraordinary where religious and social identity merge in a symbolic
stream of collective ritual affirmation. As one pilgrim testified:

> Another thing worthy of attention is the rigorous equality which obtains
> among the pilgrims, who are all subject to the same obligations and clothed in
> the same costume, not even excepting the prince and the minister. On pil-
> grimage there is neither rich nor poor, great nor small, neither honours nor
> privileges. Social class distinctions do not exist, and democracy, in the strictest
> sense of the word, is realized. Masters and servants become equals, and even the
> most humble claim their rights.[57]

"Claim their rights" – that is the ground-spring of change and reform, the distinctive prescriptive courage by which, for example, the eighteenth-century
Wahhábí reform ideas spread throughout the Muslim world where they were
taken by returning pilgrims from Mecca.[58] Wahhábism itself captured Mecca
in 1803, cleansing the Ka'ba of its images and relics, and in general infusing
a stricter, leaner tone into the pilgrimage devotions and observances.

Thus the *hajj*, particularly its Wahhábí-inspired version, is a rite of great
consequence for the Muslim world, and it is as such that it has inspired a kin-
dred theme in the *tournée pastorale* as a form of mendicant itinerancy whose
exemplary symbol is the footloose liberated friar of ascetic renown. Such individuals are the classic liminars, the ritualized embodiment of separation,
journeying, and transition. Marginality for them is a normative status, the
moral justification for their style of minority identity.

A thirteenth-century Muslim manual on initiating novices describes this
form of liminality, and does so by focusing on retreat, *khalwah*, as a precondi-
tion of personal and social transformation. This is the treatise, *al-'Awárif al-
Ma'árif* ("The Bounties of Divine Knowledge"), by Shaykh Shiháb al-Dín al-
Suhrawardí, a Qádirí *muqaddam* who was executed at Aleppo by the famous
Saladin. Al-Suhrawardí argues that itinerancy, what tour operators have popularized via Swahili as "safari," from the Arabic *safar*, produces effects that are
comparable to those produced by ritual separation and seclusion, so that the
otherwise anodyne opposites of stillness and movement join at the watershed
of change and directed transformation.

> The being separated from one's native land, from friends and familiar
> things, and the exercising of patience in calamities cause lust and nature to rest
> from pursuing their way; and take up from hearts the effect of hardness.

In subduing lusts, the effect of *safar* is not less than the effect of *nawáfil* ("supererogatory devotions"), fasting and praying.

On dead skins, by tanning, the effects of purity, of softness, and of delicacy of texture appear; even so, by the tanning of safar, and by the departure of natural corruption and innate roughness, appear the purifying softness of devotion and change from obstinacy to faith.[59]

PART III

Unbinding Identities

8

History's Forgotten Doubles

Ashis Nandy

I

However odd this might sound to readers of a collection on world history, millions of people still live outside "history." They *do* have theories of the past; they *do* believe that the past is important and shapes the present and the future, but they also recognize, confront, and live with a past different from that constructed by historians and historical consciousness. They even have a different way of arriving at that past.

Some historians and societies have a term and a theory for such people. To them, those who live outside history are ahistorical, and though the theory has contradictory components, it does have a powerful stochastic thrust. It will not be perhaps a gross simplification to say that the historians' history of the ahistorical – when grounded in a "proper" historical consciousness, as defined by the European Enlightenment – is usually a history of the prehistorical, the primitive, and the pre-scientific. By way of transformative politics or cultural intervention, that history basically keeps open only one option – that of bringing the ahistoricals into history.

There is a weak alternative – some would say response – to this position. According to their modern historians, the idea of history is not entirely unknown to some older civilizations like China and India. It is claimed that these civilizations have occasionally produced quasi- or proto-historical works during their long tenure on earth, evidently to defy being labeled as wholly ahistorical and to protect the self-respect of their modern historians. These days the historian's construction of the ahistorical societies often includes the plea to rediscover this repressed historical self.[1]

The elites of the defeated societies are usually all too eager to heed this plea. They sense that the dominant ideology of the state and their own privileged access to the state apparatus are both sanctioned by the idea of history. Many of their subjects too, though disenfranchised and oppressed in the name of history, believe that their plight – especially their inability to organize effective resistance – should be blamed on their inadequate knowledge of history. In some countries of the South today, these subjects have been left with nothing to sell to the ubiquitous global market except their pasts and, to be saleable, these pasts have to be, they have come to suspect, packaged as history. They have, therefore, accepted history as a handy language for negotiating the modern world. They talk history with the tourists, visiting dignitaries, ethnographers, museologists, and even with the human rights activists fighting their cause. When such subjects are not embarrassed about their ahistorical constructions of the past, they accept the tacit modern consensus that such constructions are meant for private or secret use or for use as forms of fantasy useful in the creative arts.

On this plane, historical consciousness is very nearly a totalizing one, for both the moderns and those aspiring to their exalted status; once you own history, it also begins to own you. You can, if you are an artist or a mystic, occasionally break the shackles of history in your creative or meditative moments (though even then you might be all too aware of the history of your own art, if you happen to be that kind of an artist, or the history of mysticism, if you happen to be that kind of a practitioner of mysticism). The best you can hope to do, by way of exercising your autonomy, is to live outside history for short spans of time. (For instance, when you opt for certain forms of artistic or spiritual exercises, perhaps even when you are deliriously happy or shattered by a personal tragedy. But these are *moments* of "freedom" from history, involving transient phases or small areas of life.)

At one time not long ago, historical consciousness had to coexist with other modes of experiencing and constructing the past even within the modern world. The conquest of the past through history was still incomplete in the late nineteenth century, as was the conquest of space through the railways. The historically minded then lived with the conviction that they were an enlightened but threatened minority, that they were dissenters to whom the future belonged. So at least it seems to me looking back upon the intellectual culture of nineteenth-century Europe from outside the West. Dissent probably survives better when its targets are optimally powerful, when they are neither too monolithic or steamrolling nor too weak to be convincing as a malevolent authority. As long as the non-historical modes thrived, history remained viable as a baseline for radical social criticism. That is perhaps why the great dissenters of the nineteenth century were the most aggressively historical.

Everyone knows, for instance, that Karl Marx thought Asiatic and African societies to be ahistorical. Few know that he considered Latin Europe, and under its influence the whole of South America, to be ahistorical, too. Johan

Galtung once told me that he had found, from the correspondence of Marx and Engels, that they considered all Slavic cultures to be ahistorical and the Scandinavians to be no better. If I remember Galtung correctly, one of them also added, somewhat gratuitously, that the Scandinavians could be nothing but ahistorical, given that they bathed infrequently and drank too much. After banishing so many races and cultures from the realm of history, the great revolutionary was left with only a few who lived in history – Germany, where he was born, Britain, where he spent much of his later life, and the Low Countries through which, one presumes, he traveled from Germany to England.

Times have changed. Historical consciousness now owns the globe. Even in societies known as ahistorical, timeless, or eternal – India for example – the politically powerful now live in and with history. Ahistoricity survives at the peripheries and interstices of such societies. Though millions of people continue to stay outside history, millions have, since the days of Marx, dutifully migrated to the empire of history to become its loyal subjects. The historical worldview is now triumphant globally; the ahistoricals have become the dissenting minority.

Does this triumph impose new responsibilities on the victorious? Now that the irrational savages, living in timelessness or in cyclical or other forms of disreputable nonlinear times, have been finally subjugated, should our public and intellectual awareness include a new sensitivity to the cultural priorities, psychological skills, and perhaps even the ethical concerns represented by the societies or communities that in different ways still cussedly choose to live outside history? Are they protecting or holding in trust parts of our disowned selves that we have dismissed as worthless or dangerous? Is ahistoricity also a form of wilderness that needs to be protected in these environmentally conscious times, lest, once destroyed, it will no longer be available to us as a "cultural gene pool" that could protect us from the consequences of our profligate ways, in case the historical vision exhausts itself and we have to retrace our steps? Before we make up our mind and answer the question, let me draw your attention to what seem to be two of the defining features of ahistorical societies.

This is not an easy task. It is my suspicion that, broadly speaking, cultures tend to be historical in only one way, whereas each ahistorical culture is so in its own unique style. It is not easy to identify the common threads of ahistoricity; I choose two that look like being relatively more common to illustrate my point. The task is made even more difficult for me because I want to argue the case of ahistoricity not on grounds of pragmatism or instrumentality (of the kind that would require me to give a long list of useful things that ahistoricity could do for us) but on grounds of diversity, seen as a moral value in itself, especially when its locus lies in the worldview of the victims.

The major difference between those living in history and those living outside it, especially in societies where myths are the predominant mode of organizing experiences of the past, is what I have elsewhere called the principle of principled forgetfulness. All myths are morality tales. Mythologization is also moralization; it involves a refusal to separate the remembered past from its ethical meaning in the present. For this refusal, it is often important *not* to remember the past, objectively, clearly, or in its entirety. Mythic societies sense the power of myths and the nature of human frailties; they are more fearful than the modern ones – forgive the anthropomorphism – of the perils of mythic use of amoral certitudes about the past.

Historical consciousness cannot take seriously the principle of forgetfulness. It has to reject the principle as irrational, retrogressive, unnatural, and fundamentally incompatible with historical sensitivities. Remembering, history assumes, is definitionally superior to forgetting. Unwitting forgetfulness, which helps a person to reconcile with and live in this world, is seen as natural and, to that extent, acceptable. Adaptive forgetfulness is also seen as human; human beings just cannot afford to remember everything and nonessential memories are understandably discarded both by individuals and societies.

The moderns are willing to go further. Since the days of Sigmund Freud and Marx, they recognize that forgetfulness is not random, that there are elaborate internal screening devices, the defenses of the ego or the principles of ideology, that shape our forgetfulness along particular lines. As understandable is unprincipled forgetfulness, the kind Freud saw as part of a person's normal adaptive repertoire, even though he chose to classify it under the psycho*pathologies* of everyday life, presumably because of the non-creative use of psychic energy they involved.

But principled forgetfulness? That seems directed against the heart of the enterprise called history. For historians, the aim ultimately is nothing less than to bare the past completely, on the basis of a neatly articulated frame of reference that implicitly involves a degree of demystification or demythologization. The frame of reference is important, for history cannot be done without ordering its data in terms of something like a theme of return (invoking the idea of cultural continuity or recovery), progress (invoking the principle of massive, sometimes justifiably coercive, irreversible intervention in society), or stages (invoking the sense of certitude and mastery over the self, as expressed in an evolutionary sequencing of it). The aim is to unravel the secular processes and the order that underlie the manifest realities of past times, available in ready-made or raw forms as historical data – textual and graphic records, public or private memories that are often the stuff of oral history, and a wide variety of artifacts.[2]

Because, as an authentic progeny of seventeenth-century Europe, history fears ambiguity.[3] The ultimate metaphor for history is not the *double entendre*; it is synecdoche: the historical past stands for all past because it is presumed to be the only past. Hence the legitimacy of psychological history as a sub-discipline of history has always been so tenuous. Psychoanalysis at its best is a game of *double entendre* loaded in favor of the victims of history – the pun is intended – but it has to be sold to the historically minded as a technology of analysis that removes the ambiguities human subjectivity introduces into history.

The enterprise is not essentially different from that of Giambattista Vico's idea of science as a form of practice. There is nothing surprising about this, for the modern historical enterprise *is* modeled on the modern scientific enterprise, whether the historian admits it or not. This is not the scientization that leads to the use of experimental methods or mathematization – though even that has happened in a few cases – but to an attempt to make history conform to the spirit of modern science (as captured more accurately, I am told, by the German word *wissenschaftlich*). I know that the idea of scientific history has acquired a certain ambivalent load ever since the great liberator of our times, Joseph Stalin, sent twenty million of his compatriots marching to their death in the name of it, with a significant proportion of the historically minded intelligentsia applauding it all the way as a necessary sac-rifice for the onward march of history. But it is also true that to the savages, not enamored of the emancipatory vision of the Enlightenment, the ortho-dox Marxist vision of history was never very distinct from that of its liberal opponents, at least not as far as the philosophical assumptions of its method-ology went. These assumptions owed much to the ideas of certitude, reliable and valid knowledge, and the disenchantment of nature to which Sir Francis Bacon gave respectability. (It is the same concept of knowledge that made history in the nineteenth century a theory of the future masquerading as a theory of the past. More about that later.)

In recent decades, there has been much talk about history being primarily a hermeneutic exercise. It is now fairly commonplace to say that there can be no true or objective past; that there are only competing constructions of the past, with various levels and kinds of empirical support. The works of a num-ber of philosophers of science, notably that of Paul Feyerabend, have in recent years contributed to the growing self-confidence of those opposing or fighting objectivism and scientism in history.[4] Contributions to the same process have also been made by some of the structuralists and postmodernists, Louis Althusser being the one who perhaps tried the hardest to bypass history.

The anti-historical stance of postmodernism, not being associated with the ahistoricity of the older civilizations, has even acquired a certain respectability.[5]

There have also been attempts to popularize other modes of time perception built on some of the new developments in science, especially in quantum mechanics and biological theory, or on the rediscovery of the older modes of knowledge acquisition, such as Zen and Yoga, and on theories of transcendence celebrated in deep ecology and ecofeminism. As important has been the growing awareness in many working at the frontiers of the knowledge industry, though it is yet to spread to the historians, that the historical concept of time is only one kind of time with which contemporary knowledge operates, that most sciences and now even a few of the social sciences work with more plural constructions of time.

Many will see all this as an exercise in self-correction, as an attempt to correct the excesses of what could be called a history modeled on the Baconian concept of science; some will identify this as an effort to incorporate into the historical consciousness crucial components of the moral universe of the ahistorical (both are implied in the work of a number of psychologists venturing new psychological utopias – eupsychias, Abraham Maslow used to call them – in the wake of the breakdown of some of the postwar certitudes in the late 1960s). A few cynical ones though will continue to say that the effort is nothing less than to capture, for preservation, what according to the moderns are the necessary or valuable components of the worldview of those living outside the post-seventeenth-century concept of history. So that the people who have kept alive the art of living outside history all these centuries can be safely dumped into the dustbins of history, as obsolete or as superfluous.

The second major difference between the historically minded and their ahistorical others is the skepticism and the fuzzy boundaries the latter usually work with when constructing the past. One thing the historical consciousness cannot do, without dismantling the historian's self-definition and threatening the entire philosophical edifice of modern history: it cannot admit that the historical consciousness itself can be demystified or unmasked and that an element of self-destructiveness could be introduced into that consciousness to make it more humane and less impersonal.[6] In other words, while the historical consciousness can grant, as the sciences do, that historical truths are only contingent, it also assumes that the idea of history itself cannot be relativized or contextualized beyond a point. History can recognize gaps in historical data; it can admit that history includes mythic elements and that theory terms and data terms are never clearly separable in practice, that large

areas of human experience and reality remain untouched by existing historical knowledge. It can even admit the idea of reversals in history. But it cannot accept that history can be dealt with from outside history; the entire
Enlightenment worldview militates against such a proposition. As a result,
when historians historicize history, which itself is rare, they do so according
to the strict rules of historiography. It reminds me of one of the fantasies Freud
considered universal, that of one's immortality. The human mind, Freud
believed, was unable to fantasize itself as dead; all such fantasies ended up by
postulating an observer/self that witnessed the self as dead. All critiques of
history from within the modern worldview have also been ultimately
historical.

Part of the hostility of the historically minded towards the ahistorical can
be traced to the way the myths, legends, and epics of the latter are intertwined with what look like transcendental theories of the past. Historians
have cultivated over the last two hundred and fifty years a fear of theories of
transcendence. And in recent centuries, what was once avoidance of the
sacred and apotheosization of the secular has increasingly become an open
fear of those who reject or undervalue the secular or who choose to use the
idiom of the sacred. This fear is particularly pronounced in societies where
the idiom of the sacred is conspicuously present in the public sphere. As some
of the major political ideologies have re-entered the political arena in the
guise of faiths, posing a threat to the modern nation-state system globally, the
nervousness about anything that smacks of faith has taken the form of an epidemic in territories where history reigns supreme. Confronted with the use or
misuse of theories of transcendence in the public sphere, historical consciousness has either tried to fit in the experience within a psychiatric framework – within which all transcendence, even the use of the language of
transcendence, acquires perfect "clarity" as a language of insanity – or it has
re-read what look like transcendent theories of the past as a hidden language
of *realpolitik* – in which all transcendence is only a complex, only apparently
ahistorical, political ploy.

Why have historians till now not seriously tried to critique the idea of history
itself? After all, such self-reflexibility is not unknown in contemporary social
knowledge. Sociology has produced the likes of Alvin Gouldner and
Stanislav Andreski; psychology Rollo May, Abraham Maslow, Roland Laing,
and Thomas Szasz.[7] Even economists, usually defensively self-certain, have
produced the likes of N. Georgesçu-Roegen and Joseph Schumacher; and
philosophers, enthusiasts of philosophical silence and the end of philosophy.[8]
Some of the self-explorations have turned out to be decisive to the disciplines
concerned, others less so; some are exciting, others tame; some are explicit,

others implicit. But they *are* there.[9] Historians have sired no such species. Occasionally, some have tried to stretch the meaning of the term "history" beyond its conventional definition; one example is William Thompson's *At the Edge of History*, which at least mentions the possibility of using myths as a means of "thinking wild" about the future by reversing the relationship between myth and history.[10] Usually, however, when historians talk of the end of history, like Karl Marx or Francis Fukuyama, they have in mind the triumph of Hegelian history.

There have also been critics of ideas of history, direct or indirect, from outside history. Ananda Coomaraswamy, philosopher and art historian, is an obvious early example, and Seyyed Hossein Nasr (the philosopher of science, who has built on the traditions of Coomaraswamy, Frithjof Schuon and René Guénon) is a more recent one.[11] And the present-day structuralists and post-structuralists also can be thought of as critics of the idea of history itself.[12] But there has emerged no radical criticism of history from within the ranks of historians. The histories of skepticism, *à la* Richard Popkins, have not been accompanied by any skepticism towards history as a mode of world construction. Or at least I do not know of such efforts. Recently, in an elegant introductory text on history, Keith Jenkins sharply distinguishes between history and the past, but refuses to take the next logical step – to acknowledge the possibility that history might be only one way of constructing the past and other cultures might have explored other ways.[13] It is even doubtful if Jenkins himself considers his essay anything more than an intramural debate, for *all* his thirty-five odd references come from mainstream European and North American thought.

I have also run across papers written by two sensitive young Indian historians who come close to admitting the need for basic critiques of history: Gyan Prakash and Dipesh Chakrabarty. The latter even names his paper "History as Critique and Critique of History."[14] On closer scrutiny, however, both turn out to be hesitant steps towards such a critique; at the moment they are powerful pleas for alternative histories, not for alternatives *to* history. Vinay Lal's two unpublished papers, which explore the entry of modern history into Indian society in the nineteenth century, both as a discipline and as a form of social consciousness, and one of Chakrabarty's more recent papers, go further.[15] Lal's paper, "The Discourse of History and the Crisis at Ayodhya," comes close to being an outsider's account of history in India. And Chakrabarty's acknowledges that "insofar as the academic discipline of history – that is, 'history' as a discourse produced at the institutional site of the university is concerned, 'Europe' remains the sovereign, theoretical subject of all histories, including the ones we call 'Indian,' 'Chinese,' 'Kenyan,' and so on." The paper goes on to say: "So long as one operates within the discourse of 'history' at the institutional site of the university it is not possible simply to walk out of the deep collusion between 'history' and the modernizing narratives of citizenship, bourgeois public and private, and the nation-state. 'History' as a knowledge system is firmly embedded in institutional practices that invoke the nation-state at every step."[16]

All three historians are exceptions and even they are basically pleading for what Sara Suleri calls "contraband history." All three leave one with the hope that some day their kind will reactivate their own cultural memories and bring in an element of radical self-criticism in their own discipline. Radicalism may not lose by beginning at home.

But the question still remains: Why this poor self-reflexibility among historians as a species? I suspect that this denial of the historicity of history is built on two pillars of modern knowledge systems. First, Enlightenment sensitivities, whether in the West or outside, presume a perfect equivalence between history and the construction of the past; they presume that there is no past independent of history. If there is such a past, it is waiting to be remade into history. To misuse David Lowenthal's imagery, the past is another country only when it cannot be properly historicized and thus conquered.[17] And the regnant concepts of human brotherhood and equality insist that all human settlements must look familiar from the metropolitan centers of knowledge and, ideally, no human past must look more foreign than one's own. On and off I have used the expression "imperialism of categories" to describe the ability of some conceptual categories to establish such complete hegemony over the domains they cover that alternative concepts related to the domains are literally banished from human consciousness. History has established such a hegemony in our known universe. In that universe, the discipline is no longer merely the best available entry into past; it now exhausts the idea of the past. In what psychoanalysis might someday call a perfect instance of concretization, it is now *the* past. (Everyone has a right to one's own clichés, C. P. Snow says. So let me give my favorite example of such a hegemony from my own discipline. When intelligence tests were first devised there was much discussion in the psychological literature on the scope and limits of these tests. Scholars acknowledged that the tests were an imperfect measure of human intelligence, that they were sensitive to, and influenced by, personal and social factors; that their reliability and validity were not closed issues. Over the decades, doubts about the reliability and especially the validity of intelligence tests have declined to nearly zero, though a debate on them raged for a while in the late 1970s.[18] Today, virtually every introductory textbook of psychology defines human intelligence as that which intelligence tests measure. IQ, once a less than perfect measure of intelligence, now defines intelligence. Other such examples are the hegemony of development and modern science over the domains of social change and science respectively. It is almost impossible to criticize development today without being accused of social conservatism of the kind that snatches milk from the mouths of hungry third-world babies. It is even more difficult to criticize modern science without being seen as a religious fundamentalist or a closet astrologer.)

History not only exhausts our idea of the past, it also defines our relationship with our past selves.[19] Those who own the past own the present, George Orwell said. Perhaps those who own the rights to shape the pasts of our selves also can claim part-ownership of our present selves. Historians have now come to crucially shape the selves of the subjects of history, those who live only with history. In the process, they have abridged the right and perhaps even the capacity of citizens to self-define, exactly as the mega-system of modern medicine has taken over our bodies and the psychiatrists our minds for retooling or renovation. We are now as willing to hand over central components of our self to the historians for engineering purposes as we have been willing to hand over our bodies to the surgeons.

Second, the absence of radical self-reflexivity in history is in part a product of the gradual emergence and spread of the culture of diaspora and the psychology of the exile as a dominant cultural motif of our times.[20] The modern world has a plurality of people who have been uprooted – from their pasts, from their cultures, and from less impersonal communities that often ensure the continuity of traditions. Modern cosmopolitanism is grounded in this uprooting. Not only have state- and nation-formation, empire-building, colonialism, slavery, pogroms, the two world wars, ethnic violence taken their toll, perhaps more than anything else, development combined with large-scale industrialization and urbanization have contributed handsomely to such uprooting. These are the "historical dislocations" that mark out, according to Robert Lifton, the "restless context" which "includes a sense of all the unsettled debts of history that may come 'back into play.'"[21]

While direct violence produces identifiable victims and refugees, social processes such as development produce invisible victims and invisible refugees. To give random examples from the twentieth century, the United States began as a nation of uprooted immigrants. Just when it began to settle down as a new cultural entity, its farming population came down from more than 60 percent to something like 5 percent in about seventy-five years. Likewise Brazil has acquired a plurality of the uprooted within two decades by going through a massive transfer of population from rural to urban settlements, probably involving as much as 60 percent of the population of the country. Independent India, which has seen colossal ethnic violence and forced movements of population during its early years, and China, which has seen in this century millions of refugees created by a world war and a series of famines, are going through similar changes at the moment. They are producing invisible refugees of development by the millions. The dams, especially the 1500 large dams built in India in the last forty-five years, presumably along with the associated major development projects, have by themselves produced nearly 22 million refugees.[22] As in the case of the environment, the sheer scale of human intervention in social affairs has destroyed cultural elasticities and the capacity of cultures to return to something like their original state after going through a calamity.[23]

This massive uprooting has produced a cultural psychology of exile that in turn has led to an unending search for roots, on the one hand, and angry, sometimes self-destructive, assertion of nationality and ethnicity on the other. As the connection with the past has weakened, desperate attempts to reestablish this connection have also grown. Paradoxically, this awareness of losing touch with the past and with primordial collectivities is mainly individual, even though it uses the *language* of collectivity. It has to use the language of collectivity because the community has in the meanwhile perished for many who are a party to the search. I have in mind something like what Hannah Arendt used to call the search for pseudo-solidarities in European fascism of the 1930s.[24]

The attempt to define history and give formal history a central place in our personality repertoire – in its conventional or dissenting sense – has its counterpart in our organized efforts to institutionalize history as the only acceptable construction of the past. History manages and tames the past on behalf of the exile, so that the remembered past becomes a submissive presence in the exile's world. The objectivity and empirical stature of history is supposed to give a certitude that alternative constructions of the past – legends, myths, and epics – can no longer give. The latter used to give moral certitude, not objective or empirical certitude; history gives moral certitude and guides moral action by paradoxically denying a moral framework and giving an objectivist framework based on supposedly empirical realities. This is what Heinrich Himmler had in mind when he used to exhort the SS to transcend their personal preferences and values, and do the dirty work of history on behalf of European civilization. He had excellent precedents in Europe's history outside Europe. His innovativeness lay in the Teutonic thoroughness and self-consistency with which he applied the same historical principles within the confines of Europe.

It is this that makes history a theory of the future for many, a hidden guide to ethics that need not have anything to do with the morality of individuals and communities. History allows one to identify with its secular trends and give a moral stature to the "inevitable" in the future. The new justifications for violence have come from this presumed inevitability. In these circum-stances, psychology enters the picture not in the sense in which the first generation of psychohistorians believed it would do – as a new dimension of history that would deepen or enrich historical consciousness – but as a source of defiance of the imperialism of history. A practicing historian, Richard Pipes, has come close to acknowledging this possibility, if not in a profes-sional journal at least in a respectable periodical. Pipes may be a distinguished retired cold-warrior and a pillar of the establishment, but in this instance at least he has chosen to identify with those uncomfortable with history, both at the center and in the backwaters of the known world:

> [H]istory may be meaningless. The proposition merits consideration. Perhaps the time has come, after two world wars, Hitler, Lenin, Stalin, Mao and Pol Pot, to abandon the whole notion of history, writ large, as a metaphysical process that leads to a goal of which people are only dimly aware. This concept, invented by German idealist philosophers in the early nineteenth century, has often been described as a surrogate secularized religion in which the will of his-tory replaces the hand of God, and revolution serves as the final judgment. As practitioner of history writ small, I, for one, see only countless ordinary indi-viduals who materialize in contemporary documents desiring nothing more than to live ordinary lives, being dragged against their will to serve as building material for fantastic structures designed by men who know no peace.[25]

There is just a hint in Pipes's essay that part of the answer to this passion for "grand history" lies in psychology, perhaps in psychopathology.[26]

II

In a well-known paper on the crisis of personal identity, psychoanalyst Erik H. Erikson, whose name is associated with most serious efforts in the once-trendy disciplinary domain called psychohistory, mentions a news report on a "smart-alecky" youth, fined twenty-five dollars for reckless driving. While in the court, the boy interrupted the judge to say, "I just want you to know that I'm not a thief." Provoked by this "talking back," the judge immediately increased the sentence to six months on a road gang.[27] Erikson suggests that the judge here ignored what may have been a "desperate historical denial," an attempt to claim that an anti-social identity had not been formed, because the judgment was not sensitive to the reaffirmation of a moral self that tran-scended in this instance the history of a moral lapse.

Can this story be re-read as a fable that redefines the role of psychology in relation to history? Can we read it as an invitation to ponder if the reaffirmation of a moral self in the present by the young man should or should not have priority over the historical "truth" of his rash driving? Can his historical denial be read as a defiance of history itself? Does his cognitive defiance have at least as much empirical and objective "truth" value as the proven history of his bad driving? Is all history only contemporary history, as Benedetto Croce suggested, or is all history psychological history – diverse, essentially conflictual, internally inconsistent constructions of the past that tell more about the present and about the persons and collectivities "doing" history? Is Erikson even *empirically* flawed because he cannot, or would not, exercise his hermeneutic or exegetic rights beyond a point? Is the unwillingness to exercise these rights fully or to share them with other civilizations determined by the same forces that we are usually so keen to invoke when we embark on historical analysis? I shall address these odd questions in a very roundabout way, not necessarily to answer them, but to tell the outlines of a story about history in what was once an unabashedly ahistorical society.

Most Indian epics begin with a prehistory and end, not with a climactic victory or defeat, but with an ambivalent passage of an era. There is at their conclusion a certain tiredness and sense of the futility of it all. The *Mahabharata* does not end with the decisive battle of Kurukṣetra; it ends with the painful awareness that an age is about to pass. The victorious are all too aware – in the words of Yudhisthira, who with his brothers has ensured the defeat of the ungodly – that they have gone through a fratricide and their victory in a war, fought in the cause of morality, is actually a glorified defeat. Even god Kṛṣṇa, the lord of lords, dies a humble death, his entire clan decimated, his kingdom destroyed.

The first non-Western psychoanalyst, Girindrasekhar Bose (1886–1953), who happened to be an Indian and like me a Bengali, wrote, among other things, a huge commentary on ancient Indian epics, *purāṇas*, which is now entirely forgotten, even in his native Bengal.[28] On the face of it, the commentary has so little to do with psychoanalysis that even the sensitive commentators on Bose, such as Christiane Hartnack and Sudhir Kakar, have mostly ignored it.[29] The book perhaps looks to them to be an attempt to construct a genealogy, which is also what it seemed to me when I first read it.

Reared in the culture of nineteenth-century science, particularly its easily exportable positivist version, Bose was in many ways an unashamed empiricist and experimentalist. That culture of science had entered India in the middle of the nineteenth century along with the European concept of history. A new space for this concept of history was created in Indian consciousness by the manifest power of the colonial regime, its self-justification in the language of science and history, and by the Enlightenment values slowly seeping into the more exposed sectors of the Indian elite, either as tools of survival under the colonial political economy or as symbols of dissent against the traditional authority system. On one side were the likes of James Mill, who mentions in his *History of British India* the "consensus" that "no historical composition existed in the literature of Hindus" and that the Hindus were "perfectly destitute of historical records"; on the other, there were Indian modernists like Krishna Mohun Banerjea who internalized Mill's estimate and Gibbon's more general belief that "the art and genius of history [was] ... unknown to the Asiatics" and that the mythological legends of India showed that the Indians had a sense of poetry, but such legends could not be confused with "historical compositions."[30] At first, it seemed that the Muslims were better in this respect. After all, Alberuni *did* say, even if politely, "Unfortunately the Hindus do not pay much attention to the historical order of things, ... and when they are pressed for information and are at a loss, not knowing what to say, they invariably take to tale-telling." But soon it became obvious to the moderns, in the language of one H. M. Elliot, who wrote a voluminous history of India, that Muhammadan histories were no better than annals.[31]

By the time Girindrasekhar Bose was writing his commentary on the Indian epics, the favorite lament of many Bengali thinkers was: *Bāngālī ātmavismṛta jāti* – the Bengalis are a people who have forgotten their self. By this was meant that the Bengalis did not have a self based on history, that the traditional depositories of Bengal's awareness of her selfhood and past – its myths, folkways, shared and transmitted memories – were no longer legitimate to the important sections of the Bengali elite. It was this Westernized elite, not the whole of Bengal, that felt it was *ātmavismṛta*, truly orphaned without a proper history. It was now looking for a different kind of construction of the past, the kind that would not humiliate them *vis-à-vis* their historically minded rulers.[32]

Yet it became obvious to Bose, after working on the subject for a while, that no modern Western historian could do justice to the *purāṇic* texts, for the modern West had lost access to certain forms of consciousness that were necessary for a more open, creative reading of the texts. If traditional India did not have access to the Enlightenment's idea of modern history, Europe also lacked access to the Indian traditions of constructing the past.[33]

Now, Bose was no ordinary nationalist trying to revalue Indian classics; he had accepted psychoanalysis as *the* mode of understanding his society as well as the cultural products of his society, including texts such as the *purāṇas*. In fact, to the best of my knowledge, he was the first non-Western psychiatrist and psychologist to do so; he began adapting the main principles of the young discipline to his culture in the first decade of the twentieth century, when hardly anything of Freud was available in English. In fact, he emerged so early in the career of psychoanalysis that he was accepted, apart from August Aichorn and of course Freud himself, as a training analyst on the basis of his self-analysis. I suspect that Bose became aware of the implicit politics of knowledge within which his work was getting located only after beginning his work on the epics of India.[34] It was as a psychoanalyst dealing with case *histories* that he deciphered some of the distinctive rules or techniques that the epics-as-*histories* followed.[35] He was a "student of pastness itself," as Ivan Illich describes the vocation.[36] Bose came to the conclusion that the *purāṇas* were themselves a form of history.[37] That formulation must not have been easy to arrive at when the Indian elite were desperately trying to create within Indian civilization a place for history as the moderns understood it.

If Bose were living today, would he talk of the *purāṇas* as alternative history or as alternatives *to* history? Do we have to interpret the *purāṇas* into history? Or should we, those who have lived through the blood-drenched history of this century, learn to cherish the few who would rather interpret history into *purāṇas* to get out of the clutches of history? Should Bose have been sensitive to the closeness of psychoanalysis to the language of myths and its ability to be a critique of history, including case *history*, at the end of the twentieth century? Let me attempt some part-answers to these questions, too, by telling a story. The "religious" violence triggered by the Ramjanmabhumi movement in India reached its climax on December 6, 1992. As we know, on that fateful day a controversial mosque at the sacred city of Ayodhya, which many claimed was built by destroying a temple that stood at the birthplace of Lord Rama, was demolished by screaming, angry volunteers eager to avenge a historical wrong.[38]

What was the nature of the history around which so much bloodshed has already taken place and what is the status of that concept of history which has so frequently been invoked by Indian historians to clinch the argument on Ramjanmabhumi one way or the other? Why did the same history not move millions of Indians for hundreds of years, not even the first generation of Hindu nationalists in the nineteenth century, not even, for that matter, the founders and ideologues of the same parties that are today at the forefront of the temple movement? Though they always claimed to be ardent devotees of the idea of history, none of them ever demanded the return of the Babri mosque to the Hindus on grounds of history: neither Balkrishna Munje, nor Keshav Hegdewar, nor Vinayak Damodar Savarkar, not even Lalkrishna Advani and Murali Manohar Joshi, the present leaders of the movement.[39]

The two questions I have raised, you may have noticed, do not lay any emphasis on the ongoing debate in India on the "truth" about the Ramjanmabhumi. They are concerned neither with the archeological and historical evidence on the controversial mosque nor with the ongoing legal battle on the judicial status of the territoriality of the birthplace of one believed to be an incarnation of Lord Viṣṇu but treated by some of his new-found political disciples as a venerable, now-dead national leader. Admittedly, the debate on the subject, particularly its style, reveals much about the psychological and cultural realities that frame the problem *today*, even if not in the sense the protagonists believe. Was there a temple which was destroyed by the builders of the Babri mosque? Is this Ayodhya really the Ayodhya of Rama? The questions *are* important for the secularized Indians, not for the millions who have trudged to the sacred city for pilgrimage over the centuries. Can we provide at least some vague clues to the point of view of the majority to whom the idea of history itself was once an encroachment on the traditional constructions of the past and some of whom have now opted to enter the dominion of history? I shall give my response as unam-biguously as I can.

History is not anthropology of past times, though it can come close to it. The growing popularity of anthropological history gives a false sense of con-tinuity between the two disciplines, for they are separated by a deep political chasm: victims of anthropology talk back in some cases and in many other cases retain the potential for doing so; the subjects of history almost never rebel, for they are mostly dead. In the first instance, the worst affliction is colonial anthropology, in the second the civilizational *hubris* that claims that not merely the present but even the past and the future of some cultures have to be reworked. The main tools in that redefinition till now have been deval-uation, marginalization, and liquidation of memories that cannot be histori-cized and, in the case of cultures that locate their utopias in the past, narrowing the range of alternatives "envisionable" within the cultures. In cultures where plural visions of the future derive from plural visions of the past, unqualified historicization has opened up new possibilities of violence to eliminate plurality, directed both outwards and inwards.

In the controversy on Ramjanmabhumi, volumes have been written by scholars, journalists, and partisan pamphleteers to prove either that there was a temple where the Babri Masjid stood since the sixteenth century or that there was no such temple. Shorn of verbiage, the Hindu nationalists have claimed that the Muslims are temple-breakers; the Muslims have denied that they are so. Two minor parties involved in the dispute are the secular and Hindu nationalist historians; they care for neither temples nor mosques, except for archeological, aesthetic, or political reasons. Some of India's respected historians such as Romila Thapar, S. Gopal, Bipan Chandra, and Harbans Mukhia have said it all on behalf of their tribe, the secular his-torians, when they wrote that there was no historical proof that Rama was ever born, certainly none that he was born in the present city of Ayodhya. And one of their main opponents, the historian S. P. Gupta, whose ambition once was to do his doctoral work in history under Thapar, has said it all on behalf of the Hindu nationalists when he claimed that he was in the archeological expedition to Ayodhya led by B. B. Lal when he was not. Both Thapar and Gupta share the belief that the conflict in Ayodhya is about historical truths and the rectification of historical wrongs which can only be solved by objective, scientific history.

On the whole, it will not be an oversimplification to say that the secular historians either claim that Hindus are also temple-breakers – they allegedly broke Śaivite and Vaiṣṇava temples in sectoral clashes as well as Buddhist and Jain temples – or that the Muslims are not temple-breakers, at least in this instance.[40] (Recently the secularists, fighting their gut reaction to Hinduism as a repository of superstitions and atavism, have added for political reasons a third angle to their viewpoint, namely that the Hindu nationalists are not true Hindus, "true Hinduism" being what the secularists find out from the traditional texts and from the writings of Hindu religious leaders through modern or postmodern textual analysis.) The Hindu nationalist historians – who claim, fittingly, that they are "positive" or genuine secularists, unlike the "pseudo-secularists" who disagree with them – demand that Indian Muslims own up to their heritage of temple-breaking and iconoclasm and atone for it by admitting that the disputed mosque should have been handed over to the Hindus for demolition or relocation in the first place and the destruction of the mosque in December 1992 was a nationalist act.[41]

The Muslim response to these demands has ranged from massive protests to violent and non-violent resistance to even early local offers to hand over the mosque to their neighbors.[42] But one possible position has not been taken: no Muslim in India has claimed till now that the Muslims broke temples *and* are proud of that past as a measure of their piety. Nor has any Muslim affirmed the right to break temples or even retain mosques built on demolished temples. No Muslim has sought protection for the Babri mosque without insisting that the mosque had *not* been built on a razed temple or without insisting that what Muslim marauders did in India was what marauders always do and such vandalism had nothing to do with Islam and that, in any case, the past was now truly past. This has been associated with a spirited denial of the accusation that they are temple-breakers. Strangely, both the *dharmaśāstras*, especially the epic vision of the *smārta* texts – the vision in which the heritage of the *Ramayana* is located – and the living traditions of everyday Hinduism, exemplified above all by a majority of the Hindu residents of Ayodhya, have customarily considered that denial an important moral statement; to them, that reaffirmation of a moral universe by the Muslims may be more acceptable than the high-pitched evangelism of the Hindu nationalists.

Traditional India not only lacks the Enlightenment's concept of history; it is doubtful that it finds objective, hard history a reliable, ethical, or reasonable way of constructing the past. The construction of time in South Asia may or may not be cyclical, but it is rarely linear or unidirectional. As in some other cultures and some of the natural sciences, the Indian attitude to time – including the sequencing of the past, the present, and the future – is not given or pre-formatted. Time in much of South Asia is an open-ended enterprise. The power of myths, legends, *itihāsas* (which at one time used to be mechanically translated as primitive precursors of history) and *purāṇas* may have diminished but is not yet entirely lost.

Elsewhere I have classified non-historical reconstructions of the past under the rubric of mythography, but it may not be an appropriate term, though politically it does seem to protect the dignity of reconstructions that are the farthest from the contemporary idea of history.[43] But whatever name or names we give to such projects, they remain part of a moral venture. What a contemporary mythographer in the West like Erikson has to establish in the guise of a clinical interpretation or the likes of Joseph Campbell in the guise of an environmentally sound practice, many of the not-entirely-recessive traditions of constructing the past in India take for granted as a part of everyday life. They take seriously the affirmation of the Indian Muslims that they are not temple-breakers, that there exist textual injunctions in Islam against even worshipping in a mosque built on forcibly occupied land. The marauders who broke temples are already in their minds marauders who "coincidentally" happened to be Muslims, and I suspect that most of their Hindu neighbors outside the reach of history have accepted that formulation. (After all, an altogether different concept of the past moved even the fiery nineteenth-century religious and social reformer, Vivekananda, from whom a majority of Hindu nationalists claim to trace their ideological lineage. As philosopher Ramchandra Gandhi tells the story, towards the end of his life, seeing evidences of desecration of Hindu temples by successive invaders in Kashmir, Vivekananda asked in anguish in a temple of Goddess Kali, "How could you let this happen, Mother, why did you permit this desecration?" Vivekananda himself records the answer Kali whispered in his heart: "What is it to you, Vivekananda, if the invader breaks my images? Do you protect me, or do I protect you?"[44])

The conventional truth value of or empirical certitude about the past is not particularly relevant from this point of view. Because once the principle of non-destruction of the places of worship of other faiths is accepted in present times, the past is "constructed adequately," the moral point has been made, and the "timeless truths" reaffirmed.

Collingwood or no Collingwood, for some ahistorical cultures at least, all times exist only in present times and can be decoded only in terms of the contemporaneous. There is no past independent of us; there is no future that is not present here and now. And therefore the model of decoding is subject to the morality of everyday life, not to the various derivatives of the Baconian worldview. This is the humbler "secular" counterpart of Coomaraswamy's proposition, made on behalf of Islam and, for that matter, the major religious worldviews, that "time ... is an imitation of eternity."[45]

In modern India, to the extent it has got involved in the controversy over the mosque at Ayodhya, history, not Ayodhya, is the terrain for which the "secularists" and the Hindu nationalists fight. Both want to capture and correct it. The former want to correct the intolerance that, they feel, characterizes all faiths; the latter want to correct the intolerant faiths and teach their followers a lesson.

Secular historians assume that the past of India has been bloody and fanatic, that the Hindus and the Muslims have been fighting for centuries, and that the secular state has now brought to the country a modicum of peace. They believe that the secular faiths – organized around the ideas of nation-state, scientific rationality, and development – are more tolerant and should correct that history (despite the more than 110 million persons killed in man-made violence in this century, the killing in most cases justified by secular faiths, including Baconian science – Darwinism in the case of colonialism, biology in the case of Nazism, and science and history in the case of communism). The Hindu nationalists believe that, except for Hinduism, most faiths, including the secular ones, are intolerant. But they do not celebrate that exception. They resent it; it embarrasses them. They, therefore, seek to masculinize Hinduism to combat and, at the same time, resemble what according to them has been the style of the dominant faiths, which the Hindu nationalists see as more in tune with modern science and technology and, above all, scientized history.[46] At the same time, they insist that the history produced by their opponents, the Indian secularists, is not adequately scientific. They believe, as their historically minded opponents do, that there is an implicit science of violence that shapes history and history itself gives us guidance about how to tame and use that violence for the higher purposes of history through the instrumentalities of the modern nation-state. Like their opponents again, the Hindu nationalists are committed to liberating India from its nasty past, by acquiring access to the state in the name of undoing the past with the help of the same kind of history. The secular historians have done it in the past; the Hindu nationalists are hoping to do so in the future.

In this "historical" battle, the two sides understand each other perfectly. One side has attacked only pseudo-secularism, not secularism; the other has attacked the stereotypy of minorities, never the concepts of the state, nationalism, and cultural integration that underpin the colonial construction of Hinduism that passes as Hindutva. It is a Mahābhāratic battle between two sets of illegitimate children, fathered by nineteenth-century Europe and the colonial empires, who have escaped from the orphanage of history.

When modern history first entered the Indian intellectual scene in the middle of the nineteenth century, many accepted it as a powerful adjunct to the kit-bag of Indian civilization. Like Krishna Mohun Banerjea, they felt that Europe had transcended its wretched past by acquiring a historical consciousness and India, which showed a "lamentable want of authentic records in … literature," could do so too.[47] The domination of that consciousness has now become, as the confrontation at Ayodhya shows, a cultural and political liability. In a civilization where there are many pasts, encompassing many bitter memories and animosities, to absolutize them with the help of the European concept of history is to attack the organizing principles of the civilization. Particularly so, given that the South Asian historians, though otherwise a garrulous lot, have produced no external critique of history, perhaps not even an authentic history of history. They have sought to historicize everything, but never the idea of history itself. For historicizing the idea of history is to historicize the historians themselves. As I have said, such self-confrontation has not been the strong suit of historians; there are very poor checks in history against the violence and cruelty that may follow from uncritical acceptance of the idea of history.

Bertholt Brecht, I am told, strongly believed that the past had to be bared to settle all accounts, so that one could move towards the future. The traditional Indian attitude to the past, as in many other such societies, is a spirited negation of that belief. That negation resists the justificatory principles on which modern, organized violence heavily depends. Provincial European intellectuals like Brecht had no clue that the construction of the past can sometimes be, as in some of the little cultures of India, guided not by memories alone, but by tacit theories of principled forgetfulness and silences. Such constructions are primarily responsible to the present and to the future; they are meant neither for the archivist nor for the archeologist. They try to expand human options by reconfiguring the past and transcending it through creative improvisations. For such cultures, the past shapes the present and the future, but the present and the future also shape the past. Some scholars feel responsible enough to the present to subvert the future by correcting the past; others are as willing to redefine, perhaps even transfigure, the past to open up the future. The choice is not cognitive, but moral and political, in the best sense of the terms.

9

Identity in World History:
A Postmodern Perspective

Lewis D. Wurgaft

Cultural identity, applied to world history, is a problematic but indispensable concept. This uneasy contention reflects not only the contorted posture one tends to assume in viewing the world through a postmodern prism, but also the seemingly impossible task of trying to write integrative and ecumenical world history while some of our most durable political and cultural constructs are in a process of dissolution. Under these conditions, in which the familiar boundaries between groups may either fragment or rigidify unpredictably, cultural identity has presented itself forcibly as a problem for historical inquiry. William McNeill, for one, has distinguished between the cultural boundedness of conventional historians who are "willing to remain safely encapsulated within a group's universe of discourse and those seeking somehow to transcend cultural boundaries."[1] "World historians," he writes, "are trying to perform a feat of intellectual prestidigitation, subordinating their own local social universe along with everyone else's to patterns and processes of which those concerned remain largely or entirely unaware."[2]

Theodore Von Laue specifically invokes the identity issue in appealing for an intercultural approach to world history. "Only by looking at ourselves from the outside, in the inter-cultural contexts, can we see how deeply enmeshed we are in the network of hidden factors that constitute our cultural identity. In that enlarged perspective we become aware that our actions are determined by an almost infinite number of forces beyond the range of our consciousness."[3] Yet, Von Laue points out, these intercultural comparisons are most often sabotaged by subtle psychological mechanisms that prevent investigators from getting beyond their own cultural assumptions. This "dense network of causative factors," largely beyond conscious awareness, most often results in incomprehension and hostility.[4]

As Von Laue suggests, no discussion of cultural identity can get very far without engaging its psychological dimension. The strategy of this essay is to pursue the identity issue along two parallel tracks, one primarily devoted to identity as a clinical or developmental phenomenon, the other focused on recent treatments of nationalism or national identity. Moving back and forth between these tracks may result in a disjointed narrative; but the intention is to create a dialogue between two separable discursive fields which, in many respects, mirror one another. Given the extent to which postmodern views of identity are embedded in a dialogical process, such a narrative approach may itself reflect the instability of the identity concept from a postmodern perspective.

It is not very surprising that the appeal for deeper psychological understanding in world history grounds itself in the problem of cultural identity. Since Erik Erikson's clinical and historical writings of the 1950s and 1960s, the notion of identity has worked as a bridge between psychoanalytic ego psychology and the psychological study of culture. Erikson used the identity concept to link Freud's treatment of introjection and identification – the building blocks of ego development and group cohesion – to a psychosocial milieu. Presented by Erikson as the crystallization of a series of partial or fragmentary identifications, the notion of identity provided a framework in which both individual and cultural development could be staged as a series of mutually reinforcing interactions. Psychosocial identity, as explored in his cultural studies, incorporated the individual life cycle, the cultural *anlage*, and the imperatives of the historical moment into an integrated, if not rigidly organized, whole. In his historical biographies, Erikson sought to demonstrate how leadership worked at the boundary of unconscious conflict and social disorder to redefine cultural identity. In contrast to the chronic warfare that Freud declared between culture and nature, Erikson articulated a relatively conflict-free zone in which subsequent investigators treated individuals and groups, interpreted the relations between leaders and followers, and constructed studies of national identity or character.

Erikson presented his notion of psychosocial identity in his landmark work, *Childhood and Society*, published in 1950; but his writings began to reach a large audience only in the 1960s in a period of acute intergenerational conflict in American society. In *Childhood and Society* he contended that the establishment of a viable identity was the primary psychological task of adolescence in industrialized societies, as well as a cornerstone of the developmental process across the life span. Erikson's awareness of adolescent turbulence was tempered by a belief in the adaptive powers of the ego, a capacity to synthesize and regenerate in the face of ongoing developmental crises. Against Freud's relative pessimism regarding the ego's integrative capacities, Erikson emphasized the depth of the individual's roots in society and his grounding in the institutionalized patterns of his culture. Erikson described ego identity as "the accrued experience of the ego's ability to integrate all identifications with the vicissitudes of the libido, with the aptitudes developed out of endowment, and with the opportunities offered in social roles."[5]

From a developmental perspective he viewed identifications and other identity elements as fragments to be molded by the ego into a mature whole. "Wholeness," he states, "seems to connote an assembly of parts, even quite diversified parts, that enter into fruitful association and organization. ... As a *Gestalt*, then, wholeness emphasizes a sound, organic, progressive mutuality between diversified functions and parts within an entirety, the boundaries of which are open and fluent."[6] A mature psychosocial identity incorporated a notion of wholeness elastic enough to maintain a complex, interactive system. At a psychohistorical level, cultures and nations struggled with these same developmental crises on a historical and evolutionary stage, adapting and broadening their identities to meet new challenges.

Heinz Kohut's writings on self psychology in the 1970s paralleled Erikson's insofar as they tried to establish a cohesive, continuous agent at the core of psychic functioning. At first, Kohut reached only the psychoanalytic establishment, but his emphasis on the self had broad cultural resonance in the 1970s and 1980s. In such works as *The Analysis of the Self* (1971), Kohut argues that the self constitutes a separate and superordinate psychic structure formed from a matrix of self-representations – the narcissistic equivalent of the identification process. Like identity theory, his psychology features continuity and cohesion as facets of subjective experience, and relates them painstakingly to issues of mirroring and idealization that are central to the qualitative aspects of the mother–child and parent–child interaction. As the contemporary psychoanalyst Stephen Mitchell writes of Kohut's theory,

> the effort to organize and maintain an integrated sense of self has been assigned a primary, superordinate motivational status. Kohut does speak of subordinate selves, trapped in what he terms vertical and horizontal splits, but these are seen as quite pathological. The central thrust within mind is viewed as integrative, and that continuous line of subjective experience forms the core of the self.[7]

For Kohut and historians influenced by his approach, the psychological mechanisms for mirroring and idealizing individual development are reproduced at the level of cultural development.[8] In his reflections on the rise of Nazism, and on charismatic leadership, Kohut has posited a notion of the group self and the cultural self-object as analogues of the representational structures encountered in his individual psychology. Emphasizing the cohesion and continuity of the group self, he extends his individual theory to a depth-psychological understanding of the foundation of cultural values. Culturally determined aspects of group identity that relate to the group's conscious or preconscious awareness of itself are distinguished from aspects that are deeply embedded in the narcissistic structures, and thus provide for its continuity and cohesion. The group self, he writes, "can be conceived of, like the self of the individual, as being laid down and formed in the energic arc between mirrored *self*-object greatness of (ambitions) and admired *self-object* perfection (ideals)."[9] He posits an analogy between the roles of the historian and the psychoanalyst, both of whom promote structure and cohesion by providing the individual and the group with a sense of continuity, or, in our terms, identity over time.[10]

Although the relationship between identity theory and psychological approaches to history is clear, its contemporary relevance has been clouded by recent discussions of the nature and authority of human subjectivity. Both from a clinical and a broadly cultural perspective, concepts like identity have been linked to a discursive strategy in Western thought that has sought to impose a sense of order and coherence on a subjective experience riddled by the contradictions and displacements inherent in language and desire. Under the influence of Jacques Lacan and other poststructuralist writers, a prominent group of American psychoanalysts have come to view their discipline as another form of cultural discourse. Since the early 1980s they have begun to take a linguistic approach to psychoanalytic knowledge, its interpretive strategies and its modes of articulation. Their focus has been on language and on narrative structure as inscribed in the classic psychoanalytic text, the case study. In *Narrative Truth and Historical Truth*, published in 1982, Donald Spence examines the influence of the desire for narrative closure on the transactions between patient and analyst, as well as on the subsequent transition from clinical dialogue into written case history. For Spence the inherent ambiguity of analytic material and the associative character of linguistic referents creates an interpretive space where the desire for narrative coherence imposes order on the otherwise fragmented data out of which the narrative is shaped. Like historical narrative, such psychoanalytic storytelling might take a variety of shapes, depending on the creativity of the analyst and the rhetorical registers in which the analysis proceeds. The analyst, Spence suggests, produces constructions rather than reconstructions, interpretations in which semantic power takes precedence over historical accuracy.[11] Along the same lines Roy Schafer argues that the logic of narration necessitates the abandonment of a single, definitive account of a life history. "What has been presented as the plain, empirical data and techniques of psychoanalysis," Schafer writes, "are inseparable from the investigator's precritical and inter-related assumptions concerning the origins, coherence, totality and intelligi-bility of personal action."[12] Without the capacity to pick objectively among narrative choices, the analyst relies on rhetorical, ethical, and aesthetic persuasiveness.[13]

Analysts have turned to Jacques Derrida's influential reading of Freud's 1925 essay, "A Note upon the 'Mystic Writing Pad,'" to underscore the inscriptive complexity of the relationships among perception, memory, and defense in the clinical setting. Likening it to the discontinuous shift from speech to writing that Derrida derives from Freud's metaphor, the analyst Evan Bellin describes the ongoing "interruption and restoration of contact between the various depths of psychical levels."[14] Under the influence of transference and resistance the psychoanalytic narrative is continually read and rewritten in the present "free play of signifiers begging for demystification and naturalization in terms of the knowable."[15] Events do not reveal them-selves, Bellin suggests, but achieve "recognizable signification only as they are woven into the fabric of idiosyncratic narration."[16]

The hermeneutic perspective welcomes a plurality of psychoanalytic mod-els. This apparent theoretical anarchy simply reflects the discipline's status as an interpretive enterprise which – like the written text – is constantly open to revision through the analytic encounter. In the most rigorously decon-structive rendering of the narrative approach, the wish for comprehensive theoretical accounts is characterized as a semantic desire for a past that needs to be mourned, and that can lead to melancholia if not analyzed. Thus, in an introduction to a volume on psychoanalysis and narration, published in 1992, Humphrey Morris writes, "Whatever sense psychoanalysis helps make of the past, facing the 'second reality' of psychoanalysis and of the past would now mean tolerating not only greater complexity, but confusion, chaos, and non-sense."[17]

One major casualty of these deconstructive readings of psychoanalytic theory and practice has been the concept of identity. Theorists of identity for-mation such as Erikson have been targeted by postmodern critics for pro-pounding a more cohesive account of personal formation than is warranted by the complexity of psychic experience. They question the association of the identification process with a fixed notion of identity that they attribute to Erikson and classical ego psychology. In fact, a reading of Erikson's notion of ego identity from this perspective reveals both an ideal of wholeness and a contrasting awareness of the centrifugal forces threatening the ego's cohesion. This conflict becomes most evident in his historical writings, in which he transposes identity theory onto a world historical stage. At this level a tension emerges between a fluid notion of wholeness, receptive to creativity and existential indeterminacy, and a more totalistic version of identity which emphasizes its rigid and absolutist elements.

When Erikson's biographies of Luther (1958) and Gandhi (1969)[18] are read together, they register the vicissitudes of the identity concept in the transposition of Western values to a colonial setting.[19] For Erikson the core of Luther's historical identity is embodied in the phrase, "Here I Stand." As Erikson acknowledges, "If Luther did not really say the words which became most famous: 'Here I Stand,' legend again rose to the occasion; for this new credo was for men whose identity was derived from their determination to stand on their own feet, not only spiritually, but politically, economically, and intellectually."[20] To the sturdy figure of Luther, Erikson attributed the authority and tenacity of the Puritan spirit. And this representation is unmistakeably gendered. His Luther is strongly masculine, and at times vulgarly so. Luther achieves a masterful identity by transforming his unconscious rage against his real and spiritual fathers into the power of speech: "He changed from a highly restrained and tentative individual into an explosive person; he had found an unexpected release of self-expression, and with it the many sided power of his personality."[21] At its best this sublimation of libidinal and aggressive strivings produced a compelling distillation of conscience, conviction, and forceful leadership. But in Luther's personality, and in its historical embodiment, such an identity structure has been vulnerable to overweening conscience and explosive violence. Acquisitiveness, racism, sadism, and authoritarianism, aspects of Western character most evident in the process of colonial expansion, have often shadowed the most masterful achievements of ego initiative.

From the perspective of transference, these biographies are offered as aspects of the history or truth of psychoanalysis itself. Thus Erikson suggests this comparison between Luther and Freud at the end of *Young Man Luther*. "Both men endeavored to increase the margin of man's inner freedom by introspective means applied to the very center of his conflicts; and this to the end of increased individuality, sanity and service to men."[22] Both men experienced self-defining struggles with their fathers and both saw in life a struggle with an external or internalized god whose gloomy message was a deep-seated moral tenacity. In their parallel search for spiritual or psychological absolutes, both could have rallied to the aphorism, "Here I Stand."

In contrast to Luther, Gandhi is treated as a much more complex and enigmatic figure. Although Erikson criticizes Gandhi harshly for his punitive personal morality, he celebrates and identifies with Gandhi's public morality inscribed in the notion of *Satyagraha*, "whereby daily living becomes an 'experiment with truth.' For what you call the relative character of truth, or what I, as a post-Einsteinian and post-Freudian, would call the *relativity of truth*, reveals itself from generation to generation."[23] By comparison with Luther's thoroughgoing absolutism, *Satyagraha* or "truth force" combined a relativistic or situational approach to knowledge with an absolute sense of commitment. Erikson characterizes this aspect of Gandhi's presence as "actualism," a term developed clinically to distinguish "what can be known because it is demonstrably correct (factual reality) from that which feels effectively true in action (actuality)."[24] Erikson measures the power of Gandhi's actualism by his political effectiveness, his command of the bargaining table and his capacity to transform apparent weakness into real strength. The actualism contained in *Satyagraha* went beyond the absolutism of Luther or Freud – as well as that of the private Gandhi – to a new, more historically responsive truth applicable both to religion and psychoanalysis. Within the transference paradigm, Luther and Freud stand together as "protestants," while Erikson identifies himself with Gandhi and *Satyagraha*.

Like his study of Luther, Erikson's treatment of Gandhi is no less influenced by gender, but in the later study identity as a gender stereotype becomes problematic. Erikson sees Gandhi's masculine competence balanced by a sense of mutuality, the element of compassionate involvement and sensitivity to the other's actuality that, according to Erikson, should also animate the analytic relationship. This quality is further perceived in Gandhi's more "maternal" approach to politics. Whether a reflection of Gandhi's origins in a culture where a less aggressively masculine sense of space and time is cultivated, or a precipitate of his complex sexual and relational conflicts, there resides in Gandhi as portrayed by Erikson "a kind of sublimated maternalism as part of the positive identity of the whole man."[25] By the same token *Satyagraha* is a form of mutuality which achieves a freer identification of the two sexes appropriate to a postindustrial society in which "the martial model of masculinity" has been devalued.

In Erikson's portrayal Gandhi presents a much more discontinuous, elusive identity structure than that of Luther, one that all but deconstructs the concept.[26] Yet Erikson remains wedded to an ideal of wholeness, a notion of universal history as the struggle against divisive "pseudo-species" in the interest of more inclusive identities. The *telos* of identity becomes the establishment of a universal history enriched by a more profound sense of mutuality; a history fostered by psychoanalysis itself, both as a tool for "diagnosing" this process and as a prime instrument in its realization. The pastoral function of psychoanalysis is to point out the dangers of repetition and regression for the stagnating social psyche, so that it can turn to the constructive work of synthesizing new and broader identities.

If the teleological thrust of Erikson's historiography encouraged him to pre-serve a concept of identity in the face of its apparent eclipse, contemporary clinical theorists – especially those influenced by postmodern approaches – are more receptive to its dissolution. Robert May, for instance, writes that the notion of identity "can imply a sense of self too final, smooth and conflict-free"[27] to do justice to the levels of disorganization and disjunction of self-representations typically encountered in the adolescent or adult. For May, psychic experience is more adequately characterized by its uncertainty, fluid-ity, and discontinuity than by its coherence. Identity is less a psychic state positively experienced than one resorted to for protection against conflicting wishes and conflicting aspects of the self.

Not surprisingly, identity theory has been most frequently applied and most heatedly critiqued in the study of gender. Over the last twenty-five years the debate among feminist writers has shifted from the denial of gender dif-ference to an emphasis on representations of difference as a pivotal, if subtle, parameter of individual development. The studies of Kate Millett and Betty Friedan, which became influential in the late 1960s and 1970s, sought to establish an area of "androgyny" on which to construct a non-sexist culture.[28] They were followed in the late 1970s by works by scholars such as Nancy Chodorow and Carol Gilligan which acknowledged female developmental differences and sought to integrate them into a broader cultural understand-ing of family structure and moral development.[29] Contemporary feminist scholars and clinicians deal with both the actuality of difference and its rep-resentation as an instrument of social and cultural control. They argue that essentialist treatments of gender identity work to naturalize gender differ-ences and to promote an exclusionary cultural ideal of heterosexual comple-mentarity. Insofar as Freud collapsed the distinctions among sex, sexuality, and gender, they suggest that psychoanalysis has viewed the range of differ-ences between men and women as natural, as constitutionally based rather than socially or culturally derived. Virginia Goldner contends that the construct of gender identity serves as a socially instituted norm which "pathologizes any gender-incongruent act, state, impulse or mood."[30] The naturalization of gender under the rubric of identity serves to obscure the reality "that gender is fundamentally and paradoxically indeterminant."[31] Nonetheless, the idea of a unified gender identity remains deepseated. In Jacqueline Rose's reading of Lacan on gender, she stresses how the conflicts and obscurity that mark subjectivity are reflected in the ambiguities of gen-der identity. Rose views gender identity as a law imposed on the child repress-ing aspects of its own desire. Developmental accounts of the acquisition of sexual identity rest on a myth of subjective cohesion which the unconscious continually subverts. "For Lacan," Rose writes, "the descripton of sexuality in

developmental terms invariably loses sight of Freud's most fundamental discovery – that the unconscious never ceases to challenge our apparent identity as subjects."[32] The recognition of the mirror stage which bestows the
image of coherence is read as a misrecognition insofar as it masks the fragmentation and alienation of desire in a frozen image of the self.[33]

For contemporary feminist theorists the naturalization of gender identity
has been articulated through a binary system of gender-driven dichotomies
that have been culturally constructed. Goldner has pointed out how gender
dichotomy has set the terms for other constructed polarities: culture versus
nature, reason versus unreason, subject versus object, active versus passive.
These polarities are coded in gender terms, with masculinity appropriating
the favored side of the opposition.[34] To deconstruct these gendered
dichotomies, feminist critics focus on the tendency to define the terms of
these polarities as essences – as things – rather than as fluid signifiers that take
on meaning only in relation to one another. As Muriel Dimen writes, "In theoretical terms, looking at either masculinity or femininity without looking at
the contrasts between them encourages us to imagine fixed essences, hard and
fast polarities."[35] By contrast, Dimen argues, gender appears to be less a
determinate category than something resembling a force field.

> Much like the atom, once thought of as a substance but now constructed as a
> set of interacting forces, so gender appears not to consist of essences but of com-
> plex and shifting relations among multiple contrasts or differences. Sometimes
> these contrasts remain distinct, at other times they intersect, and at still other
> times they fuse and exchange identities.[36]

From this point of view binary notions of gender and heterosexuality are
linked, not as evolutionary imperatives, but as psychosocial processes that
require and imply one another.

In this spirit Jessica Benjamin argues that the rigid opposition of gender
identities, which, viewed developmentally, she characterizes as Oedipal, is
constituted by the splitting and projecting of unwanted aspects of the self
onto the other. The effect of such psychic repudiation is to polarize gendered
subjects, and to diminish their adaptive and creative potentiality. To this
process she contrasts a post-Oedipal form of opposition constituted by
sustaining the tension between contrasting elements. In this tension the
opposition between them can be experienced as pleasurable, rather than as
dangerous or forbidden.[37]

This line of reasoning leads Benjamin to a critique of the identity concept.
Applied to gender, identity suggests a simple axis of sameness–difference that
rigidifies into a discourse of opposites. The term identity suggests a coherence

and uniformity that is belied by the multiplicity of self-representations apparent in the exploration of unconscious processes.[38] Benjamin would give up
the notion of identity, "reified as thing," but preserve the concept of identification as a vital aspect of internal dynamics. Identification focuses attention
both on the multiplicity of self-representations in the course of development,
and on the mechanisms by which they play off and alter one another. It is
concerned less with what the self *is* than *how* it responds within a field of
plural and sometimes contradictory representations. "The idea that self identifies as belonging to a sex," Benjamin states, "should not be equated with the
idea of an unambiguous and coherent *identity*. ... Core identity only makes
sense if we conceptualize it as a background for future gender ambiguity and
tension, a repetitive base line against which all the other instruments play
different, often conflicting or discordant, lines."[39] Identity can produce only
a single theme, while identification commands a richer, if more ambiguous,
register of responses.

A similar anti-essentialist critique has been directed at Heinz Kohut's concept of the self. In contrast to Kohut's emphasis on cohesion, post-classical
theory focuses on the discontinuities in the experience of the self. As
Christopher Bollas has written, "The person's *self* is the history of many internal relations. ... There is no one unified mental phenomenon that we can
term self. ... The concept of self should refer to the positions or points of view
from which and through which we sense, feel, observe and reflect on distinct
and separate experiences in our being."[40] Although the experience of the self
as distinct and separate from others appears as a universal feature of subjectivity in Western culture, contemporary psychoanalysis focuses greater attention on the relational context in which that experience is embedded. The
relational approach employs free association to produce a degree of disorganization in which the individual strands that constitute experience can
become differentiated. As Stephen Mitchell suggests, one paradox of the analytic process is that the greater the capacity of patients to experience multiple versions of themselves, the more resilient they experience themselves as
being. At its best, Mitchell states, psychoanalysis "makes possible an appreciation of the self as continually regenerated in time; and an appreciation of the
multiplicity within the integrity of self-organizations enriches the tapestry of
subjective experience."[41] Observing the vicissitudes of the self from an evolutionary perspective, Malcolm Slavin and Daniel Kriegman have recently
described the adaptively divided character of the self. What might appear as
the practical difficulty of achieving inner integration or cohesion, they spec-
ulate, may be understandable as an evolved strategy, a structured division
designed to promote context-dependent flexibility and adaptive change.[42] As
Mitchell notes ironically, insofar as patients' psychic worlds become more

fluid, complex, and subtly textured, they are "actually less known at the end of analysis than at the beginning."[43] Anti-essentialism in both psychoanalytic theory and clinical practice is only one aspect of a more general trend. Critiques of fixed or primordial "unities" in the historical realm parallel those of identity and self.

Since the early 1980s the issue of how we know or experience the nation has become as contentious a topic as how we know or experience ourselves. In the introduction to his pathbreaking study *Imagined Communities*, published in 1983, Benedict Anderson addressed the putative universality of nationalism by noting that "in the modern world everyone can, should, will 'have' a nationality, as he or she 'has' a gender."[44] The comparison of nationality and gender is both noteworthy for our discussion and ironic. By placing the predicates for both of these conditions within quotation marks, Anderson suggests that national identity and gender identity belong on the same footing as cultural constructs. In fact, in recent years the notion of identity has been scrutinized from a historical perspective as well as from a psychological one, an examination undertaken in an environment increasingly sensitized to the constructed or manipulated aspects of cultural or national forms of cohesion or integration.

Within an Indian framework Ashis Nandy has characterized such a process of "traditionalization," a quality of permeability in Indian culture that allows new influences to be integrated as a set of age-old traditions while existing values are discarded.[45] From a Western point of view Eric Hobsbawm has described the "invention of tradition" as a self-consciously created set of practices "which seek to inculcate certain values and norms of behavior by repetition, which implies continuity with the past."[46] Given the instability of the modern world, the effort to exalt some aspects of social or political life as immutable would seem extraordinary. Yet these very conditions encourage the political use of symbolism and ritual to impose a sense of group identity on otherwise disparate communities. Historians participate in these identity-conferring practices, Hobsbawm reminds us, insofar as all invented traditions employ history "as a legitimator of action and cement of group cohesion."[47] One paradox of this process, he notes, is that modern nations, although clearly constructed of heterogeneous elements, typically assert a natural, self-evident right to exist.[48] Similarly, Ernest Gellner points out that nationalism treats itself as a self-evident principle, although it owes "its plausibility and compelling nature" to the very special historical circumstances imposed by modernization and industrialization. Paradoxically, Gellner notes, nationalists preach tradition and continuity but owe their influence to the decisive break in human history embodied in the modernizing nation-state.[49]

This critique of nationalism and national identity is composed at "the edge of psychology."[50] It is reflective of the suggestive power of psychological metaphors for contemporary historians when Tom Nairn describes national-ism as "the pathology of modern developmental history, as inescapable as 'neurosis' in the individual, with much the same essential ambiguity attach-ing to it, a similar built-in capacity for descent into dementia, rooted in the dilemmas of helplessness thrust upon most of the world and largely incur-able."[51] The "essential ambiguity" Nairn attributes to nationalism has re-cently been examined through its narrative strategies, strategies in which the deconstructive logic of difference and the vicissitudes of identity play with and through one another. In *Imagined Communities* Anderson cites the "imag-inative power of nationalism" for its capacity to weld the heterogeneous ele-ments of the modern nation into a series of images that convey homogeneity and cohesion.[52] He cites a number of strategies in writings on the nation in which the individual is subsumed to the general through the narrative assumption of belonging or commonality. The narrative function of the newspaper – its fictive quality – according to Anderson, is to provide a serial form for the expression of collective identity, an unfolding plot doubly punc-tuated by the daily rhythm of mass participation and mass reading.[53]

The historian Anne McClintock has recently explored the construction of the national narrative in nineteenth-century Britain from the perspective of gender stereotypes. The influence of Social Darwinism, she argues, shaped Britain's nationalist discourse around the image of the Family of Man. Under the Darwinian umbrella, the family metaphor sanctioned the subordination of women as a natural right, and also naturalized other hierarchical structures of class and race that supported Britain's rise to global prominence.[54] By the same token, McClintock suggests, British nationalism employed gendered metaphors to resolve what Gellner cited as nationalism's anomalous rela-tionship to historical time. Male metaphors embodied nationalism's forward thrusting, progressive, or revolutionary dimension of discontinuity. Female metaphors, on the other hand, expressed the passive, regressive stereotypes of female character, and represented nationalism's rootedness in an archaic, continuous temporal framework.[55]

For Homi Bhabha the narrative of the nation reflects the postcolonial condition, the chronic dissonance engendered by discordant interests, entrenched minorities and ongoing patterns of migration. Bhabha's stated aim is to displace the historicism that has dominated discussions of the nation with a narrative that reflects the liminal status of the nation as a fractured artifact of cultural modernity.[56] The ambivalence he attaches to the nation is partly a function of postcolonial heterogeneity. But it also belongs to the play of language in national discourse, a process equally hostage to the logic of difference and to the ambiguities and uncertainties inscribed in the cultural unconscious. Borrowing a term from Fanon, "the zone of occult instability where the people dwell," Bhabha suggests a double narrative movement in which the people are at once the objects of a nationalist pedagogy based on a historical genealogy, and the subjects – the sources – of a process of significa-tion that erases originary principles with the "repetitious, recursive strategy of the performative."[57] The conceptual ambivalence that emerges in the act of writing the nation takes the shape of "counter-narratives of the nation that continually evoke and erase its totalizing boundaries – both actual and con-ceptual – and disturb those ideological maneuvers through which 'imagined communities' are given essentialist identities."[58]

In contesting the essentialist identity of the nation, Bhabha draws the same line as Jessica Benjamin between identity and identification. He associ-ates cultural identity with the pedagogical process of historical sedimenta-tion, to which he contrasts the shifting identifications evoked in the perfor-mative process of signification. Such cultural identifications could be said to constitute a loss of identity, a submission to the undecidability of culture that crystallizes in its hybridity. It is reflected not so much through "identity as identification (in the psychoanalytic sense). I try to talk about hybridity through a psychoanalytic analogy, so that identification is a process of iden-tifying with and through another object, an object of otherness, at which point the agency of identification – the subject – is itself always ambivalent, because of the intervention of that otherness."[59] As in psychoanalysis the process of cultural identification is dialogical or transferential, constituted through the locus of an other in "a process of substitution, displacement or projection."[60]

The struggle for cultural identity has had its most poignant expressions in the colonial encounters of the past century. But while, in the postwar period, attention has largely been directed to identity formation among newly liber-ated nations, more contemporary critics have argued that the need to forge viable Western identities has been at the heart of the colonial enterprise from the outset. Citing Hegel's and Marx's universalizing texts, they suggest that the underlying project of world historical narrative has been the creation and domination of Europe's "others."[61] Colonial expansion produced or promised not only political and economic expansion, but also the opportunity to culti-vate and impose a universal identity and a complementary value system, an enterprise reinforced by binary oppositions such as reason versus unreason, advanced versus primitive, and masculine versus feminine. Ashis Nandy, for one, has pointed to the social and cultural costs of this undertaking to the col-onizing powers: for Britain a false sense of cultural homogeneity that discour-aged criticism of the class system; and the creation of alternate channels of social mobility that promoted nationalist sentiment and again blunted social consciousness.[62] Colonialist ideology itself, Nandy notes, encouraged gender stereotypes as homologues of political and cultural stratification: the colonizer as "the tough, courageous, openly aggressive, hyper-masculine ruler" and the colonized as "the sly, cowardly, passive-aggressive womanly subject."[63]

Bhabha, predictably, views the colonial arena as the locus par excellence where Western identity and desire were simultaneously imposed and deflected. He depicts the colonialist as tethered to rather than confronted by "his dark reflection, the shadow of colonized man."[64] This shadow, the mark of the colonists' ambivalent identification with the colonized, had the effect of splitting his presence and obscuring his sense of boundaries. For Bhabha the term hybridity best captures "the revaluation of the assumption of colonial identity through the repetition of discriminatory identity effects. ... It unsettles the mimetic or narcissistic demands of colonial power but reimplicates its identifications in strategies of subversion that turn the gaze of the discriminated back upon the eye of power."[65] To the degree that hybridization, rather than repression, is the actual product of the imposition of colonial power, it generates its own subversion in the form of ambivalence and uncertainty.

Nandy makes a very similar point without resort to the elaborate scaffolding of deconstructionist logic. Even when they seemed totally controlled, he argues, Indians under British rule retained some indeterminateness and freedom.[66] For him the oppressed is never a pure victim. While one part of him collaborates and adjusts, another part subverts or destroys under the guise of collaboration. By refusing to embrace the same values – the same cultural identity – as their masters, the colonized could tease and defy them, subverting their dignity and identity as paternalist rulers.[67] That space of "indeterminateness and freedom" was, of course, embodied in Mahatma Gandhi. By affirming the primacy of myths over history, Nandy writes, "he thereby circumvented the unilinear pathway from primitivism to modernity, and from political immaturity to political adulthood."[68] By the same token, Gandhi rejected the hypermasculinity of the West in favor of a more androgynous stance rooted in Indian traditions. In contrast to the West's pursuit of categorical values, Indian culture has displayed the capacity to tolerate cultural ambiguities and to deploy them as defenses against cultural invasion.[69]

Despite the critique of identity as a viable psychological or cultural construct, its critics often find themselves drawn to it recursively, as a notion that resists deconstruction. In viewing identity as a "necessary defense," Robert May formulates it as a "universal expression of the psychic need for order and coherence in one's view of oneself."[70] Other clinicians have been alert to the dangers posed by identity diffusion. Jane Flax, a clinician and feminist sympathetic to postmodern deconstructions of the cohesive self, is unwilling to abandon all discourses rooted in a sense of continuous or integrated subjectivity. Drawing on her experience with borderline patients, she writes that "those who celebrate or call for a 'decentered' self seem self-deceptively naive and unaware of the basic cohesion within themselves that makes the fragmentation of experiences something other than a terrifying slide into psychosis."[71] She rejects any reified notion of a unitary self, but insists that a coherent core self is required to explore the transitional space of postmodern practice in which the boundaries between self and other are obscured.

An analogous point has been made by Stephen Mitchell with regard to the phenomenon of multiple personality. Alongside his advocacy of the multiplicity of the self, he distinguishes those who suffer from multiple personalities or major dissociative states from other people in that there is no recognition of a continuous, enduring subjectivity. "The discontinuities," he notes, "are too discontinuous."[72] Although the self changes over time, the continuous experience of self serves an evolutionary and psychological function. The self as multiple and discontinuous refers to the patterned variability of multiple configurations of self in different relational contexts. The self as integral and continuous describes the subjective experience of forming patterns over time and across different organizational frameworks.[73] In the context of gender development, Jessica Benjamin appeals to the symbolization process to reconcile the multiplicity of positions underlying the appearance of a single identity. For her, development should not dictate a unilinear trajectory to a fixed gender identity, but the ability to return to earlier, more flexible and inclusive gender representations without compromising the knowledge of difference. In this scheme the need for both gender identity and multiplicity are acknowledged.[74]

If, from a contemporary perspective, identity appears impossible to justify conceptually or experientially, it also seems indispensable as a measure of agency or internal cohesion. The same paradoxical condition pertains to identity in its sociocultural or historical manifestations. Benedict Anderson cites three so-called paradoxes that relate to nationalism: its objective modernity to the historian against its subjective antiquity to the nationalist; its universality as a sociocultural concept opposed to its manifest particularity in practice; and its political hegemony in contrast to its philosophical poverty or incoherence.[75] The reader, in fact, hesitates between Anderson's insightful unveiling of the shallow roots of national identity, and his representation of the power or authority of the concept in spite of its "poverty." Anderson acknowledges the strong affinity of nationalist imaginings and religious imaginings, with their fluent response "to the overwhelming burden of human suffering."[76] He reminds us that the dawn of the age of nationalism was also the dusk for religious modes of thought. "What then was required," he writes,

> was a secular transformation of fatality into continuity, contingency into meaning. As we shall see, few things were (are) better suited to this end than an idea of nation. If nation-states are widely conceded to be 'new' and 'historical,' the nations to which they gave political expression always loom out of an immemorial past, and still more important, glide into a limitless future. It is the magic of nationalism to turn chance into destiny.[77]

Bhabha's treatment of the nation struggles with this same disparity. On the one hand the incoherence of the nation as narrative is all around us. Its totalizing boundaries are constantly being displaced and erased by the plurality of narrative voices at work in the postcolonial community. Even as Bhabha documents the "insurmountable ambivalence" of postcolonial culture, he continues to cite the *will* to nationhood as a powerful force in contemporary society. "It is the will," he writes, "that unifies historical memory and secures present day consent. The will is, indeed, the articulation of the nation-people."[78] For Bhabha, of course, the enunciation of such a will is inherently fractured or equivocal. His discourse pivots around his own unanswered question, "In what historical time do such configurations of cultural difference assume forms of cultural and political authority?"[79] It suggests an ongoing desire for an "imagined community" undercut by the very conditions of its enunciation.

Bhabha's focus on national will leads back to the critique of identity in a psychological context, particularly to Jane Flax's observation that postmodern intellectuals who would proscribe any coherent discourse on subjectivity have not witnessed or experienced the terrifying depersonalization of borderline regression. On the one hand, Bhabha's essays can be read as a sophisticated rendering of the multiple identities of the modern nation. On the other, the paradoxical thrust of his argument appears to undermine the minimal conditions for articulating viable forms of group cohesion. His stance reflects the cosmopolitan detachment of the postcolonial intellectual elite, as much as the needs of oppressed peoples within these societies. In other circumstances, in developing or fractured societies, the emotional or political need for national identity may preclude such intellectual luxuries, even at the cost of postponing the salutary disillusionment embraced from a postmodern position.

These reflections on identity and identification take us directly back to Von Laue's concern with the psychological obstacles to writing world history, to the "hidden factors that constitute our cultural identity." His appeal to look "at ourselves from the outside, in the intercultural contexts," I would hope, takes on more resonance from this discussion. I would further suggest, however, that our identities as world historians are constituted neither inside nor outside our culture or any other, but within the intercultural contexts themselves. The re-examination of identity theory suggests that the barriers between groups are at least partly constructed out of a process of projection. As many writers have argued, these projective mechanisms extrude unacceptable or ambivalently regarded aspects of the self or group and attribute them to an external individual or collective other.[80] In this regard psychoanalysis has a critical contribution to make to the study of identity formation within a world-historical framework. Although the role of projection as a dynamic factor in social life has been appreciated outside a clinical context,[81] psychoanalysis has developed the most exacting account of projection through its study of individual development and the mechanisms of defense. Through the medium of transference an array of projective defenses has been observed clinically and categorized in terms of the degree of defensive distortion required to restore narcissistic equilibrium.[82]

These insights have been adapted from a clinical setting to help explain the consolidation of racial prejudice or virulent national feeling at a group level. During the period of imperial expansion particularly, this projective process has crystallized in a set of culturally or racially derived oppositions through which Western thought has tended to structure the global experience. The ideologies of domination that have flourished in these circumstances have by now been well documented. At a less obvious level, however, the desire or need for a categorical distinction between self and other has generally blunted our awareness of the depth of cultural miscegenation that marks the global condition. In his recent study *The Black Atlantic*, Paul Gilroy underscores the extent to which modern identity has been shaped by the interaction of discourses of the center and the margins, a process that transcends and refigures national and cultural boundaries. Exploring the interwoven experiences of black and white cultures, he describes the discontinuities endemic to modern life and the inescapably plural character of modern identity.[83] The ambiguous suspension between cultures, the deflection from categorical convictions, opens the way to more penetrating historical inquiry, even as it widens the margins of uncertainty.

The psychoanalytic treatment of projection and related defenses, applied at the group level, helps to clarify the ambiguities bound up in the intercultural and international encounter. Yet contemporary psychoanalysis, like other forms of cultural discourse, has recently been undergoing an identity crisis of its own in coming to terms with the ambiguities bound up in the linguistic or rhetorical dimension of the clinical encounter. When the clinical process is read as a text, its ambiguities are not regarded simply as the fallout from psychic conflict, but rather as integral to the truth of psycho-analysis itself. Approached through its language, psychoanalysis is shaped by the clinical dialogue. To the extent that psychoanalysis is fundamentally dia-logical or transferential, constituted through the locus of another, it replicates and models the ambivalent process through which cultural identification crystallizes and fragments. Such identifications, as Bhabha argues, must pass through the other, "always constituted in a process of substitution, displace-ment or projection." The focus on process in cultural identification is mir-rored in the attention to process in recent psychoanalytic discussion. Emphasis has moved from theoretical models as such to the theory implicit in clinical practice – driven by the dynamics of the unconscious and the uni-versality of transference. The movement toward a hermeneutics of practice not only recognizes but hinges on the permeable boundaries of self and other in the clinical dialogue, a condition of intersubjectivity energized by the ambivalent play of introjective and projective mechanisms. As the discussion of identity theory has suggested, this approach to psychoanalysis points less to the consolidation of identity than to the unbinding of a multiplicity of actual or potential selves. As such it constitutes a discursive practice whose method overlaps with and deepens other forms of cultural analysis.

Such a perspective on psychology and culture will disappoint those who are seeking a master narrative for world history, an overarching theoretical construct from which the enterprise of world history can proceed. The objec-tives of this essay are more limited, directed less to psychohistory – to the psychological interpretation of history – than to exploring the grounds for a psychologically informed world history. By suggesting the ways in which psy-choanalytic discourse is embedded in cultural formations, it endeavors to render the cultural barriers that appear to obstruct world-historical inquiry more surmountable, even if more susceptible to ambiguous effects.

PART IV

Charting Trajectories

10

Reflections on *The End of History,* Five Years Later

Francis Fukuyama

I Introduction

When I showed a draft of my original article "The End of History?" to a political theorist friend in early 1989 and asked for his opinion, he said: "You will be misunderstood." This judgment proved quite prophetic: after its publication in *The National Interest* that summer, it elicited a flurry of misinterpretations, many related to its supposed relevance to American foreign policy (it had none). Part of the reason that I enlarged the article into *The End of History and the Last Man* was to correct these misinterpretations by presenting the argument at much greater length. Surely, I thought, a 400-page book would go a long way to setting the record straight. I should have known better, of course; what you are is what you are *recognized* as being, to use one of the book's central concepts. We exist not "in ourselves," but only in an intersubjective social context; and in that context, what I said was that events would somehow stop happening, or there would be perpetual peace.

Nonetheless, I have been asked to look again at my arguments in 1994, in light of both the significant events that have taken place in the real world since 1989, and in light of the criticisms that have been made of my article and book. While I have little confidence that a third attempt to clarify will actually serve that purpose, I will nonetheless try.

My book consisted of two distinct parts, the first an empirical investigation of various events, both contemporary and historical, and the second a "normative" or theoretical one that sought to evaluate contemporary liberal democracy.[1] The empirical part has been attacked the most relentlessly. Virtually every week I read a story in the papers that contains some variant on the words, "As we can see, history has not ended but is only now beginning. ... " (This phrase has now been used by Margaret Thatcher, Mikhail

Gorbachev, George Bush, Hosni Mubarak, Anthony Lake, and a host of lesser lights; I propose a moratorium as it now represents the total bankruptcy of the speechwriter's art.) The normative or theoretical part has been attacked also, usually by a different and more serious group of readers, who argue that I got Hegel wrong, or Kojève, or Nietzsche, or one of the other philosophers mentioned in the book. And finally, as Greg Smith points out, there is a major question as to the way that the two parts of the book relate to one another.[2] The normative part of the book has been criticized for being based on "mere" empiricism and vulnerable to changes in a turbulent world scene. Alternatively, I have been charged with moving to inadmissible normative arguments when the empirical analysis failed.

I will take on each of these groups of criticisms, beginning with the relationship of the empirical to the normative argument, then moving to the empirical argument itself, and finally to the most difficult issue, the normative or theoretical question.

II THE RELATIONSHIP BETWEEN THE EMPIRICAL AND NORMATIVE ARGUMENTS

Perhaps the most common misunderstanding of my argument (of which I am sure none of the readers of the current essay is guilty) is that the phrase, "the end of history," is a simple empirical statement describing the current condition of the world. These critics believe I was asserting that there would be no more war, struggle, or conflict, and their criticism takes the form: "As we can see, history has not ended because X happened," where X is something they regard as bad: the Gulf War, the Yugoslav conflict, famine in Somalia, a coup in Moscow, the LA riots, poverty, drug use, you name it. A colleague of mine who is working for the Agency for International Development in Bangladesh sent me what is probably the ultimate of this form of critique: a local Dhaka columnist denounced the idea of the end of history because a Bangladeshi had been bumped off a British Airways flight (this evidently showed that racism still existed in the world).

A somewhat more sophisticated version of this criticism asserts that the reality of the post-cold war world is not democracy, but virulent nationalism. By this account, everyone was euphoric in 1989 after the fall of the Berlin Wall thinking that the world was turning democratic and capitalist, but in fact it was returning to a premodern world of tribalism and ethnic passion run amok. Bosnia proved that modernity was a thin veneer; even in Western Europe, the upsurge in anti-foreigner violence showed that liberal democracy rested on very weak foundations. The institutions of world order like the

UN, EC, or NATO proved to be woefully inadequate in maintaining a common level of civilized behavior, and the future was likely to look much uglier than the past.

These sorts of issues are not irrelevant to the argument (and will be dealt with at greater length in the following section), but they fundamentally miss the point of the phrase, "the end of history." The latter is not a statement about the *is*, but about the *ought*: for a variety of *theoretical* reasons, liberal democracy and free markets constitute the best regime, or more precisely the best of the available alternative ways of organizing human societies (or again, if one prefers Churchill's formulation, the least bad way of doing so). It most fully (though not completely) satisfies the most basic human longings, and therefore can be expected to be more universal and more durable than other regimes or other principles of political organization. It does not *completely* satisfy them, however, which means that the resolution of the historical problem cannot be brought to a close.

This is a normative, not an empirical statement, but it is a normative statement based in crucial ways on empirical evidence. It is of course possible to construct a best regime "in speech," as Socrates did in the *Republic*, that has no chance of ever being realized on earth. Most college students (at least, before they became so earnestly careerist) have sat around their dorm rooms late at night imagining a perfectly just society that would be just as perfectly impossible to bring into being, for reasons they will come to understand in another ten or fifteen years. No one likes the moral implications of capitalism, or imagines that the way it distributes gains is perfectly just. Socialist schemes of distribution are arguably fairer in a moral sense.[3] Their chief problem is that they don't work. The latter is not something one can determine theoretically or on *a priori* grounds. When writing *Capitalism, Socialism, and Democracy* in 1943, Joseph Schumpeter argued that there was no reason why socialist economic organization should not be as efficient as capitalism. He dismissed the warnings of Hayek and von Mises that centralized planning boards would face problems of "unmanageable complication," gravely underestimated the importance of incentives in motivating people to produce and innovate, and falsely predicted that centralized planning would reduce economic uncertainty.[4] None of this could have been known without the experience of real-world socialist societies trying to organize their economies according to socialist principles and failing. If the Soviet Union had entered on an era of explosive double-digit growth in the 1970s and 1980s while Europe and the United States stagnated, our view of the respective normative merits of capitalism and socialism would be very different. The normative argument, therefore, is crucially and obviously dependent on empirical evidence.

The normative assertion that liberal democracy is the best available regime depends, then, not simply on a theoretical view of the adequacy of its moral and political arrangements, but also on empirical verification of its workability. If liberal democracies all failed shortly after being established (as European conservatives like Joseph Demaistre believed the American experiment would fail), or if liberal democracy proved successful only on Kiribati or Vanuatu, but nowhere else, we would not take it seriously as a moral alternative. On the other hand, its moral adequacy is not simply dependent on its workability, durability, or power: there have been a variety of bad regimes (or at least, regimes constructed on principles diametrically opposed to those of liberal democracy) that have been very successful as historical enterprises. Might does not make right, though might may be a *condition* for right.

The assertion, then, that liberal democracy constitutes the "end of history" does not depend on the short-term advances or setbacks to democracy worldwide in 1994 (or 1989, or 1939, or 1806, for that matter). It is a normative statement about the principles of freedom and equality that underlay the French and American revolutions, to the effect that they stand at the end of a long process of ideological evolution, and that there is not a higher set of alternative principles that will in time replace them. This normative statement, to repeat, cannot be divorced from empirical fact. Empirical fact alone cannot prove or disprove its validity, except perhaps at the very unlikely extremes (that is, the complete disappearance of liberal democracy, or the total universalization of it, or the appearance of an angel announcing the millennium). Empirical fact does not and cannot arm us with a deterministic methodology for predicting the future. What empirical fact can do, on the other hand, is to give us a greater or lesser degree of *hope* that the normative statement is true. In this respect, empirical fact plays the same role that Kant's proposed "universal history" does in his essay of the same name. As Susan Shell points out, the purpose of this reading of history for Kant is to give us hope, and therefore perhaps to assist in the accomplishment of moral and political progress in the world. I have been accused, particularly in France, of being the "last Marxist"; of having a linear, deterministic, or mechanical understanding of history; or generally of espousing some "strong" version of historicism. If one goes back to *The End of History and the Last Man*, however, it should be clear that I was proposing a very *weak* version. I asked whether "it makes sense for us once again to speak of a coherent and directional History of mankind that will eventually lead the greater part of humanity to liberal democracy." To "speak of History" is only to say that the question is once again meaningful, and not that it is possible to answer the question with a strong version of historical progress.

Thus the truth of the assertion of the "end of history" did not in any way depend on the events of 1989. It could have been asserted with equal validity ten years earlier, at the height of the Brezhnev era; it was asserted in the late 1930s on the eve of World War II (by Alexandre Kojève); and in the aftermath of the Battle of Jena in 1807 (by Hegel himself). The statement was not absurd in any of these cases, despite the turbulent and bloody "history" (in the conventional sense of the word) that took place before and after each was enunciated, for in each case they signified that the principles of the French revolution were normatively the best available principles of political organization. Indeed, the flow of empirical events has given us greater *hope* that it is true with each repetition: in 1807, there were only three working democracies; in 1939, there were thirteen; while in 1989 there were over sixty. Thus, if the question is asked "Have the events of the past few years (the Gulf War, Bosnia, Somalia, and so on) made you rethink the hypothesis?" the answer is obviously no. There may be somewhat less hope, but the normative argument concerning liberal democracy is not affected by the short-term flow of empirical events, but rests on other, broader grounds. Nor is there empirical evidence that an alternative set of normative principles is taking hold: fascism may be winning politically in Serbia, but no one (even, I would guess, in Belgrade) sees Serbia as an attractive generalizable model for the future.

There is, of course, a higher-level question to be answered concerning the relationship of the empirical to the normative question, namely, how does one arrive at normative statements at all? The whole thrust of modern thought teaches us that there can be no such thing as a rational derivation of values from facts, or values grounded on a concept like nature. How one resolves this conundrum is of course the essence of the Strauss–Kojève debate, which will be taken up in section IV below.

III THE EMPIRICAL ARGUMENT

The empirical case that there is such a thing as "History" in the Marxist–Hegelian sense is perhaps the easiest to demonstrate of the various points made in *The End of History and the Last Man.* It is of course not fashionable to speak of History in this sense, particularly among professional historians who are trained to be narrowly empirical. But I would argue that virtually everyone believes in the existence of a directional history (though not necessarily in an "end" of history) on some level, and that the burden of proof is in fact on those who argue that history in this sense does not exist.

First, to define our terms, by "History" or "universal history" we mean a coherent and directional transformation of human societies that affects the whole, or nearly the whole, of mankind.

The starting point for a discussion of whether History in this sense exists is emphatically *not* in the events of the past few years, but in the concept of economic modernization. Prior to the scientific revolution of the sixteenth and seventeenth centuries in Europe, there could be a high degree of continuity in history: Chinese civilization, whether one looks at political organization, family life, or economic production, did not look terribly different in the Han dynasty than it did in the Sung or even Ch'ing periods. But with the development of the scientific method, a process of economic development began that has encompassed virtually the whole of humanity.

The logic of this development process is determined by the progressive nature of scientific knowledge and its embodiment in technology through research and development. Science unfolds, once the scientific method is discovered, out of what is at least a twofold process: on the one hand, there is something like the desire for "utility maximization" described by neoclassical economists, and on the other a desire for recognition that leads human beings to seek mastery over nature. But while this process serves human ends and occurs through human agency, the internal logic of the process is determined ultimately by the laws of nature, which impose upon it a certain regularity. The second law of thermodynamics is not culturally determined; it is no different in Japan or Rwanda than it is in the United States. Technology provides a uniform horizon of production possibilities at any given level of scientific knowledge, and forces all societies employing technology to organize themselves in certain ways. It is now clear, forty years after the elaboration of "modernization theory," that there are a variety of paths to modernity, and that all societies will not necessarily resemble England or the United States in their development histories (indeed, in certain respects England's and the United States' differed considerably from one another). Late developers do things differently from early ones; there are cultural aspects to economic organization; the state can play varying roles in promoting or retarding the process. But the broad outlines of the process – urbanization, rational authority, bureaucratization, an ever-ramified and complex division of labor – can be found in all developing cultures.

What is remarkable about the process of economic modernization is its universality as a goal. For a while, Burma was the only nation that explicitly stated that it did not want to modernize, but now, even "Myanmar" has gotten on the treadmill. The only parts of humanity not aspiring to economic modernization are a few isolated tribes in the jungles of Brazil or Papua New Guinea, and they don't aspire to it because they don't know about it.

Societies that at one point did not want to modernize or rejected further social change (for example, Japanese renunciation of certain types of new weapons in the Tokugawa period) were eventually forced to adopt technology with all it implied because of the decisive military advantage that technology conferred. There are, of course, small communities in the developed West like the Amish who keep alive an earlier level of technology (not, I would note, neolithic but nineteenth-century), and ideologically committed environmentalists, who want to reverse the process of industrialization. But the aspiration to economic modernization is one of the most universal characteristics of human societies one can imagine.

Though the tendency toward capitalism has historically been much less universal than the desire for economic modernization *per se*, I argued in *The End of History and the Last Man* that technology necessarily points toward market-oriented forms of economic decision making. What is even less universal than capitalism is the preference for liberal democracy. Nonetheless, as a purely empirical matter, there is an extraordinarily strong correlation between high levels of industrial development and stable democracy.[5] With modernization, there has been a corresponding growth in the legitimacy of the idea of human equality, the phenomenon noted by Tocqueville at the beginning of *Democracy in America*. There has been considerable argument as to why this correlation exists: at one extreme, the case has been made that democracy is culturally determined; it flows in some sense from Christian cultural systems and it is merely an accident that the world's earliest developed countries were also Christian nations.[6] On the other hand, it can be argued that there is a certain hierarchy of goals, with the satisfaction of economic needs preceding in some sense the need for recognition. With advancing socioeconomic status comes an increasing demand for recognition in the form of political participation. As an empirical matter, the most interesting test cases are now in Asia: Japan, Korea, Taiwan, and other Asian countries are not culturally Christian, and yet there has been a distinct correlation between level of economic development and stable democracy there as well. This suggests that while there may be cultural elements to the correlation, the correlation itself is not ultimately culturally determined but applies universally.

As noted earlier, the argument for the existence of a universal history would have to be made in a relatively weak form. That is to say, there is nothing necessarily linear, rigid, or deterministic about saying that the progressive unfolding of modern natural science determines in broad outline the economic modernization process, which in turn creates a predisposition toward liberal democracy. Marxists tended to state their theories of history in a very strong form: feudalism *inevitably* gives way to capitalism, which *inevitably* collapses from its own internal contradictions and gives way to socialism, and so

on. The misuse of such deterministic theories to legitimize political terror by
Lenin and Stalin has justifiably given them a bad name. On the other hand,
many people who reject Marxism would accept a weak form of this theory, for
example that put forth by Max Weber, which accepted the fact that history
had a directionality, but which allowed for vast discontinuities like the
Reformation not explainable by any unitary theory.

A universal history understood as modernization can and has been
attacked from a postmodernist perspective. Why "privilege" the story of economic development, or identify it with History itself? Is this not a Euro-,
phallo-, or whatnot-centric story? Why not tell another story, say, the story
of indigenous peoples crushed by modernization, or the story of women, or
the story of family life, each of which would follow a very different trajectory? What about the story of all those years prior to the invention of the scientific method; were these not worthy of being called history? Who is the
teller of the Universal History, and what are his interests in telling the story
in this manner?

Modernization theory collapsed in the 1970s under the weight of such
attacks, but it should not have. The transition from a premodern to an industrial society is one that affects virtually every other "story" in a fundamental
way, and it affects virtually all societies in some manner, whether or not they
have modernized successfully. The postmodernist professor who asserts that
there is no coherent direction to history would most likely never contemplate
leaving his comfortable surroundings in Paris, New Haven, or Irvine, and
move to Somalia, or raise his children under the hygienic conditions prevailing in Burundi, or teach postmodernist philosophy in Teheran.

While there is a reasonable empirical basis for constructing a directional
universal history, the empirical grounds for arguing that the historical process
has an end or goal are much weaker. To begin with, the phenomenon of modern natural science is open-ended; it does not, as far as we know, have an end
point where we will know everything there is to know about the physical universe. And if our lives and our forms of social organization are governed by
the inner logic of the development of science, we cannot know with finality
what social arrangements will be dictated by a given level of scientific knowledge in the future.

Moreover, while it might be possible to assert that something broad like
economic modernization is a virtually universal goal, any particular set of
political arrangements like liberal democracy is rather unlikely to emerge out
of the merely empirical data as the immanent goal of the historical process.
The present confusion over the nature of the post-communist world order is
testimony to the lack of consensus on how to interpret the data. Some will
deny that there has been any particular trend toward democracy. Others, like

G. M. Tamàs, will assert that what Western liberals have identified as democracy in contemporary Eastern Europe is actually a depoliticized version of democracy that rests on very different normative roots. Others will assert that individualistic democracy has been stripped of any real meaning in Japan and other places in Asia where the form of democracy has been observed. And finally, there will always be reasonable doubts about the cohesiveness and irreversibility of democracy in places, such as Western Europe or even the United States, where it already exists by common consensus.

Thus, empirical fact can lead us to assert that there is such a thing as History. Empirical fact can probably also falsify the notion of liberal democracy as an "end of history" under several conditions: if liberal democracies around the world collapsed as communist systems did in the late 1980s; if a society based on genuinely different principles arose somewhere in the world and looked like it was a going concern over a long period of time (my candidate is an Asian "soft authoritarian" state); or if some earlier non-liberal principle returned and gained widespread legitimacy (for example, if American women lost the right to vote or slavery became legal once again). Empirical fact by itself, however, does not provide us a basis for talking about an end of history. As stated above, all it can do is give us a certain basis for hope.

IV THE NORMATIVE ARGUMENT

The first question that arises is how, at the end of the twentieth century, anyone can put forward a serious "normative" argument concerning the goodness (or badness) of liberal democracy. God having been killed off in the nineteenth century, the entire thrust of twentieth-century philosophy from Heidegger to the postmodernists has been to kill God's secular replacement, enlightenment rationalism, as well. Modern thought has sought to undermine the very notions of metaphysics, nature, natural right, and the like, on which any philosophical concept of "the good" could be built. This, I take it, is the reason for Peter Fenves's unhappiness with my "forays into the problem of 'man as man'" or the "doses of metaphysics" that appear in the book:[7] I use them, in his view, as illegitimate buttresses to an empirical argument, as if I hadn't heard the news that metaphysics is no longer permissible – somewhat like a modern social scientist using biblical authority to cover a gap in his survey data.

It is not my purpose here, nor was it my purpose in *The End of History and the Last Man*, to defend traditional metaphysics against its modern critics. This is certainly well beyond my abilities. I find, however, that many of the epigones of Nietzsche and Heidegger themselves assume the impossibility or

falsity of traditional metaphysics and spend their careers playfully deconstructing the Western philosophical tradition, without thinking through the
disastrous consequences of their actions. Richard Rorty is a telling case in
point. Anyone listening to Rorty understands that he is very committed to a
certain set of rather conventional liberal values: he does not like what
Ronald Reagan did to the poor, he does not favor totalitarian regimes, he is
against "ethnic cleansing" and other atrocities in Yugoslavia. Yet he is equally
if not more committed to demonstrating that there is no philosophical basis
for these commitments: they are just a matter of sentiment, of the surrounding moral climate, of education, of pragmatic adjustment to experience.
Fortunately, his surrounding moral climate is the relatively benign one of
Charlottesville. The country in which he lives is a liberal democracy; the
politics, for all its problems, are moderate, and a Jamesian pragmatism may
indeed be sound moral and political advice. But what if one were growing up
not in Charlottesville, but in Novotny's post-1968 Prague? While Rorty
claims Václav Havel as a "postmodern" politician, his own advice would have
led the young Havel not to jail and dissidence, but to a career as a reform
communist. For an individual living in the even less benign environments of
Hitler's Germany or the Serbia of 1993, the "sentimental education" provided by the local environment might have led to even less palatable moral
choices. They would be unpalatable from Rorty's own point of view, yet
Rorty's attack on the possibility of philosophy and moral knowledge leaves
him no ground on which he can criticize a phenomenon like "ethnic
cleansing."[8]

Many postmodernists seem to think that their critique of traditional philosophy leads to a kind of depoliticized, de-ideologized *faute de mieux* liberalism. A postmodernist liberalism would rest not, like the American
Declaration of Independence, on the "self-evident" truths of human equality
or natural rights, but rather on the mutual exhaustion of all other fundamentalisms, ideologies, or philosophies, and would do no more than give free play
to the individual's self-creation (or in the case of Havel, his moral being).
This, and not a universalist enlightenment doctrine, seems to be what G. M.
Tamàs argues was the meaning of democracy for his generation of Eastern
European dissidents. Their common cause with traditional American liberals
on a human rights agenda during the days of communist tyranny, he argues,
was more an accident than a real convergence of thought. This also seems to
be the meaning of Peter Fenves's "tower of Babel": contemporary liberal
democracy is actually a cacophony of different languages, but since the "language of liberal democracy" is the only one left standing in the ring, it has
convinced itself that it is a universal language.

This line of argument seems to me to be very problematic insofar as its proponents do not have the courage or the resolution of either Nietzsche or Heidegger in seeing this line of thought to its logical conclusions. For any doctrine that undermines the "ideologized" version of liberalism undermines the egalitarian principles on which that liberalism rests, as well. A postmodernist liberalism may remain safe from external threat in a world populated exclusively by other such liberal states – in other words, if postmodernists knew they were living at the end of history. But by their own premises they do not and cannot know this. They have no reason in principle not to expect the rise of new "fundamentalisms" (whether traditional or modern, at home or abroad), and have only the very weak armor of their own intellectual premises to protect them once they do. The denial that there can be any knowable concept of "man as man," no consensus on the question of human nature or the basis of human dignity, means that any discussion of liberal rights will simply amount to "rights talk," with no principled way of adjudicating the conflicts and contradictions that will inevitably arise.[9] While such a society will continue to thrive for a time on the basis of pre-postmodernist habits, I do not understand how it could defend itself from external enemies in the short run or sustain either polity or community over the long run.

The "crisis of modernity" then is a very real one. Both Leo Strauss and Alexandre Kojève were both aware of the *aporia* of modern thought, and both believed that a way out was the most urgent of problems. This is why I believe the Strauss–Kojève debate was one of the most important of twentieth-century discussions, because these two thinkers tried to address this problem from diametrically opposite positions, those of history and of nature.

Without reviewing that very complicated discussion in detail, it seems to me that Strauss shows quite convincingly that history does not in the end provide a way out. As pointed out in section III above, the empirical facts of history provide us with nothing more than a *hope* that it is directional and purposeful. While Hegel asserts that history is radically different from nature, the product of free human self-creation, we cannot know whether this history is unique without a larger teleological theory of nature: perhaps there is another universe or another time in which our history has unfolded in an identical manner, not the product of free human creation but of a natural process of which we are simply not cognizant.

Moreover, we have a major problem with the knowability of "the end of history." As Tom Darby points out, the end of history for Hegel lies not in the appearance of Napoleon as such, but in the appearance of the dyad Napoleon–Hegel.[10] That is, Hegel is the philosopher who truly understands Napoleon's significance; he is not speculating about "imaginary kingdoms" but understands the underlying rationality of the world's seemingly meaningless flow of events. He understands that Napoleon is not just another ambitious adventurer, but is ushering in the universal homogeneous state that will realize the possibility of universal recognition. In doing so, human beings as such achieve a self-knowledge that they are beings that seek recognition and are satisfied by universal recognition. And Napoleon becomes something more than an adventurer by the fact of his having been "interpreted" by Hegel.

But how do we know that Hegel was right about Napoleon? The end of history is not immanent in the empirical facts of history, as noted above. Hegel would argue (with considerable empirical justification, even with the hindsight of nearly two hundred years) that the French Revolution and Napoleon ushered in the principle of universal recognition. But how, then, does one know that human beings seek recognition, and are satisfied by universal recognition? It is possible to regard universal recognition as a kind of Kantian rule of transcendental reason (or, in the language of a contemporary Kantian like Rawls, something like the rule that arises out of the "original position") that would be valid regardless of our knowledge of empirical facts about the world, and would apply to rational beings whether they were human or not. For Hegel to represent much of an advance over Kant in this regard, we would have to understand and accept much of the argument of the *Science of Logic* and the critique it contains of Kantian metaphysics, a task that seems at once formidable and dubious. It is dubious not simply because I have never succeeded in working my way through this book, but because it seems to me very unlikely that humanity's final knowledge of itself should rest on a book so obscure, and about which there is so little consensus even among Hegel specialists.

It seems to me that one of the sources of Kojève's great appeal is that he offers a highly anthropologized reading of Hegel, in which our understanding of the role of recognition in history does not depend on our knowledge and acceptance of the *Science of Logic*, but rather on the degree to which Kojève's anthropology corresponds with our own observation or intuition of "man as man." That is, its appeal lies in the plausibility of his explanation of man as a being that works and struggles over pure prestige, and in the degree to which this explanation is revealing of a deeper level of motivation when we view the empirical facts of history. The adequacy of this highly anthropologized Hegel stands or falls on the basis of what amounts to an account of human nature, that is, the transhistorical concept of man as a being that seeks and is satisfied by recognition. This, in the end, is why I was driven back to Plato and his tripartite account of the soul, because Plato's account of *thymos* seemed to provide an alternative language in which we could discuss recognition as an *anthropological* phenomenon.

Victor Gourevitch and other critics are undoubtedly right that one cannot reconcile unreconcilables: Plato and Hegel, nature and history. Orthodox Hegelians will argue, doubtless correctly, that this highly anthropologized version of Hegel is not, in fact, Hegel. They may further argue that it is not Kojève, either, and therefore could not be the synthetic philosopher Hegel–Kojève. The charge that I am not seeking to understand Hegel as Hegel understood himself, that I am using bits and pieces of this most systematic of philosophers, is doubtless true, and is one that I accepted in the book itself. But one can still make an argument about a universal history without use of the concept of history in the Hegelian sense (that is, of the human being's free self-creation in opposition to nature). I would argue that this procedure is implicit to some degree in Kojève's work itself, when it calls on us to understand man as a being for whom recognition is primary. Whatever Hegel's self-understanding, it is both an interesting and an important question to uncover the degree to which the historical process can be properly understood as the result of an "anthropologized" struggle for recognition.

A much more central criticism of this argument is the one made in the essays by Tim Burns, Victor Gourevitch, and in a somewhat different framework, Peter Lawler.[11] The question can be put simply: how is it possible to have *recognition* without a prior *cognition*?[12] That is to say, what is the value of the universal recognition underlying liberal democracy that is not based on a knowledge of what it means to be a good or excellent human being? Recognition as it appears in Hegel or Kojève is a purely formal matter. One is recognized equally and universally for being a human being, that is, a free being undetermined by nature and therefore capable of moral choice. There can be no other formal solution to the problem of recognition, because no other form of recognition can be universalized and therefore made rational. One might wish to say that being a brilliant physicist or concert pianist or even a devoted father is a worthy way of life deserving of recognition; but recognition of such qualities cannot be universalized because all human beings are not brilliant physicists or pianists or fathers. To recognize those qualities means to denigrate those who do not possess them. All forms of *megalothymia* are hostile, ultimately, to the *isothymia* on which liberal democracy is based. One is reduced, then, to recognizing a kind of moral lowest common denominator, a free being that can negate nature. By this Hegelian scheme, one can distinguish between a human being and a rock, a hungry bear, and a clever monkey, but one cannot distinguish between the first man who kills his fellow human being in a battle for pure prestige, and a Mother Teresa who sacrifices her worldly happiness to follow the dictates of God.

Tim Burns and Victor Gourevitch make similar points about my comparison of Hobbes and Hegel. In *The End of History and the Last Man*, I argued that Hegel provides a broader and deeper understanding of human motivation, not because Hobbes does not understand the desire for recognition, but because he seeks to subordinate it to rational desire. Hegel, I argued, understood that in modern polities men did not live for the rational pursuit of bread alone, but sought recognition, and that the Hegelian universal homogeneous state honored this honor-seeking side of modernity by making universal recognition the basis of all rights. Both Burns and Gourevitch argue, properly, that in this respect both Hobbes and Hegel share the narrowing of perspective characteristic of modern thought. Hobbes and Hegel deny the possibility of an original cognition, that is, they both deny the existence of cognizable human goodnesses or excellences, goodnesses or excellences that exist "by nature," that are inherently worthy of recognition. While Hegel's point of view may be broader than Hobbes's in the sense that he understands the irreducibility of *isothymia*, and honors it politically, he shares with Hobbes the principle that rights must be formal and not substantive. The state, in other words, can only recognize the right to *free* speech, not good or excellent speech.

While I accept this criticism (and indeed anticipated much of it in *The End of History and the Last Man*), I still believe that the distinction between Hobbes and Hegel is crucial in one key respect. Tocqueville in *Democracy in America* talks about the American "passion for equality": how equality is the founding principle of democracy, how the passion has spread ineluctably over the centuries, and how it comes to affect all aspects of the social life of a democracy over time. Yet he never really explains what is meant by the "passion for equality." Surely it does not mean a passion for physical equality: Americans do not aspire to be equally strong or tall or handsome. It does not refer exclusively to equal political or legal rights, since these were *in principle* established with the founding of the country (with the well-known and ever-narrowing circle of exceptions: the propertyless, racial minorities, women, tomorrow perhaps homosexuals). Nor does it refer to an equality of economic station: Lockean principles of property have been widely accepted, and therefore Americans have accepted a fair degree of economic inequality throughout their history. The "passion for equality" refers, above all, to a passion for equal recognition, that is, an equality of respect and dignity. I believe that the major currents of contemporary American politics – feminism, gay rights, the rights of the handicapped or of Native Americans – are merely the logical present-day manifestations of the same *isothymia* that Tocqueville described in the 1830s. Contrary to most economists and rational-choice theorists, this desire for equal recognition cannot be reduced to economic motives; instead, much of what passes as economic motivation has to be understood in terms of the struggle for equal recognition. In this respect alone, Hegel is a better guide for understanding our politics than is Hobbes.

None of this, however, speaks to the legitimate question of what the original cognition is that underlies recognition. Is not "man as man" something more than a being capable of negating nature? And if this is indeed the central question, should not the faculty of cognition have been emphasized to a much greater extent relative to the desire for recognition?

The centrality of the issue of cognition underlies, I assume, Peter Lawler's repeated question of whether it is possible to have a sense of human dignity without God, or without making the distinction between man and God. His own answer to his rhetorical question is, I assume, no: only God can provide us with the original cognition to know what is truly worthy in His sight, and therefore only God can open the way for our moral beings to express themselves in something other than the blind fury of Hegel's "first man" and his struggle for pure prestige.

My answer to Lawler's question is: If the question of man's dependence on God is meant in a practical sense, that is, if he is asking whether a liberal society is conceivable without religion and other premodern sources of constraint and community, the answer is probably no. If his question is meant in a theoretical sense (that is, are there other sources of cognition besides God), the answer is, I don't know. In answering the latter question, it may be that God is the only possible source for such knowledge; if that is true, and if God has indeed died, then we are in a lot of trouble and need desperately to find another source on which to base our belief that human beings have dignity. Enlightenment rationalism is not the solution, it is part of the problem: Hobbes and Hegel are constitutive thinkers in that tradition, but the self-undermining character of their thought is what has landed us in this predicament in the first place. Tim Burns, following Leo Strauss, suggests another approach which some have labeled "zetetic": to start as Socrates did not with abstractions like the first man, or man in the state of nature, but to engage in a reasonable dialogue with human beings engaged in political life on questions like the nature of justice or the nature of the good, and from there to lead them to understand the problems and self-contradictions of their positions. It is certainly the case that while postmodernists believe that there is no rational systematic philosophical view of the whole that would allow us to come to a consensus on what constitutes specific human excellences, virtually everyone (postmodernists included) has opinions as to what those excellences are. We live in a world dedicated to *isothymia*, and yet see evidence of *megalothymia* all around us: While all of us believe we are entitled to equal respect, no one in their heart of hearts believes equal respect is all there is to life, or thinks that life would be worth living if there was no room for unequal respect based on some degree of excellence or achievement. And since, in Peter Fenves's words, the content of that respect is constituted by *logos*, there remains the possibility that *logos* can be subject to rational discussion and ultimately some measure of consensus.

Let me turn for a moment to a different question. I am accused by both Theodore von Laue and Peter Fenves of, as odd as it may seem, being insufficiently reductionist in my analysis of the underlying forces of history on the one hand and the nature of desire on the other. These critiques are quite different. Von Laue asserts that "The most crucial flaw is Fukuyama's blindness to the centrality of power," which he notes is "a common failure among Americans." He then goes on to draw up his own thumbnail "universal history," in which all the varied phenomena of history, from power politics to economics to religious enthusiasm to family relations can be seen as manifestations of an underlying struggle for power.[13] Fenves, on the other hand, takes me to task for distinguishing between simple desire, which I portray as something like the "utility maximization" of traditional "economic man," and the desire for recognition, which is attached not to material but to ideal objects. Fenves's point, as I understand it, is that all desire is constituted by language, and all desire therefore partakes of a "non-material" quality, even those desires that are conventionally thought of as material or economic in nature.

Any attempt to construct a universal history necessarily involves a high degree of abstraction and simplification from the enormous mass of empirical historical fact, and therefore will always be open to the charge of reductionism. Much of my book was implicitly an attack on the economic reductionism of Marxism and an attempt to recover the greater richness of human motivation embodied in the concept of the struggle for recognition. It seems to me that in constructing any kind of universal history, one should as a matter of course prefer less reductionist to more reductionist theories, consistent of course with the need to construct a general theory in the first place. In this respect, trying to reduce the larger patterns of history to a simple struggle for power seems to me a step backwards rather than a step forwards, one that I criticized at some length in my discussion of power politics. Those who seek to reduce everything to power forget to ask the question, power for what? Is it desired for its own sake, or is it a fungible commodity to be converted into other goods? I doubt seriously that it is the former: Can one understand Luther's motives in launching the Protestant Reformation, or those of the American founding fathers, without reference to the ends that they sought to achieve, and for which power was only a means? If, alternatively, power is simply a fungible commodity sought as a means to other ends, then one hasn't advanced a theory of history by saying that everyone seeks power. In the absence of a discussion of ends, the statement becomes tautological, just like those of economists who define "utility" so broadly that it includes any end actually pursued by human beings.

Fenves's critique is considerably more subtle. I had tried to decompose economic motivation into what was truly economic in a conventional sense (that is, the satisfaction of basic needs like food and drink), and an ideal dimension in which people sought recognition of their dignity through the acquisition of material goods. I thought this added a layer of nuance to our understanding of desire. Fenves seems to be arguing that I didn't go far enough: Economic motivation in the former sense doesn't exist at all – as he says, "remaining alive, keeping one's body in motion, may very well be a matter of pride – and nothing else."[14] I doubt it – at least, the "and nothing else" clause, which makes things a bit too subtle. While there is potentially a thymotic dimension to virtually everything, sometimes one eats because one is hungry.

I would like to conclude with the question raised by Peter Fenves, as to why I raised the question of the end of history at this particular juncture in history.[15] He (and a legion of others, including Theodore von Laue) asserts that I am an "optimist," and tries to uncover the position from which an optimist might understand his own activity. If history is indeed over, there is no historical necessity for optimism: The proclamation of an optimistic point of view becomes a matter of vanity, of one's reputation as a historiographer. I do not have the serious purpose or self-understanding of Kant, who by raising the question of progress in history hoped to contribute to the end of progress.

The problem with this analysis is that it begins with the assumption that I am fundamentally optimistic. In fact, Susan Shell is much more correct in characterizing *The End of History and the Last Man* as a "most pessimistic of optimistic books."[16] As noted earlier, one can be optimistic in the sense of being able to discern a "universal history" in the mass of empirical data, and one can be optimistic concerning the long-term prospects for liberal democracy. But to be optimistic in any philosophical sense requires that one know that liberal democracy is a good thing. This, as I stated at several points in the book, is not something we can take for granted. One can conclude, provisionally, that liberal democracy satisfies the different parts of the soul more completely than its competitors, but one has to know whether the soul exists, and if so, of what it consists. The question that is prior to the empirical one is an epistemological one. There has to be a ground for the "original cognition," and one can at least begin the search by revisiting the debate between Strauss and Kojève.

The present *aporia* brings me to the larger reasons for writing the book. We are at a unique juncture in history when, most people would admit, liberalism does not have many serious competitors. There is only "one language," that of liberal democracy. But our preference for liberal democracy was conditioned for many years by the enemies of liberal democracy. We knew that liberal democracy was better than communism or fascism, but we deferred addressing the question of whether liberal democracy was choiceworthy in itself, or whether we could conceive of preferable arrangements, if not among actual regimes, then among some that could only now be imagined. The time for that discussion has come, and it seems to me that our initial attempts to address the question show the nakedness of our position. It is clear to me that the postmodernist answer, that no ground exists, either for an original cognition or for liberal democracy itself, is politically, morally, and humanly intolerable. And in this respect, it is impossible to be anything but pessimistic.

11

World History, Cultural Relativism, and the Global Future

Theodore H. Von Laue

Our grasp of the human condition depends on the distance from which we examine it. On the ground floor of life we proceed from personal observations of concrete detail through our eyes and ears amidst the familiar contexts of daily life. Rising higher in our imagination to a view of our country, or highest to a look at the entire world, we visualize reality increasingly through our minds, with the help of copious abstractions and generalizations premised on theoretical considerations. "The nation" is a theoretical construct covering a relatively small territory; "globalism," covering the entire world, is an even more copious construct. The more inclusive our perspectives become, the more we depend on abstract summaries made meaningful by simplifying theoretical considerations. Given its overweening ambitions, world history demands ceaseless intellectual experimentation with theoretical analyses. Never before has history, the sum total of the human experience, been in such need of theory ("theory" here being broadly defined as "a belief that guides action or assists comprehension or judgment.")

This essay ventures a few theoretical perspectives for the study of world history designed to help teachers and their students cope more effectively with the problems they will face in their lives. From its elevated perspectives – and therefore rather impressionistically – it seeks to convey a strong sense of the diversity of the human experience; aware of the intellectual risks, it searches for the most suitable approach for assessing the complex realities of the global age. An immigrant in American society, I consider myself an "in-between" person prompted to see in every conflict the justifications on the other side. That approach provides the best access to the forces at work in the contemporary world as in the past. We need better control over reality in order to advance human life – my ultimate ideal balancing my cultural relativism.

In pursuit of that goal, let me start from the fact which should impress every thinking person. In the global age the human multitudes have become interlocked to the point of cultural disorganization or even dissolution. Traditional guidelines evolved in the isolated cultural and linguistic envelopes of the pre-global age are outdated in the relentlessly advancing global interaction. Aware of our ignorance in this unprecedented age in human experience, we have to try out novel approaches to human relations, in our political and economic affairs, in our lives, and in our historical interpretations as well. We cannot afford in these critical times to get immersed in the infinite details of the past. We need a present-and-future-oriented historical awareness, an activist mentality, and a forward-looking sense of command over human destiny. That is the reason why this essay probes at length into the present and foreseeable future, the most important times in world history.

I

To begin with an assessment of the basic motivation of human nature, the motor of history: Everywhere and at all times we are prompted by an urge for power, for dominating the setting in which life is conducted. In order to overcome the perennial uncertainties of life and to survive, we crave to expand our control in all directions, an unending and highly complex effort.

The primary target throughout history has been the natural environment, to be dominated for providing food, shelter, tools and weapons, for vital sources of energy assisting us in our effort to survive. There is no lack of opportunity to prove the persistence of the human urge to draw strength from nature, now with heightened awareness of the ecological perils involved; power over nature should not mean power against nature.

Next the inward-turned struggle for power: command over our physical vitality for the sake of better chances of survival. Shifting bodily energy into cerebral activity has been a long process in collective evolution, as it is in individual education. Intellectual skills like reading and writing, or abstract thinking as in mathematics, are needed for mastering the knowledge that assures human command over reality. The buildup of human knowledge in the past has been impressive, yet it is always insufficient in the face of ever new uncertainties. We demand of each new generation a more extended effort of personal self-discipline and intellectual achievement for the sake of solving the complex problems in the new age of global interdependence.

And finally, the even more crucial – and poorly understood – form of human power: shaping human behavior at the deepest level of human motivation. In the persistent insecurity of life the human psyche must be trained to increase individual resilience and working capacity. As social creatures forever dependent on community support, we must be socialized in the depths of our subconscious, in order to increase spontaneous civic cooperation. The power skills conditioning the innermost core of human behavior have been most effectively developed in the form of religion.

Religious institutions have historically provided the crucial techniques for controlling the relentless struggle in the human mind (whether described as a struggle of reason, feeling, will, and conscience, subordinating the flesh to the spirit). Selfishness (or sinfulness) has to be subordinated to the harmonizing rules controlling the supporting community and the natural environment in the name of an all-powerful divine force. Admittedly, religious creeds were shaped differently in different cultural and geographic settings, but they always aimed at the innermost core of human motivation.

Throughout history the awareness-raising techniques guiding the lifelong inward power struggles have been perfected, advancing from polytheism to more potent and ascetic monotheistic creeds. The founders of the major world religions have been the most powerful figures in history, dominating individual lives and collective destinies through the ages. What could be more central to human survival than inspiring weak and fallible individuals to maximum creativity in facing both the adversities of personal life and the responsibilities of social cooperation? Responsible history has to emphasize at all times the crucial role of religion; its ability to shape the human psyche has been the central guarantee of human survival. Admittedly, the competition between different religions has often led to deadly conflicts; religion too is part of the competition for power. Yet the central message of all major religions has been the advancement of human life, which puts peace above war. In European history, the Sermon on the Mount has subtly promoted peaceful cooperation amidst the often violent competition for power within state and society. After the Age of the Enlightenment the hold of organized religion declined, but spiritual values persisted as part of civilized life, invisibly perpetuating themselves through the benefits of constructive cooperation.

Human beings forever compete for political power, enviously comparing themselves with others and trying to surpass their accomplishments, in communities ranging from tribes to modern nation-states. They cooperate under compulsion, as in tyrannies and dictatorships, or under democratic rule compelled by their own civic discipline. Inevitably, the need for civic discipline increases as the community grows in size; a modern state with tens or even hundreds of millions of citizens has to exert extensive social controls for the sake of civic cooperation. With all their obvious flaws, functioning modern democracies are built on a massive unconscious civic conformity enforced by a minimum of compulsion.

Whatever their form of government, all states are set into the largest context of power struggles, into the international – and now global – arena. In international relations power has traditionally assumed the rawest form in wars for expansion – with modern visions of global domination from the eighteenth century onward.[1] The perpetual competition within regional or worldwide networks has led to the perfection of military skills and state power. It has also affected the spiritual and intellectual underpinnings of society, the key factors in human evolution.

Envious comparison is provoked by all human accomplishments from brute force to saintliness; what counts is whatever contributes to success. International relations have both hard and soft components. Regarding the latter, enemies learn from each other in trade and commerce; religion crosses political boundaries; respect for human dignity wins friends. Varied international and intercultural frameworks mixing hard and soft power in human interaction have always shaped individuals and societies at their core.

Different societies present different mixtures of hard and soft power – lucky are those peoples among whom power is exercised peacefully through self-restraint; they possess an advantage over rivals ruled by compulsion. Competitive strength grows from peaceful civic cooperation. Historians therefore have to pay close attention to that crucial capacity, analyzing the moral values sustaining it.

II

In addition, we need to study another basic aspect of human evolution: the physical settings of the human power struggles. Looking at the globe, we become aware of the great variations in the earth's land surfaces and their climates, each shaping the lives, culture, and religion of a given population; historical studies have to proceed from a strong sense of geographical and ecological determinism. The influence of climates, commonly disregarded, deserves special emphasis. Cool climates stimulate human energies and ambitions; the northerners have been the most active and cerebral agents in global power politics. As many Europeans working in tropical Africa have testified, hot and humid climates create more sensuous and passive ways of life; they also breed more life-destroying diseases.

Geography has also shaped routes of communication and transportation, inhibiting or promoting human interaction. Fertile soils and mineral deposits furnish valuable assets; deserts impede human contact; land-bound peasants are at a disadvantage compared with sea-going people living along ocean fronts. For millennia the inhabitants of the vast Eurasian plains lived dangerously on open highways traversed by armies as well as merchants, while mariners linked the China coast with the mid-East, all disseminating vital skills and instruments of power.

Diverse geographic conditions have prompted a bewildering variety of cultural responses, of different languages (6,170 by a 1990 count), different religions and histories. Viewed in all-inclusive historical perspective, the early "world systems" described by various theorists have not prevented the creation of a geographically determined profusion of human associations often at bitter war with one another. Even more significantly by the same perspectives, geography and climate have produced stark contrasts in cultural resources and political power, responsible for the glaring inequalities in the human condition around the world increasingly revealed since the days of Columbus and burdening the contemporary world. The ultimate cause for this tragic inequality lies not in human design but in the diversity of the world's land surface; the blame, one might facetiously argue, falls on "Mother Earth." In any case, geography will remain important also in the future, resisting, although at a diminishing rate, the growing uniformity of the new globalism. One of the global challenges of the future, for instance, is "Asia's empty tank," the shortage of natural oil resources at a time of increasing demand, especially in China, Japan, and South Korea.

III

Moving now from the basic factors just outlined to a survey of the power centers in different parts of the world, historical accounts should proceed comparatively, concentrating on the power-creating human interaction within a given geographic and climatic setting. Throughout we should search, with heightened sensibilities beyond the boundaries of academic disciplines, for the totality of factors at work. What counts are all the forces, many of them invisible, shaping the attitudes and beliefs of the human raw material on which states and countries are built.

Unfortunately, given the shortage of space, it is not possible here to trace the historical evolution of the human power centers in various parts of the world.[2] Let us merely recognize the fact that wherever we look, people sought to expand their domain, subject to the opportunities and limitations mandated by their location on earth. The greatest mobilization of power occurred in the areas of the keenest human interaction on the rim of the vast Eurasian space, in China, the mid-East, and eventually most prominently in Western Europe. The peoples in sub-Saharan Africa or in the western hemisphere, all expansionist in their own ways, found themselves overpowered when confronted with invaders trained in the Eurasian power competition, tragically suffering from the inequality caused by geography and climate.

Our present-and-future-oriented world history needs to concentrate on the winners in the global power competition, who with their kin in North America, are commonly called "the West."[3] They were aided in their ascent to global power by uniquely favorable conditions beyond human control. Toughened by the ceaseless struggle for power in the Eurasian space yet reasonably secure from disastrous invasions, Western Europeans enjoyed easy internal communications and open access to the oceans, creating, in a relatively small area and under an energizing climate, a network of intensely, and often brutally, competitive interaction in power politics and the arms race, as well as in the peaceful pursuits of arts, crafts, and intellectual accomplishments. Thus Western Europe emerged as a unique cultural hothouse. Drawing on the creative resources of the Fertile Crescent, the Judeo-Christian religion, the Roman Empire, and Islamic learning, it produced from the fifteenth century onward a rapid advance in all power skills to the point of dominating the rest of the world by the end of the nineteenth century. Nowhere else in the world had there emerged a power center able to match the Europeans; world history henceforth turned inevitably into the story of global Westernization.[4] The European skills, increasingly drawing on the wealth and cultural accomplishments of all humanity, covered the full gamut of human creativity, including respect for human dignity (a subtle form of power).

The Europeans' most important achievements were not capitalism, nor science and technology, nor industrialism, but the largely subconscious spiritually based discipline of social cooperation, on which all accomplishments leading to their global preeminence were premised. All analyses of the rise of European and Western power must stress the emergence, under constant social tensions and the mounting complexity of life and work, of the largely voluntary social cooperation culminating in democratic constitutions and free enterprise in a market economy.

Under the banner of freedom and liberal democracy, the Western Europeans and their North American descendants, viewed comparatively, turned into the most intensely socialized human beings on earth, reaffirmed in their civic conformity by their belief in "progress" and by their pride in their worldwide preeminence. "Freedom" is a highly complex cultural molecule deeply embedded in civic culture and therefore uncomprehended by its most ardent supporters. Where it has worked, it has combined extensive subconscious submission to unifying civic habits with opportunities for community-affirming individual initiative. A product of exceptionally favorable circumstances, Western civic culture cannot be transferred to societies more disadvantaged. Let its American ideological missionaries, the most zealous promoters of freedom, be aware of the privileged uniqueness of the American experience in the secure open lands of rich North America!

To drive home the main point: In all parts of the world people aim at power and domination, subject to the conditions imposed by nature. Westerners should always keep in mind the physical setting shaping human destiny, which enabled them to advance to unprecedented heights. Awareness of the factors beyond human control should reduce the inherent pride in Western superiority and help to soften the bitter indignation over Western supremacy in the non-Western world. Remember, it was "Mother Earth" who created that inequality.

But at the same time let us become aware of the moral responsibilities derived from our privileged condition. The Westernization of the world has ignorantly promoted profound inhumanity, forcing the non-Western peoples, the vast human majority, into alien modes of life. A responsible world history needs moral reflection, affirming that the people comparatively least favored by nature have their own moral claim to human dignity; we need to recognize their remarkable creativity. The compassionate interest in non-Western cultures fashionable among Western intellectuals and world historians is indeed justified – as long as we keep in mind the need to minimize the human differences that stand in the way of worldwide cooperation. The desire to preserve the world's cultural diversity must be fitted into the context of the ever-intensifying global interdependence.

These considerations lead to a related issue, vital in any constructive treatment of world history: the pervasive obstacles to intercultural understanding. On the ground floor of life people cannot help but judge the world and their neighbors near and far according to their own cultural conditioning; in asserting themselves they quite unconsciously universalize their limited historic experience, none more so perhaps than the Americans. As a result, ground-floor people have little comprehension of, or liking for, religious, cultural, or ideological otherness; it threatens their own identity and tends to make the others into potential enemies. Learning how to minimize that elemental gut reaction and to view the others realistically as legitimate products of different circumstances should be an essential part of world history, no easy task when we face what we consider the inhumanities in other lands. Compassionate cultural relativism bridging the differences of skin color, behavior, creeds, and ways of life, is a moral obligation for adjusting to the world in which we live; it helps to disarm hostility and to develop the common ground needed for worldwide cooperation. But let us be aware of the limitations of our best intentions. All our accounts of non-Western cultures are expressed in Western languages and concepts shaped by Western rather than indigenous sensibilities; we can only aspire to an imperfect grasp of cultural otherness.

This ethically inspired relativist approach also supports an even more con-troversial contention for the study of world history: In the absence of common ground both sides in every conflict are responsible for the human damage. In politics or even religion any assertion of superiority is bound to provoke a counter-challenge. All-inclusive global perspectives, refined by moral sensibility, have to take into account the totality of forces at work in the web of worldwide envious comparison. The challenge for a constructive world history lies in understanding the aspirations on the other side and responding in a manner reducing hostility.

IV

At this point a responsible world history has to recognize the devastating consequences of the Western impact upon the world in the first half of the twentieth century. It started the most brutal wars and mass atrocities in the history of the human race. Yet what else would one expect, given the abysmal ignorance among political leaders and their followers? They were unprepared for the new globalism they had created; it was an utterly unprecedented his-torical experience.

The Western global expansion, led in the name of a superior civilization by the two countries most favored by geographical circumstances – Great Britain and the United States – precipitously enlarged the traditional European power competition to global proportions. The British Empire served as a universal model, arousing worldwide anti-Western ambitions with unforeseen explosive consequences. The Germans, prompted by the British example to seek "a place in the sun" of global prestige, sparked World War I. The power and ideals of the winners in that war not only incited political ambitions around the world to extravagant heights, but also stirred up the irrationalities of mass politics in countries defeated or otherwise disorganized by the war.

The West thus unwittingly provoked the rise of Soviet communism and Italian and German fascism. By raising excessive expectations in unprepared countries, the West contributed to the resulting inhumanities, thereby shar-ing responsibility for them. The guiding totalitarian ideologies, Soviet Marxism and national-socialist racism, were derived from Western imports. Regarding racism, we have conveniently forgotten the widespread belief, popular before 1914 in England and the United States, in the superiority of the Anglo-Saxon race. In 1917 an American author even praised the Aryan race as superior to any other, to be kept pure in order to retain is preemi-nence.[5] And in 1919 Lord Milner, the Colonial Secretary, described himself as "a British race patriot." Admittedly, local conditions also played their part, carrying the imported ambitions to brutal extremes. And everybody remembered the slaughter of World War I. What did human lives count, when the power competition was raised to global proportions?

The prescription for organizing inadequate indigenous resources for the global power struggles was outlined by Lenin as early as 1902: "What is to a great extent automatic in a politically free country must in Russia be done deliberately and systematically by our organizations."[6] Put into updated terms: The totality of civic accomplishments achieved over centuries in the geopolitically most favored countries had elsewhere to be artificially matched as soon as possible by centrally organized political compulsion. At a time of national catastrophe and under highly adverse conditions traditional attitudes and institutions were to be totally changed. In addition, the Western political and cultural imperialism was to be challenged by the communist world revolution.

Lenin's blueprint of totalitarianism took the most extreme form under Stalin. A Russian patriot in Marxist disguise, like Lenin, he was determined to change the backward peoples of huge Eurasia into modern citizens. He conducted an utterly novel and exceedingly brutal experiment of cultural transformation on the largest scale, trying to overcome his country's humiliating weakness heightened by defeat in World War I, whatever the human costs. If Hitler had conquered the Soviet Union, the inhumanities would have been even greater, a fact overlooked by Stalin's detractors oblivious to the global context of his policies and misjudging Eurasian realities by Western standards.[7] Fascist totalitarianism – another challenge of interpretation in the study of world history – was perfected by the Aryan race patriot Adolf Hitler, an alert upstart and master of mass politics at a time of national humiliation and disorientation, but totally ignorant of the larger world. Plotting to enhance national resolve by racial purity on the road to territorial aggrandizement, he started World War II. His most tormenting atrocity was the Holocaust, the climax of political racism escalated by the anti-Semitism common in Europe and especially militant in its central and eastern parts. The Holocaust too should be viewed in the full context of the times: the scope of the new globalism; the heightened pitch of long-simmering racist tension; the ambitions of an uprooted charismatic megalomaniac appealing to a nation brutalized by the slaughter of World War I; Germany's defeat in that war and the cultural disorientation caused by it; and finally the horrors of World War II, which dehumanized human beings on a scale hitherto unknown. What else would one expect? The point in this detached approach is not to reduce our humanitarian abhorrence of Hitler's crimes, but to become aware of all the forces at work, so as to gain greater understanding and better control over reality, thereby preventing similar inhumanities in the future. But we should humbly keep in mind that outsiders can never assess the totality of factors that prompt the actions of the insiders.

In the Far East, the Japanese too were caught in the post-World War I expansionist megalomania. As their prime minister Tanaka argued in 1927, their country was to advance through Manchuria and Mongolia into China. "Having China's resources at our disposal, we shall proceed to conquer India, the Archipelago, Asia Minor, Central Asia, and even Europe."[8] Limiting themselves eventually to the "East Asian Co-Prosperity Sphere," the Japanese warlords, allied with Hitler, waged their own appallingly brutal war. They were crushed in August 1945 by the two American atom bombs, the deadliest instruments of mass destruction yet invented, another ominous landmark in the evolution of globalism. Fortunately, the destruction of Hiroshima and Nagasaki ended not only World War II – its carnage estimated to run around 55 million lives – but also the use of atomic weapons. Thus began a somewhat calmer though still perilously violent phase of global history.

V

The American-inspired vision of the new, and ever more global, era was embodied in the United Nations, a global innovation designed "to achieve international cooperation in solving international problems of an economic, social, cultural, or humanitarian character, and in promoting and encouraging respect for human rights and for fundamental freedom for all without distinction as to race, sex, language, or religion."[9] The UN was not only to prevent a repetition of the tensions responsible for two world wars by diplomatic negotiations, but also to provide an institutional framework for the peaceful evolution of Westernizing globalism. It promoted some practical advances toward that goal in the face of immense obstacles testifying to the continuing tensions of globalization. Over a hundred wars were fought between 1945 and 1992, killing millions of people, many of them civilians.

These wars were part of the cold war dominating world politics until the late 1980s. Thanks to Stalin, the Soviet Union had matched the United States as a superpower equipped with atomic weapons. In raw competition involving ruthless local wars in the name of high ideals, the two rivals offered conflicting goals for human destiny. It was either Westernization or anti-Western Westernization, either a free market economy under liberal-democratic government, or social planning and political compulsion designed to provide the benefits of Western society under a supposedly superior communism. Yet in the power competition of invidious comparison promoted by increasingly effective mass communications the outcome was foreordained. Western policymakers, overly impressed by the surface aspects of Soviet power, never grasped the underlying weaknesses of the Soviet system. In vast Eurasia the Soviet organizations were not able to arouse the voluntary cooperation prevailing in the privileged politically free countries. Communist totalitarianism became discredited at home and abroad, except in North Korea, Cuba, and China.

In China after 1949, Mao Zedong, driven by the global ambitions fostered by two world wars, had established his own theory-driven communist regime in a series of mobilizing experiments, the biggest of which was called "The Great Proletarian Cultural Revolution." It cost the lives of untold millions among China's proliferating population. Whatever the human price, Mao laid the foundation for China's rise as a nuclear power to be recognized as a force in global politics; his successor Deng Xiaoping subsequently loosened communist controls, permitting the Chinese economy to compete in the global marketplace.

Viewed in the global context, however, China has been handicapped by special hardships – including frequent natural catastrophes and the pressure of sheer numbers – that for millennia have cheapened human lives in that country. Any dogmatic imposition upon Chinese society and government of the humanitarian standards shaped by the exceptional circumstances of the West would amount to "human rights imperialism"; it prolongs and hardens traditional hostilities in a troubled country eager to join the competition for global preeminence. Increased interaction with the outside world may in time ameliorate Chinese sensibilities.

Meanwhile, global interaction has been increased by the many new states created by decolonization. The newcomers in the world's political arena were forced into forms of statehood inspired by their colonial masters, without experience of self-government; adjustment to statehood was in most cases a bloody process, the moral responsibility for which again falls on the Westerners. An obvious example is the genocidal hatred between Hutus and Tutsis sown by their former German and Belgian administrators in what is now Rwanda. In any case, henceforth the world's cultural diversity inherited from the past was cast into a political shape; the number of states in the global community rose to 179 (measured by the 1993 UN membership).[10]

The complexity of global politics has been further increased by the growth of Japan into an economic superpower, the advancing status of the "little dragons" of the Pacific rim, and China's recent economic progress. The global economy has now been extended to the Far East. By the end of the twentieth century the whole world has become a hothouse of competitive interaction, putting the leading countries, even the United States, under strain, while overburdening the lesser countries and the UN organizations.

VI

And now a look at the forces shaping, for better or worse, the present and foreseeable future in what is becoming ever more intensely "global" life, a condition of human existence utterly unprecedented in history. In the past half century the West has imposed upon the rest of the world universal standards of power in weapons, political institutions, economic and financial organizations, science and technology, ideological orientation, and communication systems. It has shaped a network of global agencies, including the United Nations, Multinational Organizations (MNCs) and Non-Governmental Organizations (NGOs) like the International Red Cross, all using English as the lingua franca. Western tastes dominate urban architecture, fashionable clothing, and lifestyles generally. Envious comparison, encouraged by worldwide communications and rising literacy, ranks everybody against everybody else: Who does not want to be at the top and enjoy the good life advertised by Americans?

In addition, the ideals of freedom and democracy, propagated around the globe, have everywhere politicized collective life as never before. Yet lifted out of the restraining contexts of civic discipline these ideals tend to promote anarchy. While Westernization is disseminating essential material benefits around the world, it does not spread the spiritual underpinnings of civic discipline needed for effective state-building. It even undermines the traditional discipline of non-Western cultures.

Westernization, now generally universalized as "modernization," proceeds by its own momentum as a profound worldwide challenge. People eager to improve their circumstances can achieve a higher standard of living, develop their intellectual resources, and introduce their considerable achievements into the global mainstream. Yet in order to secure these benefits of Westernization, we also have to keep in mind its negative effects. While the progressive West continues to export its cultural standards as absolutes upon the diverse non-Western peoples, their cultures continue to throb underneath the Westernized surface, humiliated, discredited, and yet still bound to their past creativity. Yet nowhere in the non-Western world do we still find original indigenous cultures. All have lost their past integrity. Contemporary world politics, therefore, cannot be viewed as a struggle between civilizations (to use Samuel Huntington's terminology).[11] The Japanese seem to be an exceptional case, safeguarding their cultural continuity while absorbing and even advancing Western achievements, despite their disastrous defeat in World War II.

The majority of non-Westerners have been shaken to their depths, especially in sub-Saharan Africa. Suspended between the discredited norms of their past and the uncomprehended realities of Western ways, where are people to find effective guidance for their personal lives and collective existence? Corrupt political leaders aim at Western lifestyles, complete with Mercedes-Benz cars; ambitious intellectuals emigrate to the West, inventing, with the help of sympathetic Western scholars critical of their own society, an idealized version of their traditional ways. The bulk of the people are caught in civil unrest bordering on violent anarchy, most distressingly so in some West African countries.[12] But crisis persists also in Russia, now liberated from its artificial unity under Soviet rule. How can its disoriented and divided peoples build an effective polity in their vast country? And look at India, Pakistan, or even China,[13] let alone Afghanistan, or the troubled republics in Central America!

Cultural disorientation is even advancing in the heartlands of the West, mirrored among intellectuals in their discussions of postmodernism, a school of thought undermining traditional verities. In daily life the influx of non-Western immigrants and migrating workers has added a vigorous cultural pluralism, intensifying the long-standing agitation for equality among African-Americans and Native Americans. The traditional democratic consensus is weakening. The dynamics of Western life have introduced further tensions, as in the feminist protest against masculine domination, or the controversies over abortion and homosexual rights. Finally, the escalating global disarray has separated the young people from their more sheltered elders; the generation gap is widening alarmingly. Under the impact of more permissive, more body-oriented cultural trends, Western society's civic discipline and its religious foundations are obviously declining; violence, crime, and anti-social behavior are growing, encouraged in part by the media.

Perhaps the most disturbing aspect of the escalating disorientation is what may be called "the global overload," a novel aspect in world history. People are overwhelmed by the ever-increasing human multitudes intruding into their lives, by the profusion of stimuli thrust at them locally, nationally, and globally. In the vast unstructured openness of the global cultural bazaar they desperately seek refuge in narrow traditional bonds like nationality, ethnicity, religious fundamentalism, or even small-scale gangs – in any form of human bonding no matter how primitive. As a challenge to intellectuals globalism is a source of inspiration as well as of disagreement or even bewilderment; among the average and often overworked citizens it tends to shrink social awareness and lead to civic discord and violence.

Adding to the global overload, the intensified worldwide competition for markets and jobs causes additional strains, even in the most advanced countries. Just consider the anxieties caused by rapid economic change in contemporary American (or Japanese) society and the violence which they promote. Is it surprising that American self-styled "patriots" think of "world government" as the biggest threat to their lives, justifying extreme violence, as in the Oklahoma City bombing on April 19, 1995? Precisely a month earlier, in Japan the Aum Shinrikyo cult driven by Shoko Asahara's apocalyptic vision of a Third World War had planned to wipe out Tokyo by dropping poison gas from the air; a rehearsal at a subway station killed eleven people and hospitalized around 5,000 others. Explosive irrationality is a sign of our times, with ominous prospects for the future.

VII

In this stressful culturally disoriented phase in world history the eternal power struggles continue, in some ways more subtly. In the age of nuclear weapons, it seems safe to predict (at least for the foreseeable future), world wars are unlikely. Within global interdependence the rivalry between the major power centers – North America, Europe, East Asia – is essentially economic. However intensive the competition, worldwide economic relations demand peaceful methods of transacting business under common regulations (as enforced hopefully by the World Trade Organization). Economic rivalries continue within enlarged frameworks of regional cooperation, as under the expanding European Union, North American Free Trade Association (NAFTA), and comparable associations on the Pacific Rim, in Africa or South America. Yet while globalism condemns the irrationality of world wars, it has not ruled out local wars. It has even intensified the use of violence by terrorism or mafias all along the paths of Westernization.

In the worldwide cultural power struggle the major states try to expand their sway by "developing" "underdeveloped" countries in their own image; yet the official approach of "structural adjustment" suffers from appalling incomprehension of the cultural and physical obstacles; geography and climate stand in the way, reaffirming the validity of traditional ways. Modernization cannot reshape the earth's surface. Can the gap between the rich and the poor be significantly narrowed? Not surprisingly, Westernizing modernization provokes continuous and often violent resistance, as tradition-oriented distraught people try to affirm their customary ways. The most dramatic challenge is currently mounted by Islamic fundamentalists, who have declared war on the Western Satan with a persuasive message: A simple lifestyle based on religious values is a sounder foundation for social stability and spiritual satisfaction than materialistic self-indulgence. Yet even these fanatic crusaders are vulnerable. They cannot allow too great a contrast in lifestyles and cultural sophistication between their followers and the modern world. In addition, their violence hardly fits the spiritual message of the Koran.

Other long-simmering power conflicts promoting violence are in the foreground of the contemporary news. Cultural diversity inherited from the past thrives. Everywhere ethnic and religious minorities stand up for their rights: Irish Catholics in British Northern Ireland; ethnic separatists in England, Belgium, and Spain; Greek Orthodox, Roman Catholics, and Muslims in Bosnia; Kurds in Turkey, Iraq, and Iran; Chechens in Russia; Armenians and Azeris, together with smaller ethnic minorities, in the Caucasus area; Tibetans under Chinese rule; Tamils in India and Sri Lanka, Muslims and Hindus in India; Palestinians in Israel; and tribal groups throughout Africa. The profusion of unmanageable local conflicts derived from the cultural diversity of the world's peoples testifies to the intensity and complexity of contemporary global politics.

Looking from a high altitude at the global power politics at the end of the twentieth century, we can discern two conflicting tendencies. The first, stressed by optimists, predicts that worldwide interdependence promotes an ever more intense globalism under the auspices of the United Nations assisted by a profusion of non-governmental agencies and transnational corporations (TNCs, also called MNCs). According to the United Nations, "at the beginning of the 1990s, there were about 35,000 parent TNCs, with some 175,000 affiliates, covering all sections of the economy and regions of the world."[14] Hopeful observers even cite mounting evidence of an emerging global civil society outdating the nation-state. Yet they are overlooking one crucial fact: All global agencies, as indeed all forms of globalism, depend on effective states and governments taking care of life on the ground floor of human existence.

On this troubled level we observe the countertrend. States and societies in dissolution, or riven by civil discord, undermine all progress toward global cooperation. Without law and order maintaining a productive economy, governments cannot fund the United Nations, nor can they provide the institutional security that allows transnational agencies to run their offices within state borders; multinational corporations are threatened by labor troubles in their home countries. In short, effective globalism presupposes effective Western-style government in disciplined societies with material and intellectual resources allowing a peaceful outreach abroad.

In assessing the present phase of world history let us therefore always examine the conditions of domestic politics, aware that disorientation combined with the search for equality and human dignity is promoting a worldwide surge of violence threatening peaceful civic cooperation where it counts most, on the ground floor of life. If the tempo of change runs too fast, if people are confronted with cultural, social, and political complexities beyond their comprehension, they are likely to respond irrationally and violently. Globalism promotes an anarchic counter-globalism; the contest will continue for a long time.

And now for an additional cloud over the human landscape: a brief reference to the non-political consequences of the Westernization of the world that call for political action – the over-rapid population increase starting in the nineteenth century and ominously carried into the future, and the resulting drain of the earth's vital resources, evident in the disappearance of tropical rainforests, the shortage of water in dry lands, the pollution of the air, global warming – to mention but a few items under current anxious discussion. Huge problems loom ahead.

VIII

What, then, in the light of the mounting violence and the record of world history generally, are the challenges for the foreseeable future? A responsible world history should end with a constructive vision based on our highest ideals. Peaceful global interaction within the earth's limited resources requires heightened moral sensibilities and expanded intellectual capacities. At the deepest level of human consciousness we need to evolve universal values promoting global cooperation. We have to integrate a compassionate cultural relativism with the vision outlined in the Charter of the United Nations. A morally alert future-oriented global history should help us move toward the transcendent universal truth of loving our neighbors – and our natural environment – as we love ourselves. The human experience through time teaches one supreme lesson: Human life and happiness depend on the moral skills promoting peaceful cooperation. A global history without moral reflections, however controversial, is an irresponsible venture.

Looking back over the long course of world history, I would like to offset my prophylactic pessimism by suggesting an encouraging conclusion. Let us keep in mind the advance of human skills throughout the past millennia. Despite continuous crises and wars, despite outrageous inhumanities, human beings have developed impressive resources for sustaining life. The Westernization of the world, admittedly at a high cost in human misery, has offered people everywhere novel opportunities for advancing their potential. In times of profound misery the common desire to survive by exercising power over the human destiny is bound to reaffirm the priority of the spiritual techniques that have advanced human cooperation in the past. I am confident that in the future human beings will be able to perfect these techniques for constructively meeting the awesome challenges of the utterly novel global phase of human existence. It will take many generations and much suffering to reconcile the world's persistent cultural diversity with the need for effective global cooperation. But there is encouraging evidence around the world of human efforts working in that direction. Human beings are edging toward the freedom of willingly submitting to all the restraints that make possible their peaceful survival in global interdependence.

Meanwhile we might derive courage from Salman Rushdie, who in *The Satanic Verses* "celebrates hybridity, impurity, intermingling, the transformation that comes of new and unexpected combinations of human beings, cultures, ideas, politics, movies, songs. ... *Mélange*, hotchpotch, a bit of this and a bit of that, is *how newness enters the* world."[15] Let us join him in affirming that elemental human vitality.

IX

May I add, as a postscript, a personal concern? I am afraid that my all-inclusive overview has moved me away from the human sense of reality prevailing on the ground floor of life. In addition, I fear that looking at Hitler's Germany or Stalin's Soviet Union – or at all the other atrocities and catastrophes in recent or current history – from an all-inclusive macrostructural perspective, minimizes both the cruelties of the victimizers and the agonies of the victims; viewed in large contexts individuals cease to matter. Global perspectives thus tend to depersonalize history, which puts me into a quandary. On the one hand, global perspectives seem justified; they help improve human control over the course of events and thereby diminish violent tensions, saving lives in the future. On the other hand, they reduce human beings to virtual insignificance, each one a nonentity among almost six billion others, with a yearly increase of several hundred million more. What do individuals count in a world that has, by my reckoning, grown over everybody's head? And what of my tendency to charge well-meaning Westernizing missionaries with moral responsibility for the world's miseries by applying novel criteria beyond their comprehension? My all-inclusive global perspectives are likely to antagonize Americans loyal to their traditional optimistic righteousness.

Of course, I, too, am tied to my family, my community, and to my country with an immigrant's admiration for the American way of life. I have read the heart-wrenching accounts of the survivors of Auschwitz and the Gulag; I follow the news and see pictures of human suffering in the media; I have looked into the eyes of people in distant parts of the world. And yet, as an "in-between" person circulating between everyday life and global perspectives, I have become a theorizing academic who has risen above the ground-floor consensus, thereby adding further discord to the growing existential disorientation. What counts: the local familiarities or the global vastness? For me "living locally and thinking globally" is a glib formula of good intentions that conveys no sense of the immense distance between daily life and an awareness of global interdependence in all its complexity, between my familiar neighborhood and the competing alien multitudes around the globe. I seek my consolation in the realization that my uneasiness is part of the human condition in the emerging full-scale globalism.

Notes

INTRODUCTION: THE THEORY AND PRACTICE OF WORLD HISTORY

1   In a pamphlet written for Michael Adas's series, *Essays on Global and Comparative History*, Jerry H. Bentley shows that despite its unpopularity, "many scholars continued to draw inspiration from modernization analysis. ... Indeed, in some ways it seems that a renewed and reformulated modernization analysis has recently begun to take shape in the works of scholars like E. L. Jones." Bentley, *Shapes of World History in Twentieth-Century Scholarship* (Washington, DC, 1996), 10.

2   Michael Geyer and Charles Bright, "World History in a Global Age," *American Historical Review* 100 (October 1995): 1057.

3   Ibid., 1054.

4   Although historians attuned to history as literature attend to the construction of historical narrative and the role of semiotic factors in shaping the writing of history, those more heavily invested in the social sciences tend to think in terms of structural principles, the most prominent of which is the systemic architectonic. An overarching system might include genetic, epigenetic, dialectical, and catastrophic (meaning, here, a principle of discontinuous change) structural features.

5   The word "ideology" made its debut in 1796 in the circle around Destutt de Tracy, a *philosophe* whose influence spread from France to such distant places as the United States (Thomas Jefferson) and Imperial Russia (the Decembrists). Distinctly a product of the Enlightenment, "ideology" signified a comprehensive science of ideas with progressive goals. Napoleon Bonaparte attacked de Tracy's group and made *ideologue* a term of opprobrium. For some recent discussions of ideology, see Raymond Geuss, *The Idea of a Critical Theory* (Cambridge, 1981); John B. Thompson, *Studies in the Theory of Ideology* (Berkeley, 1984); Raymond Boudon, *The Analysis of Ideology*, trans. Malcom Slater (Chicago, 1989); Terry Eagleton, *Ideology, an Introduction* (London, 1991).

6   Janet Lippman Abu-Lughod, chapter 4 in this volume, 77.

7   William H. McNeill, chapter 1 in this volume, 24.

8   R. R. Palmer and Joel Colton, *A History of the Modern World*, 3rd edn (New York, 1950). In later editions the chronological tables at the end include Asia and

Africa as distinct entities only beginning in 1945. By contrast, McNeill's *The Rise of the West* (1963) bears a title suggesting Eurocentrism, yet places the West in a genuine world context both before and after its global ascendancy.

9 It should be noted that "the West" can be narrowed or expanded in the discourse of historians. Von Laue, for example, excludes eighteenth-century Germany from the West in *The World Revolution of Westernization* (New York, 1987), 37–43.

10 *The Intimate Enemy, Loss and Recovery of Self Under Colonialism* (Delhi, 1988).

11 Michael Adas, chapter 5 in this volume, 100.

12 S. N. Eisenstadt, chapter 6 in this volume, 111.

13 William A. Green, chapter 3 in this volume, 56.

14 Erik H. Erikson, *Childhood and Society* (New York, 1963), 261–2.

15 Lewis D. Wurgaft, chapter 9 in this volume, 181.

16 Foucault wrote an introduction for the most influential single work, by Gilles Deleuze and Felix Guattari, *Anti-Oedipus: Capitalism and Schizophrenia*, trans. Robert Hurley, Mark Seem, and Helen R. Lane (Minneapolis, 1983).

17 Eisenstadt, chapter 6, 109.

18 McNeill, chapter 1, 40.

19 Bruce Mazlish, chapter 2 in this volume, 51.

20 McNeill, chapter 1, 40.

1 THE CHANGING SHAPE OF WORLD HISTORY

No notes

2 CROSSING BOUNDARIES: ECUMENICAL, WORLD, AND GLOBAL HISTORY

1 Perhaps a more authoritative voice than Humpty Dumpty's is to be found in the following lines: "Words strain, / Crack and sometimes break, under the burden, / Under the tension, slip, slide, perish, / Decay with imprecision, will not stay in place, / Will not stay still" (T. S. Eliot, *Burnt Norton* V).

2 The eighteenth-century French *philosophe*, Condillac, put it well when he remarked that "Every science requires a special language because every science has its own ideas. It seems that one ought to begin by composing this language, but people begin by speaking and writing and the language remains to be composed." Quoted in Fernand Braudel, *The Wheels of Commerce* [Vol. 2 of *Civilization and Capitalism*], trans. Sian Reynolds (New York, 1982), 234.

3 Cf. Walter L. Adamson, "Marx's Four Histories: An Approach to his Intellectual Development," *History and Theory*, Beiheft 20 (1981). Also, my own brief discussion in *The Meaning of Karl Marx* (New York, 1984), 143–5.

4 Paul Costello, "The Ecumenical Ideal and the Mission of Twentieth Century World Historians," unpublished manuscript prepared for the World History Conference held at Wesleyan University on March 25–6, 1994, especially p. 4. For an excellent and informed review-essay, properly critical, of Costello's full book, *World Historians and Their Goals: Twentieth-Century Answers to Modernism* (DeKalb, IL, 1993), see Raymond Grew in *History and Theory* 34 (1995): 371–94.

It should be noted, as my friend Philip Pomper points out, that ecumenical history in a pre-scientific (i.e., modern scientific) era was a brave attempt to deal with the anxiety aroused in a world otherwise presenting itself as a scene of chaotic change. Further, ecumenical history was written in many hybrid forms, in which, as Pomper adds, "Christian and pagan, linear and cyclical approaches are combined ... to produce progressive spirals, heavenly cities, etc." My concern here, obviously, is with the attempts at ecumenical history in the recent past and present, as reflected, for example, in Costello's presentation.

5 Charles Norris Cochrane, *Christianity and Classical Culture* (New York, 1957).

6 Civilization, for Spengler, is the inevitable conclusion, the destiny of every Culture (*Kultur*). It is the phase of the Culture in which the thing-become succeeds the thing-becoming, death follows life, and the petrifying world-city replaces mother earth. In short, it is the last phase of a culture-form which is dying.

   As with other slippery words, civilization and culture take on special meanings in nineteenth- and twentieth-century Germany (see, for example, Norbert Elias's treatment of this subject in his *History of Manners. The Civilizing Process*: Volume I, trans. Edmund Jephcott [New York, 1978]). What I am suggesting is that there is a certain synonymy in Spengler's use of culture with Toynbee's of civilization, and that we not be thrown off this trail by Spengler's special use of the term "civilization."

7 Gerald Holton, "Science and Progress, Revisited," p. 15 in a paper prepared for the volume *Progress: Fact or Illusion*, ed. Leo Marx and Bruce Mazlish (Ann Arbor, forthcoming).

8 Arnold J. Toynbee, *A Study of History* (New York, 1962), 284.

9 In this regard, it may be useful to note Hans Blumenberg's learned and difficult work, *The Legitimacy of the Modern Age*, trans. Robert M. Wallace (Cambridge, MA, 1983). In enormous detail and depth, Blumenberg questions the assumption that modernity and the idea of progress are secularized versions of Christian eschatology. In fact, he believes modernity to have arisen out of its own challenges, i.e., its own phenomenological conditions, though strongly influenced by its medieval heritage. The latter ensured, however, that modernity was burdened with the false need to explain history in teleological terms. On this account, modernity as a new beginning was necessarily opposed to the Christian claim to novelty and finality – and, of course, in turn, opposed by it as well (see especially p. 74).

10 For fuller treatments of Spengler and Toynbee, which, at least in the case of Spengler, strike a more positive note, see my *The Riddle of History: The Great Speculators from Vico to Freud* (New York, 1966), chapters IX and X.

11 A printed mailing from Richard Rosen, Executive Director, World Historical Association, no date.

12 Jerry Bentley, review of *Conceptualizing Global History*, ed. Bruce Mazlish and Ralph Buultjens (Boulder, CO, 1993), on H-NET BOOK REVIEW (August 1995), 1. Of especial interest on my topic here are the chapters by Wolf Schafer and by Manfred Kossok in *Conceptualizing Global History*. The volume itself is part of a series, whose co-editors are Carol Gluck, Raymond Grew, and myself.

13   William H. McNeill, chapter 1 in this volume, 27.

14   Immanuel Wallerstein, *The Modern World-System II: Mercantilism and the Consolidation of the European World Economy 1600–1750* (New York, 1980).

15   Janet Lippman Abu-Lughod, *The World System in the Thirteenth Century: Dead-End or Precursor?* (Washington, DC, 1993), 2. The next quotation from Abu-Lughod is on p. 6. See also her book, *Before European Hegemony: The World System A.D. 1250–1350* (New York, 1989).

16   This is not to say that a number of world historians do not have activist interests. Clearly, for example, William McNeill is concerned with environmental trends, and Immanuel Wallerstein's Marxist inclinations implicitly push him in a predictive direction.

17   See, for example, the Foreword to Abu-Lughod's volume, *The World System in the Thirteenth Century*, vii.

18   McNeill, chapter 1, 40. It should be noted that this is a very recent comment; as I interpret it, contextually, McNeill is talking about the need for a new definition of world or global history rather than about one of his previous "transmutations."

     Incidentally, McNeill was a participant in the first international conference on Global History, as I shall be defining it here, held at Bellagio in 1991. Though he denied then any difference between World and Global History, it would appear that what was said at that meeting may have rubbed off inadvertently. I am aware that others may find my inference hazardous, but I hold to it based on my personal acquaintance and knowledge of McNeill.

19   Michael Geyer and Charles Bright, "World History in a Global Age," *American Historical Review* 100 (October 1995): 1037 and 1041.

20   Bruce Mazlish, "An Introduction to Global History," in *Conceptualizing Global History*, ed. Mazlish and Buultjens, 1–2.

21   See further ibid., 17–20. Incidentally, over 3 billion people are said to have seen on TV the Coca-Cola commercials accompanying the 1996 Olympic games.

22   The demise of the Soviet Union must itself be seen in a global context. As Charles Maier has written, "The Communist collapse was a reaction to forces for transformation that have gripped West and East alike, but which Western Europeans (and North Americans) had responded to earlier and thus with less cataclysmic an upheaval." ("Why Did Communism Collapse in 1989?," *History Workshop* [Spring 1991]).

23   Samuel Huntington's notion of an apocalyptic clash between Islamic and Western civilizations is a recent, and ill-informed, attempt to view world history in such terms. One might note also a version of the notion of conflict of civilizations in Russia, where it takes the form of a "Eurasian" ideology, and has been embraced by many nationalist/communist opponents of Boris Yeltsin and others perceived as "reformers." Eurasian ideology has deep roots in Russian history.

24   See, for example, Roland Robertson, *Globalization: Social Theory and Global Culture* (London, 1992).

3 PERIODIZING WORLD HISTORY

1 William A. Green, "Periodization in European and World History," *Journal of World History* 3 (1992): 13–53.
2 For a brief comprehensive analysis of theories of progress, see Kenneth E. Bock, "Theories of Progress and Evolution," in *Sociology and History: Theory and Research*, ed. Werner J. Cahnman and Alvin Boskoff (Glencoe, IL, 1964), 21–41.
3 Karl Jaspers, *The Origin and Goal of History*, trans. M. Bullock (New Haven, 1953), 1–21.
4 Hodgson observed that spiritual and intellectual advances since the axial age have, in the main, arisen inside the cultural traditions laid down in that period. See Marshall G. S. Hodgson, *The Venture of Islam: Conscience and History in a World Civilization*, 3 vols (Chicago, 1974), I:48–53, 105–20.
5 Benjamin I. Schwartz (among others who wrote on the theme), "Wisdom, Revelation, and Doubt: Perspectives on the First Millennium B.C.," *Daedalus* 104 (1975); *The Origins and Diversity of Axial Age Civilizations*, ed. S. N. Eisenstadt (Albany, 1986).
6 Benjamin I. Schwartz, "The Age of Transcendence," *Daedalus* 104 (1975): 3; S. N. Eisenstadt, "The Axial Age Breakthroughs – Their Characteristics and Origins," in Eisenstadt, ed., *Origins and Diversity*, 2.
7 Geoffrey Barraclough, *Main Trends in History* (New York, 1979), 164.
8 Janet Lippman Abu-Lughod, *Before European Hegemony: The World System A.D. 1250–1350* (New York, 1989).
9 William H. McNeill, "*The Rise of the West* after Twenty-Five Years," *Journal of World History* 1 (1990): 1–21.
10 André Gunder Frank and Barry K. Gills, "The Cumulation of Accumulation: Theses and Research Agenda for 5000 Years of World System History," *Dialectical Anthropology* 15 (1990): 19–42; Frank, "A Theoretical Introduction to World System History," *Review* 13 (1990): 155–248; Frank, "A Plea for World System History," *Journal of World History* 2 (1991): 1–28.
11 Frank and Gills, "The Cumulation of Accumulation," 27.
12 André Gunder Frank, "Transitional Ideological Modes: Feudalism, Capitalism, Socialism," *Critique of Anthropology* 11 (1991): 171–88.
13 For example, in his *Economic Theory of the Feudal System* (1962) Witold Kula demonstrated that early modern Polish aristocrats were poor representatives of "economic man," at least as defined by classical economists. They did not relentlessly pursue profits; they sought steady, if comfortable, income. When grain prices fell, they squeezed the peasants; when prices rose, they relaxed the squeeze. Similar examples abound among subsistence or near-subsistence peoples in precolonial Africa.
14 J. H. Parry, *The Age of Reconnaissance: Discovery, Exploration and Settlement 1450–1650* (Berkeley, 1963), 35–6; Daniel Boorstin, *The Discoverers* (New York, 1985), 161–2.
15 Pauline Moffitt Watts, "Prophecy and Discovery: On the Spiritual Origins of Christopher Columbus's Enterprise of the Indies," *American Historical Review* 90 (1985): 73–102.

16 McNeill, "*The Rise* After Twenty-Five Years," 12–18.
17 An early attempt at such history is Clive Pointing's *A Green History of the World: The Environment and the Collapse of Great Civilizations* (New York, 1991).

4 THE WORLD-SYSTEM PERSPECTIVE IN THE CONSTRUCTION OF ECONOMIC HISTORY

> An earlier version of this essay was delivered to the Norwegian National Sociology Conference held in Lofoten, Norway, June 17–21, 1992, and printed in the limited circulation of their proceedings. It was substantially revised for its original publication in *History and Theory*.

1 I am indebted to Dr Steven Hutchinson for providing me with this translation taken from pp. 143–4 of Argentinian novelist Jorge Borges's *El Hacedor*. This work, which purports to be a seventeenth-century account attributed to Suarez Miranda, *Viajes de varones prudentes*, fourth book (Lerida, 1658), chapter XLV, is, of course, a wise satire on, *inter alia*, science's attempt to "reflect" the world accurately.
2 Full title is *Before European Hegemony: The World System A.D. 1250–1350* (New York and London, 1989).
3 See J. M. Blaut, *1492: The Debate on Colonialism, Eurocentrism and History* (Trenton, NJ, 1992). Blaut's thesis is that the "West" did *not* rise *before* its ability to harness the bullion, and then the resources and labor of the "New World." He goes to the opposite extreme of Eurocentered historians by granting no intrinsic value to Western culture.
4 Alan K. Smith, *Creating a World Economy: Merchant Capital, Colonialism, and World Trade, 1400–1825* (Boulder, CO, 1991).
5 Unbeknown to each other, Smith and I had evidently been researching our books at roughly the same time, although I infer from the frequency distribution of publication dates of sources he examined, he began and ended his research a few years before I did. Not unexpectedly, we were consulting many of the same books and articles for the time period covered in *Before European Hegemony*. Indeed, a glance at his bibliography revealed that we had read at least fifty sources in common for that period. Despite our overlapping sources and our similar questions, however, we came out with entirely different interpretations and narratives.
6 Jerry H. Bentley, *Old World Encounters: Cross-Cultural Contacts and Exchanges in Pre-Modern Times* (New York and Oxford, 1993), which I reviewed for the *American Historical Review* in June of 1993.
7 Bentley's approach is exemplary in its non-Eurocentrism. This allows him to give the Mongols, the Arabs, the Ottomans, the Indians, and the Chinese credit for their accomplishments and permits him to reconceptualize the period between 600 and 1000 AD as more active than any previous period in history (ibid., 110).
8 See, for example, Leslie Sklair, *The Sociology of the Global System* (Baltimore, 1992).

9   My major criticism of his work is that, in the concluding pages of the last chapter when Bentley steps beyond the boundaries of his period, he actually undermines the theoretical premises he has worked so hard and so eruditely to establish by attributing the "rise of the West" in the post-fifteenth century to two factors: technological superiority and biological immunities. These are clearly inconsistent with his earlier arguments giving primacy to culture and religion. One would have expected a more Weberian interpretation.

10 Namely, Kajsa Ekholm, "On the Limitations of Civilization: The Structure and Dynamics of Global Systems," *Dialectical Anthropology* 5 (July 1980): 155–66; Philip D. Curtin, *Cross-Cultural Trade in World History* (Cambridge, 1984); Janet Abu-Lughod, *Before European Hegemony*; and most recently, *The World System: From Five Hundred Years to Five Thousand*, ed. André Gunder Frank and Barry Gills (London, 1993).

11 I contributed an article to a book entitled *Remaking History*, ed. Phil Mariani (New York, 1989). It was a revised version of a paper delivered at the annual meetings of the American Sociological Association that year, entitled "Did the West Rise or Did the East Fall? Some Reflections from the Thirteenth Century." (See note 14.) At that time I was less concerned with the issues raised in this current essay, or perhaps more "self-righteous" about the superiority of my approach. The quotation from John Fairbank, reproduced in note 39, in which with great humility he confesses his own uncertainty, gives me some consolation.

12 *American Journal of Sociology* 36 (May 1931).

13 I am quoting here from the reprint of this piece that appears on pp. 190–5 in Stanford Lyman, *Militarism, Imperialism, and Racial Accommodation: An Analysis and Interpretation of the Early Writings of Robert E. Park* (Fayetteville, AR, 1992), 194.

14 The title of both an article of mine, "Remaking History: The Thirteenth Century World System," and the book in which it appeared: *Remaking History*, ed. Mariani.

15 See *Writing Culture: The Poetics and Politics of Ethnography*, ed. James Clifford and George Marcus (Berkeley, 1986).

16 See Hans Georg Gadamer, *Truth and Method*, trans. Joel Weinsheimer and Donald Marshall (New York, 1989); see also *Hermeneutics and Modern Philosophy*, ed. Bruce R. Wachterhauser (Albany, NY, 1986). My understanding of Gadamer's argument has been greatly enhanced by a paper given by philosophy professor Gail Soffer, "Gadamer, Hermeneutics and Objectivity in Interpretation," to the Graduate Faculty of the New School for Social Research in 1992.

17 (New York, 1987), 93–4.

18 (New York, 1940), vii. Wright's work is now experiencing a long-overdue revival in American literature, I suspect because in the post-Soviet period his Communist party association is no longer considered a threat.

19 This, of course, is one of the major strains in Thomas Kuhn's argument in *The Structure of Scientific Revolutions* (Chicago, 1962). It is important, however, to acknowledge a second and not quite compatible strain in his work, namely, the

recognition that academic "power politics" also plays its role in the struggle for paradigmatic privilege.

20   Namely, his two-volume work on the Mediterranean (*The Mediterranean and the Mediterranean World in the Age of Philip II*, trans. Sian Reynolds [New York, 1972]), which appeared in English translation just at the time I was researching my book on Moroccan urbanization (*Rabat: Urban Apartheid in Morocco* [Princeton, 1980]). I had found that it was impossible to study Moroccan history without paying detailed attention to the linkages between the Maghreb and the other side of the Mediterranean, as well as those between the Maghreb and Africa south of the Sahara. Thus, I was already a "world-system" person before I ever met Wallerstein. The third volume of Braudel's *Civilization & Capitalism, 15th-18th Century*, 3 vols (New York, 1982–4), entitled *The Perspective of the World*, was even more significant, even though I did not know about it until the English translation appeared in 1984.

21   For example, Smith's book referred to above (note 4) struck me as having failed to pay sufficient attention to the influence of wars on the changes in the world system. Furthermore, he had a tendency to back up into individual regions and subsystems for his explanations, rather than address the global system itself.

22   I am not alone in this "prejudice" for systemic explanation. A good justification for this approach can be found in Sklair, *The Sociology of the Global System*, 93. Sklair argues forcefully for the distinction between attention to parts and focus on the system itself, or what he calls transnational practices. Failure to pay attention to the impingement of the world on any of its subregions is also critiqued by George Marcus in his "Contemporary Problems of Ethnography in the Modern World System," in *Writing Culture*, ed. Clifford and Marcus, 165–93.

23   See especially the English translation of the second edition of Gadamer's *Truth and Method*, trans. Weinsheimer and Marshall. In this section of the essay I am indebted to an unpublished paper by Gail Soffer, entitled "Gadamer, Hermeneutics and Objectivity in Interpretation" (see note 16).

24   *Writing Culture*, ed. Clifford and Marcus, addresses itself to some of the issues my essay tried to raise, although I have my quarrels not only with some of what it contains but with what it fails to address.

25   Kurt H. Wolff, *Surrender and Catch: Experience and Inquiry Today*, Boston Studies in the Philosophy of Science 51 (Dordrecht and Boston, 1976).

26   This is why we insist that students "write down everything" in their field notes – even items and events that appear at the time to have no "meaning" or significance. In fact, we caution them against attributing meaning even to events and items that appear to have *prima facie* significance and *self-evident* meaning.

27   A nice illustration of how this works can be found in the recent book edited by Michael Burawoy, *Ethnography Unbound: Power and Resistance in the Modern Metropolis* (Berkeley, 1991).

28   See Paul Deising, *How Does Social Science Work? Reflections on Practice* (Pittsburgh, 1991), 247.

29   Obviously, I take for granted an earnest effort to apprehend the "real" world!

30   For example, if the outbreak of disease was viewed, in an "exotic" source, as being

evidence of God's displeasure at moral failures, I might note this but tend to ignore it in favor of an epidemiological explanation for the operation of contagious diseases. My favorite quotation comes from a medieval exchange between a religious Muslim and a more "scientific" inquirer. "The thing you ask of me is both difficult and useless. Although I have passed all of my days in this place, I have neither counted the houses nor have I inquired into the number of inhabitants; and as to what one person loads on his mules and the other stows away in the bottom of his ship, that is no business of mine. ... God only knows the amount of dirt and confusion that the infidels may have eaten before the coming of the sword of Islam. ... O my lamb! Seek not after the things which concern thee not!" (quoted in *Before European Hegemony*, 26). The trouble was that these were *exactly* the things my "ideology" alerted me to seek.

31 See David Faust, *The Limits of Scientific Reasoning* (Minneapolis, 1984).

32 See *Criticism and the Growth of Knowledge*, ed. Imre Lakatos and Alan Musgrave (Cambridge, 1970).

33 Richard Nisbett and Lee Ross, *Human Inference: Strategies and Shortcomings of Social Judgment* (Englewood Cliffs, NJ, 1980).

34 Deising, *How Does Social Science Work?*, 247.

35 Again, this idea is not new. Recall Carl Becker's compelling argument in *The Heavenly City of the Eighteenth-Century Philosophers* [1932] (New Haven, 1973).

36 For me, that biography included following my (then) husband to Cairo in 1958, where I became enamored of history. Who could resist history in a country with a civilization as old as Egypt's? In the ten years I spent researching and writing a book on the history of Cairo, *Cairo: 1001 Years of the City Victorious* (Princeton, 1971), I became convinced that the periodicity of European narratives was fatally flawed with respect to "the rest of the world" (what I came to call, with irony, TROTW, the regions of the globe containing 80 percent of the world's population), and that there were many more connections in a preexistent international system than European medievalists seemed to acknowledge. That work planted in me deep seeds of disaffection for one of the "gods" in sociology, Max Weber, and left me with an unquenchable interest in the high cultures outside Europe. Travels to many countries, museum visits, and books I subsequently read, among others the corpus of William McNeill and, even before its publication, the outlines of the world-systems approach which Immanuel Wallerstein had presented in an early lecture at Northwestern around 1972, deepened my commitment to rethinking the premodern period. All of these lay germinating until 1982 when I began more systematic work on what eventually became *Before European Hegemony*.

37 See, for example, the fascinating accounts in George Johnson, *In the Palaces of Memory* (New York, 1992).

38 It is interesting that critics of Wallerstein's world-system work have felt free to "minimize" his achievements *because* they appeal politically to third-world scholars, without recognizing the equally "political" agendas of Max Weber's corpus, not to mention those of other "Orientalists." Thus, in an otherwise fair article evaluating "Periodization in European and World History," Green notes, a bit

condescendingly to my mind, that "Wallerstein's ... model ... was warmly embraced in the Third World ... [where scholars] seek explanations for their dependency, for their poverty, for the decimation of local institutions, tradition-al values, and collective self-esteem ... [from this theory] that assigns moral cul-pability to the West." See William A. Green, "Periodization in European and World History," *Journal of World History* 3 (1992), 47–8.

39   Since preparing the text, I came across a statement by John Fairbank, the author-itative historian of China, in which he expressed similar misgivings. I am grate-ful to André Gunder Frank for calling this to my attention. Unfortunately, I do not have the original and would therefore appreciate a more complete reference.

5 Bringing Ideas and Agency Back In

Valuable suggestions for refining this essay were provided at various stages by Sarah Buck, Kevin Deuschle, Matt Guterl, Al Howard, Richard Keller, Dina Lowy, Denise Quirk, Todd Uhlman, and especially Phil Pomper.

1   For Leibniz's celebration of Kangxi and the vast Chinese bureaucracy as models for the West, see R. F. Merkel, *Leibniz und China* (Berlin, 1952) and Donald Lach, "Leibniz and China," *Journal of the History of Ideas* 6/4 (1945): 436–55. Voltaire's *Essai sur l'histoire générale et sur les mœurs et l'esprit des nations* (Paris, 1756) not only begins and ends with chapters on the wonders of China under the second Qing emperor, but touts the celestial empire as the exemplar of overall civiliza-tional development to that point in human history. See also his *Lettres chinoises, indiennes et tartares à monsieur Paw (un Bénédictin)* (London, 1776).

2   The cumulative dimension of this sustained effort is critical, setting the *philosophes'* forays into world history off from earlier, individual efforts, such as Ibn Khaldún's brilliant *Muqaddimah* and the cross-cultural history of the Muslim world that follows.

3   Quote taken from his invited reply to Charles Beard's address on "Written History as an Act of Faith," *The American Historical Review* 39/9 (1934): 230. For an elaboration of this viewpoint, see Croce's *History: Its Theory and Practice* (New York, 1921).

4   They have been brought together in a collection, edited by Edmund Burke III, entitled *Rethinking World History: Essays on Europe, Islam, and World History* (New York, 1993). For an assessment of Hodgson's views on the writing of world history, see Edmund Burke, III, "Marshall G.S. Hodgson and the Hemispheric Interregional Approach to World History," *Journal of World History* 6/2 (1995): 237–50.

5   From his early lectures on "Beyond Western Civilization: Rebuilding the Survey," and "A Defense of World History," published in *Mythistory* (Chicago, 1986) to his recent "*The Rise of the West*, Twenty-Five Years After," *Journal of World History* 1/1 (1990): 1–21.

6   See especially his essays on "History and the Social Sciences in the Twentieth Century," and "The Revival of Narrative: Reflections on a New Old History," both reprinted in *The Past and the Present* (Boston, 1981).

7 The best introductions to the *annales* approach available in English can be found in Traian Stoianovich, *French Historical Method: The Annales Paradigm* (Ithaca, 1976) and Peter Burke, *The French Historical Revolution: The Annales School, 1929–89* (Stanford, 1990).

8 The most debated and emulated studies of the links between peasant societies and agrarian revolutions with explicit comparisons and global ramifications include Barrington Moore, Jr, *Social Origins of Dictatorship and Democracy* (Boston, 1966); Eric Wolf, *Peasant Wars of the Twentieth Century* (New York, 1969); John Dunn, *Modern Revolutions* (Cambridge, 1972); Jeffrey M. Paige, *Agrarian Revolution* (New York, 1975); Theda Skocpol, *States and Social Revolutions* (London, 1979); and Jack Goldstone, *Revolution and Rebellion in the Early Modern World* (Berkeley, 1991).

9 Particularly that of Fernando Henrique Cardoso and André Gunder Frank. See Cardozo, "The Consumption of Dependency Theory in the United States," *Latin American Research Review* 12/1 (1977) and Cardozo and Enzo Faletto, *Dependency and Development in Latin America* (Berkeley, 1979); and Frank, *Capitalism and Underdevelopment in Latin America* (New York, 1969).

10 See especially the successive volumes (now up to four) of *The Modern World-System*, the first of which was published in 1974. For a sense of the range and number of historians and scholars in related disciplines who have contested or followed his world-systems lead, see the essays in *Review*, the journal connected to Wallerstein's Braudel Center.

11 "Rentier State and Shi'a Islam in the Iranian Revolution," *Theory and Society* 11 (1982): 265–83.

12 With the major exceptions of Wolf's *Peasant Wars of the Twentieth Century*, which skillfully combines social movements, ideologies (both failed and successful), and pivotal leaders with the processes of political economy on a global scale, and Dunn's *Modern Revolutions*, which was so concentrated on ideologies and political movements that it was virtually ignored by those writing on revolutions in this period. As his terminology suggests, Jack Goldstone's "residualist" approach to the cultural dimensions of revolutions does little to alleviate his determinedly structural analysis, and Barrington Moore's occasional references to contingency and human agency more or less reflect the theoretical chaos that prevails through much of *Social Origins*.

13 The limitations of cross-cultural comparison that does not give serious attention to cultural factors, including values and ideological commitments, are manifest in Frances Moulder's *China, Japan and the Modern World Economy* (New York, 1977), which adopts the world-systems approach discussed below.

14 There are important exceptions to the preoccupation with Europe and structuralist analysis in works influenced by Wallerstein's version of world-systems theory. These include Bruce Cumming's skillful blending of world-systems perspectives and diplomatic historical techniques, which allow for human agency and contingency and focus on the east Asian segments of the evolving capitalist world system (see *The Origins of the Korean War* [Princeton, 1981, 1990], and Richard White's *Roots of Dependency*, which is discussed below). For alternative

approaches to world-systems analysis, see the writings of Janet Abu-Lughod (also discussed below) and John Obert Voll, "Islam as a Special World-System," *Journal of World History* 5/2 (1994): 213–26.

15   See *The Road to Independence: Ghana and the Ivory Coast* (Paris, 1964).

16   See especially, *Peasant Wars*, and *Sons of the Shaking Earth* (Chicago, 1959).

17   *Europe and the People without History* (Berkeley, 1982).

18   Including, C. G. F. Simkin, *The Traditional Trade of Asia* (London, 1968); O. W. Wolters, *Early Indonesian Commerce* (Ithaca, 1967); K. N. Chaudhuri, *Trade and Civilization in the Indian Ocean* (Cambridge, 1985); M. A. P. Meilink-Roelofsz, *Asian Trade and European Influence in the Indonesian Archipelago* (The Hague, 1962); and Niels Steensgaard, *The Asian Trade Revolution of the Seventeenth Century* (Chicago, 1973).

19   See especially chapters 2 and 3 of *L'expansion européenne du xiiie au xve siècle* (Paris, 1969).

20   Akin to the term stereotyping that was once widely employed in studies of representation and cross-cultural interaction, essentializing and essentialism involve the process of defining the basic attributes that are seen to characterize a particular people or culture. Where the term stereotype emphasized the ways in which individuals came to epitomize nations, races, and ethnic groups, the concept of essentialism focuses on discourses and popular perceptions in which whole cultures and peoples are abstracted and categorized according to generalized and timeless essences.

21   Particularly in his influential and provocative *Orientalism* (London, 1978). In his more recent *Culture and Imperialism* (London, 1993), Said has softened a number of his earlier arguments about the possibility of cross-cultural understandings, but continues to see essentializing as a peculiarly Western vice.

22   As David Kopf argued most persuasively in an early review essay on *Orientalism* in *Journal of Asian Studies* 39/3 (1980): 495–506.

23   For some of his most direct thinking on these linkages, see *Discipline and Punish* (Harmondsworth, 1982 edn), 24–31 *et passim*.

24   Most famously, or infamously depending on one's point of view, in Gayatri Spivak's "Can the Subaltern Speak?" in *Marxism and the Interpretation of Culture*, ed. Cary Nelson and Lawrence Grossberg (Champaign-Urbana, 1988), 271–313.

25   For a critique of these tendencies on the part of writers identifying themselves with the Subaltern "school," which emerged, of course, precisely to write the history of hitherto voiceless lower-caste and class groups, see Ramachandra Guha's review article on "Subaltern and Bhadralok Studies," *Economic and Political Weekly* (August 19, 1995): 2056–8. For incisive questioning of postcolonial literary studies more broadly, see Rosalind O'Hanlon and David Washbrook, "After Orientalism: Culture, Criticism and Politics in the Third World," *Comparative Studies in Society and History* 34/2 (1992): 141–67; and Russell Jacoby, "Marginal Returns: The Trouble with Post-Colonial Theory," *Lingua Franca* 5/6 (1995): 30–7.

26   See, for example, Spivak, "Can the Subaltern Speak?," or Zakia Pathak and Rajeswari Sunder Rajan, "Shahbano," *Signs* 14/3 (1989): 558–92.

27 One does not have to agree with all of Stephen Greenblatt's arguments to see in his historicist methodology an effective antidote to the postmodernist malaise. Superb starting points with special relevance to world historians can be located in *Learning to Curse: Essays on Early Modern Culture* (New York, 1990); and *Marvelous Possessions: The Wonder of the New World* (Chicago, 1991).

28 For a broadly conceived and cogent statement of this position, see Anthony Pagden, *The Fall of Natural Man: The American Indian and the Origins of Comparative Ethnology* (Cambridge, 1986).

29 For a detailed account of this transition, see Michael Adas, *Machines as the Measure of Men: Science, Technology and Ideologies of Western Dominance* (Ithaca, 1989), especially chapters 1 and 2.

30 *Ecological Imperialism: The Biological Expansion of Europe, 900–1900* (New York, 1986).

31 Ian Inkster, "Scientific Enterprise and the Colonial 'Model': Observations on Australian Experience in Historical Context," *Social Studies of Science* 15 (1985): 687.

32 For elite responses in China, see, among a number of fine studies, Guy S. Alitto, *The Last Confucian: Liang Shu-ming and the Chinese Dilemma of Modernity* (Berkeley, 1979) and Joseph R. Levenson's brilliant *Confucian China and Its Modern Fate* (Berkeley, 1968), which can be extended into the nationalist era by Maurice Meisner's fine study on *Li Ta-Chao and the Origins of Chinese Marxism* (Cambridge, 1967). See also the recent essay by Joanna Waley-Cohen on "China and Western Technology in the Late Eighteenth Century," *The American Historical Review* 98/5 (1993): 1525–44. For the Islamic world, it is difficult to top Tim Mitchell's *Colonizing Egypt* (Cambridge, 1988) or volume three of Hodgson's *Venture of Islam*. On African epistemologies and responses to the West, see Wyatt MacGaffey's recent essay on "Dialogues of the Deaf: Europeans on the Atlantic Coast of Africa," in *Implicit Understandings*, ed. Stuart B. Schwartz (Cambridge, 1994), 249–67, and the now-classic essays of Robin Horton on "African Traditional Thought and Western Science," *Africa* 37 (1967): 50–71, 155–87. For the Gandhian revival of ways of perceiving and thinking indigenous to pre-colonial South Asia, see Ashis Nandy, *The Intimate Enemy: Loss and Recovery of Self under Colonialism* (Delhi, 1983). Works dealing with African and Asian influences on European thinking and popular responses are cited in the footnotes for the arguments on contextualization and reconfiguration that follow below.

33 On the mix of these factors in different areas and time periods and the representations that resulted, see, for example, Philip Curtin, *The Image of Africa* (Madison, 1964); A. C. Cairns, *Prelude to Imperialism* (London, 1965); Alden Vaughn, *The Roots of American Racism* (New York, 1995); Roy Pearce, *The Savages of America* (Baltimore, 1953); Greenblatt, *Marvelous Possessions*; Bernard Smith, *European Vision in the Pacific, 1769–1850* (Oxford, 1960); and Basil Guy, *The French Image of China* (Geneva, 1963). For broader overviews, see Annemarie de Waal Malefijt, *Images of Man* (New York, 1974) and Margaret Hodgen, *Early Anthropology in the Sixteenth and Seventeenth Centuries* (Philadelphia, 1964).

34 For differing approaches to the rise of racism, see Vaughn, "The Origins Debate:

Slavery and Racism in Seventeenth-Century Virginia," in *Roots of American Racism*; William B. Cohen, *The French Encounter with Africans* (Bloomington, 1980); Gérard Leclerc, *Anthropologie et colonialisme* (Paris, 1972); and George Fredrickson, "Toward a Social Interpretation of the Development of American Racism," in *Key Issues in the Afro-American Experience*, ed. Nathan Huggins et al. (New York, 1971), 240–54.

35 Adas, *Machines*, chapter 4.

36 To mention just a few of the more influential, Pierre Chaunu (noted above), Robert Lopez, J. H. Parry, and Carlo Cipolla.

37 It should not be inferred from my arguments here regarding European excep-tionalism that I believe that themes connected to the process of Western expan-sionism are the only possible organizing principles for world history since *c*.1400 or that there was no *real* world history before the early modern epoch. For a direct statement of these assumptions, which have often been expressed as uncon-testable givens by historians of Europe, see Ernst Breisach, *Historiography: Ancient, Medieval, & Modern* (Chicago, 1983), 399–400.

38 In *The Economy of Early Renaissance Europe, 1300–1460* (Englewood Cliffs, 1969), especially, pp. 132–8.

39 A superb introduction to the impact of scientific advances on overseas explo-ration and extraction can be found in the essays in *Scientific Aspects of the European Expansion*, ed. William Storey (Aldershot, 1996).

40 For concise surveys of the impact of Islamic civilization on an expanding Europe, see the essays by G. M. Wickens in *Introduction to Islamic Civilization*, ed. R. M. Savory (Cambridge, 1976), and the relevant portions of Chaunu, *Expansion européenne*; and for China, see Joseph Needham, *Clerks and Craftsmen in China and the West* (Cambridge, 1970), and *The Great Titration: Science and Society in East and West* (London, 1969).

41 For some responses by non-Western specialists, see Angus McDonald, Jr, "Wallerstein's World Economy: How Seriously Should We Take It?," *Journal of Asian Studies* 38/3 (1979): 535–40; and Frederick Cooper, "Feudalism, Capitalism, and the World-System in the Perspective of Latin America and the Caribbean," *African Studies Review* 33 (1990): 1–120.

42 For an even fuller response to Wallerstein than that found in *Before European Hegemony*, see her recent essay on "The World System in the Thirteenth Century: Dead-End or Precursor?," in *Islamic and European Expansion: The Forging of a Global Order*, ed. Michael Adas (Philadelphia, 1993), 75–102.

43 In this time-frame there is considerable support for Robert DuPlessis's contention that there was no true Europe-centered, capitalist *world system* until the eigh-teenth century, and that the emergence of that system had as much to do with protoindustrialization and industrialization as the spread of capitalism. See "The Partial Transition to World-Systems Analysis in Early Modern European History," *Radical History Review* 39 (1987): 11–28.

44 Including K. N. Chaudhuri, *Asia before Europe: Economy and Civilization of the Indian Ocean from the Rise of Islam to 1750* (Cambridge, 1990); M. N. Pearson, *Before Colonialism: Theories on Asian–European Relations 1500–1750* (Delhi,

1988); Anthony Reid, *Southeast Asia in the Age of Commerce, 1450–1680* (New Haven, 1988); and Sanjay Subrahmanyam, ed., *Merchants, Markets, and the State in Early Modern India* (Delhi, 1990).

45 Much of the work of the Cambridge school of Indian history has been devoted to the study of the ways in which the British Raj was built and maintained through alliances with indigenous notables and local functionaries. Their contributions are surveyed with great insight in Howard Spodek, "Pluralist Politics in British India: The Cambridge Cluster of Historians of Modern India," *The American Historical Review* 84/3 (1979): 688–707. For classic accounts of these patterns of colonizer dependence in other areas, see Charles Gibson, *The Aztecs under Spanish Rule* (Stanford, 1964); Leslie Palmier, *Social Status and Power in Java* (London, 1960); and John Phelan, *The Hispanization of the Philippines* (Madison, 1967). This dependence has also been chronicled in numerous literary works written by the colonizers and colonized, but perhaps never as brilliantly as in Eduard Douwes Dekker's (pseudonym Multatuli) *Max Havelaar* (Amsterdam, 1860; English language edition, London, 1967).

46 Again, some of the best work on these forms of dependence has been done on India, most notably Philip Mason's *A Matter of Honour* (London, 1974), but see also J. A. de Moor and H. L. Wesseling, eds, *Imperialism and War: Essays on Colonial Wars in Asia and Africa* (Leiden, 1989) and Marc Michel, *L'appel à l'Afrique* (Paris, 1982).

47 See, especially, Deepak Kumar, *Science and the Raj, 1857–1905* (Delhi, 1995).

48 In his essay on "Feudalism, Capitalism, and the World-System in the Perspective of Latin America and the Caribbean," *The American Historical Review* 93/4 (1988): 829–72.

49 "Maritime Asia, 1500–1800: The Interactive Emergence of European Domination," *American Historical Review* 98/1 (1993): 83–105.

50 Alan Smith, *Creating a World Economy: Merchant Capitalism, Colonialism and World Trade 1400–1825* (Boulder, CO, 1991).

51 "Between Global Process and Local Knowledge: An Inquiry into Early Latin American Social History, 1500–1900," in *Reliving the Past: The Worlds of Social History*, ed. Olivier Zunz (Chapel Hill, 1985), 115–90 (quoted portion p. 126). Wallerstein's neglect of the state has proved a problem even for Europeanists, despite the fact that he gives considerably more attention to political structures in his analysis of the succession of European nation-states which center the core of the world system at various stages. For sample questions raised in this regard, see DuPlessis, "World Systems Analysis," 22–3 on Fernand Braudel's responses to Wallerstein's model; and, especially, Theda Skocpol, "Wallerstein's World-Capitalist System: A Theoretical and Historical Critique," *American Journal of Sociology* 82 (1977): 1075–90.

52 Ibid., 127, 132–8, 141–2. For the world historian, James Scott's comparative analyses of patron–client systems and the process of colonial domination are exceedingly informative and conceptually apt. See, for example, "Patron–Client Politics and Political Change in Southeast Asia," *Political Science Quarterly* 66/1 (1972).

53　Nor for Eric Wolf's archetypical peasants in world history. See his *Peasants* (Englewood Cliffs, NJ, 1966) and the case studies in *Peasant Wars of the Twentieth Century*.

54　"Marking: Race, Race-making and the Writing of History," *American Historical Review* 100/1 (1995): 1–20.

55　See Gramsci, *Selections from the Prison Notebooks*, ed. Quintin Hoare and Geoffrey Nowell Smith (New York, 1971), especially pp. 12–13, 52–63, 260–4, and 416–18.

56　In *Marxism and Literature* (Oxford, 1977), especially pp. 55–82, 108–14.

57　"The Concept of Cultural Hegemony: Problems and Possibilities," *The American Historical Review* 90/3 (1986): 567–93.

58　Compare Skocpol, *States and Social Revolutions*, 31–2, 42 on the Iranian revolution in "Rentier State," and the observations in *Revolutions in the Modern World* (New York, 1994), 334–7.

59　Though the concept gives White's much-lauded, second book its title – *The Middle Ground: Indians, Empires, and Republics in the Great Lakes Region, 1650–1815* (Cambridge, 1991) – that work is heavily devoted to matters political and military, and hence much less attentive to the critical cultural and intellectual dimensions of the process of cross-cultural interaction. Nonetheless, human agency is evident in White's exhaustively researched and engaging narrative.

60　Respectively, *Payson and Revolution: Popular Movements in the Philippines, 1840–1910* (Manila, 1979) and *Contracting Colonialism: Translation and Christian Conversion in Tagalog Society under Early Spanish Rule* (Ithaca, 1988).

61　"Culture of Terror – Space of Death: Roger Casement's Putumayo Report and the Explanation of Torture," *Comparative Studies in Society and History* 26/4 (1984): 467–97; and *The Myth of the Lazy Native* (London, 1977).

62　"The Invention of Tradition in Colonial Africa," and "Representing Authority in Victorian India," in *The Invention of Tradition*, ed. Eric Hobsbawm and Terence Ranger (Cambridge, 1983).

63　See, for superb examples from different areas, David Lan, *Guns and Rain* (Berkeley, 1985); Douglas Haynes, *Rhetoric and Ritual in Colonial India: The Shaping of Public Culture in Surat City* (Berkeley, 1992); C. A. Bayly, *Rulers, Townsmen and Bazaars: North Indian Society in the Age of British Expansion, 1770–1870* (Cambridge, 1983); Richard Fox, *Lions of the Punjab: Culture in the Making* (Berkeley, 1985); Hue-Tam Ho Tai, *Millenarianism and Peasant Politics in Vietnam* (Cambridge, MA, 1983); and Florencia Mallon, *Peasant and Nation: The Making of Post-colonial Mexico and Peru* (Berkeley, 1995).

64　See Scott's seminal article on "Gender: A Useful Category of Historical Analysis," *The American Historical Review* 91/5 (1986); and the essays by Joan Kelly on "The Social Relation of the Sexes," and "The Doubled Vision of Feminist Theory," in *Women, History and Theory* (Chicago, 1984).

65　For an incisive overview of some of the approaches and the questions at issue, see Jane Haggis, "Gendering Colonialism or Colonising Gender?," *Women's Studies International Forum* 13/1&2 (1990): 105–15. For case examples, see the essays of

Ann Stoler, particularly "Rethinking Colonial Categories: European Communities and the Boundaries of Rule," *Comparative Studies in Society and History* 31/2 (1989): 134–61; and the essays by Julia Clancy-Smith, Mrinalini Sinha, and Antoinette M. Burton in *Western Women and Imperialism*, ed. Nupur Chaudhuri and Margaret Strobel (Bloomington, 1992).

66   For some of the best of these revelatory investigations, see part three of Leila Ahmed, *Women and Gender in Islam* (New Haven, 1992); Dagmar Engels, "The Limits of Gender Ideology: Bengali Women, the Colonial State, and the Private Sphere, 1890–1930," *Women's Studies International Forum* 12/4 (1989): 425–37; Partha Chatterjee, "Colonialism, Nationalism, and Colonialized Women: The Contest in India," *American Ethnologist* 16/4 (1989): 622–33; and Luise White, "Separating the Men from the Boys: Colonial Constructions of Gender in Central Kenya," *International Journal of African Historical Studies* 23/1: 1–26.

67   *Distant Companions: Servants and Employers in Zambia, 1900–1985* (Ithaca, 1989).

68   Though as Margaret Villanueva and others have shown, the extensive pre-contact participation of women in sectors such as textile production could strongly influence the labor preferences and extraction systems introduced by the most male-privileging of colonizers. See "From Calixqui to Corregidor: Appropriation of Women's Cotton Textile Production in Early Colonial Mexico," *Latin American Perspectives* 13/1 (1985): 17–40.

69   Joan Scott has correctly, I believe, identified this tendency to construct binary oppositions with regard to gender attributes and relationships as a persistent feature of male-dominated discourse. See "Gender: A Useful Category," 39–40 and 43.

70   See "The Great War and the Decline of the Civilizing Mission," in *Autonomous Histories; Particular Truths: Essays in Honor of John Smail*, ed. Laurie Sears (Madison, 1993); and the chapter on "Contesting Hegemony," in *War of the Empires: World War I as a Global Conflict* (New York, forthcoming 1999).

71   With some notable exceptions, including James C. Scott's *Weapons of the Weak* (New Haven, 1985) and the micro-studies of Carlo Ginzburg that have global applications, most especially *The Cheese and the Worms* (New York, 1984).

72   For a provocative assessment of the nature of this process with great relevance to world historians, see Peter Novick, *That Noble Dream: The "Objectivity Question" and the American Historical Profession* (Cambridge, 1988).

73   In their essay on "The Uses of Comparative History in Macrosociological Inquiry," *Comparative Studies in Society and History* 22/2 (1980): 174–97. On these issues, see also Arthur Kallenberg, "The Logic of Comparison: A Methodological Note on the Comparative Study of Political Systems," *World Politics* 19/1 (1966): 69–82.

74   A listing of even the most influential of these works would require an additional essay. For a sense of the variety and significance of the works in question, see Raymond Grew, "The Case for Comparing Histories," *The American Historical Review* 85/4 (1980): 763–78; George Fredrickson, "Comparative History," in *The Past Before Us*, ed. Michael Kammen (Ithaca, 1980); Carl Degler, "Comparative

History: An Essay Review," *Journal of Southern History* 34/4 (1968); Philip Curtin, "World Historical Studies in a Crowded World," AHA *Perspectives* 24/1 (1986); and Victoria E. Bonnell, "The Uses of Theory, Concepts and Comparison in Historical Sociology," *Comparative Studies in Society and History* 22/2 (1989): 156–73.

75 For suggestive variants of this approach, see Marshall Sahlins, "Cosmologies of Capitalism: The Trans-Pacific Sector of 'The World System,'" *Proceedings of the British Academy* 76/1 (1988): 1–51 and *Islands of History* (Chicago, 1985). In recommending Sahlins's work, I am fully aware of the vehement critique of his approach recently mounted by Gananath Obeyesekere in *The Apotheosis of Captain Cook: European Mythmaking in the Pacific* (Princeton, 1992). Whatever Obeyesekere's reservations about Sahlins's ability to reconstruct indigenous cosmologies and responses to the Europeans, Sahlins's comparative, trans-cultural, culturally based approach and emphasis on the incorporation and appropriation of expansive influences from the West by non-Western peoples and societies impresses me as exemplary.

76 R. G. Collingwood's arguments for the centrality of these procedures to the discipline of history remain the most powerful marshalled to date. See *The Idea of History* (Oxford, 1946), especially pp. 235–46.

77 These problems have been emphasized by John Goldthorpe with special reference to the tensions inherent in efforts to meld historical and sociological approaches. See John H. Goldthorpe, "The Uses of History in Sociology: Reflections on Some Recent Tendencies," *British Journal of Sociology* 42/2 (1991), especially pp. 219–25.

78 "Emerging Agendas and Recurrent Strategies in Historical Sociology," in *Vision and Method in Historical Sociology*, ed. Skocpol (Cambridge, 1984), 382–3.

6 WORLD HISTORIES AND THE CONSTRUCTION OF COLLECTIVE IDENTITIES

This research was supported by grants from the Israel Science Foundation and the Chiang-Ching-Kuo Foundation for International Scholarly Exchange.

1 See also S. N. Eisenstadt, *Power, Trust and Meaning* (Chicago, 1995), chapter 13.

2 This part of the discussion is based on S. N. Eisenstadt and B. Giesen, "Construction of Collective Identities," *European Journal of Sociology* 36 (1995): 72–102.

3 Such codes are somewhat akin to what Max Weber called *Wirtschaftsethik*. Unlike contemporary structuralists, Weber did not consider such an ethos, like the economic one, to be a purely formal aspect of the human mind which generates only a set of abstract, symbolic categories. He saw such an ethos as given in the nature of man, in his social existence and carrying a direct implication for the order of society. Weber conceived of such codes as variant expressions of the symbolic orientation of human beings towards the facts of their existence in general and towards the problems of social interaction in particular. Thus, a *Wirtschaftsethik* does not connote specific religious injunctions about proper

behavior in any given sphere; nor is it merely a logical derivative of the intellectual contents of the theology or philosophy predominant in a given religion. Rather, a *Wirtschaftsethik*, or a status or political ethos, connotes a general mode of "religious" or "ethical" orientation, focused on the evaluation of a specific institutional arena, and with broad implications for behavior and distribution of resources in such an arena. The orientation is rooted in premises about the cosmic order, about the nature of ontological reality and its relation to human and social existence. See on this, in greater detail, Eisenstadt, *Power, Trust and Meaning*, chapters 1 and 13.

4   E. Shils, "Primordial, Personal, Sacred, and Civil Ties," in *Center and Periphery: Essays on Macrobiology* (Chicago, 1975), 111–27.

5   See Shils, *Center and Periphery*; C. Geertz, "The Integrative Revolution: Primordial Sentiment and Civil Politics in the New States," in *The Interpretation of Cultures* (New York, 1973), 255–310.

6   E. Shils, *Tradition* (Chicago, 1981).

7   This of course is due to the fact that tacit and formal knowledge are not of the same order. Cf. M. Polanyi, *Personal Knowledge: Towards a Post-Critical Philosophy* (Chicago, 1962), 87ff.

8   F. H. Tenbruck, *Die kulturellen Grundlagen der Gesellschaft* (Opladen, 1989).

9   See S. N. Eisenstadt, ed., *The Origins and Diversity of Axial Civilizations* (Albany, NY, 1983); and Eisenstadt, *Kulturen der Achsenzeit: Ihre institutionelle und kulturelle Dynamik*, 2 vols (Frankfurt am Main, 1987).

10   See on this, in greater detail, Eisenstadt, ed., *The Origins and Diversity of Axial Civilizations*.

11   Geertz, *The Interpretation of Cultures*, 93–4.

12   D. M. Schneider and R. T. Smith, *Class Differences and Sex Roles in American Kinship and Family Structure* (Englewood Cliffs, NJ, 1973).

13   E. Durkheim, *The Division of Labour in Society* (New York, 1933). The construction of collective identity or consciousness is also closely related to the distinction, recognized long ago by Durkheim, between the sacred and the profane, and to the different combinations of these two dimensions of social order.

14   See, in greater detail, Eisenstadt, *Power, Trust and Meaning*, chapters 12 and 13.

15   For a general discussion of these processes and the relevant references, see S. N. Eisenstadt, Michel Abitbol, and Naomi Chazan, "The Origins of the State Reconsidered," 1–27; and "State Formation in Africa, Conclusions," 168–200, in S. N. Eisenstadt, Michel Abitbol, and Naomi Chazan, eds, *The Early State in African Perspective: Culture, Power and Division of Labor* (Leiden, 1988).

16   See Eisenstadt, ed., *The Origins and Diversity of Axial Civilizations*.

17   See S. N. Eisenstadt, "Introduction," chapters 3–8, in S. N. Eisenstadt, ed., *Political Sociology* (New York, 1971).

18   See Eisenstadt, ed., *The Origins and Diversity of Axial Civilizations*.

19   Robert Redfield, *Fieldwork: The Correspondence of Robert Redfield* (Boulder, CO, 1991).

20   Shaye J. D. Cohen, "Religion, Ethnicity and 'Hellenism' in the Emergence of Jewish Identity in Maccabean Palestine," in *Religion and Religious Practice in the*

Seleucid Kingdom, ed. Per Bilde, Troels Engberg-Pedersen, Lise Hannestad, and Jan Zahle (Aarhus, Denmark, 1990), 204–24.

21 See on this S. N. Eisenstadt, *Jewish Civilization – The Jewish Historical Experience in a Comparative Perspective* (Albany, NY, 1992), chapters 1 and 2.

22 See Bilde et al., eds, *Religion and Religious Practice*, passim.

23 This analysis is based on S. N. Eisenstadt, *Japanese Civilization: A Comparative View* (Chicago, 1996), especially chapters 12, 13, and 15.

24 In greater detail, see J. M. Kitagawa, *On Understanding Japanese Religion* (Princeton, NJ, 1987); G. Rozman, *The East Asian Religion, Confucian Heritage and Its Modern Adoption* (Princeton, NJ, 1991); M. Waida, "Buddhism and the National Community," in *Transactions and Transformations in the History of Religions*, ed. F. E. Reynolds and T. M. Ludwig (London, 1980); C. Blacker, "Two Shinto Myths: The Golden Age and the Chosen People," in *Themes and Theories in Modern Japanese History*, ed. C. Henny and J.-P. Lehman (Atlantic Highlands, NJ, 1995); J. R. Werblowsky, *Beyond Tradition and Modernity* (Atlantic Highlands, NJ, 1976).

25 See on this Eisenstadt, *Japanese Civilization: A Comparative View*.

26 See S. N. Eisenstadt, "Heterodoxy, Sectarianism and Dynamics of Civilization," *Diogenes* 120 (1982): 5–26.

27 See S. N. Eisenstadt, *European Civilization in a Comparative Perspective* (Oslo, 1988).

28 M. Lipset and Stein Rokkan, eds, *Party Systems and Voter Alignments* (New York, 1967).

29 See S. N. Eisenstadt, "Barbarism and Modernity," *Transactions* 33 (May–June 1996): 31–9.

30 A rather parallel emphasis on territoriality developed also in the realm of Islam in the Ottoman Safavid and Mogul Empires; in China with the Ming and Vietnam; and even in Southeast Asia. See Alexander Woodside, "Conceptions of Territoriality and the State in Confucian Asia: Especially China and Vietnam, 17th–19th Centuries," paper submitted to the Conference on "From Empires to Nations and States: Collective Identity, Public Sphere and Political Order in Early Modernity. The Civilizations of Europe, the Islamic, Hindu and Confucian World Japan," held in Uppsala, June 11–14, 1996.

  See also Frederic E. Wakeman, "Boundaries of the Public Sphere in Ming and Qing China," ibid.; M. E. Berry, "The Construction of the Public Sphere under the Tokugawa," ibid.; Sariga Subrahmanyan, "Jonah and the Whale: On Transformations in Individual and Collective Identities in South (and Southeast Asia) in the 15th–18th Centuries," ibid.; Serif Mardin, on Islamic Civilization, ibid.

31 G. Hoston, *Marxism and the Crisis of Development in Pre-War Japan* (Princeton, 1989); Hoston, "IKKOKU Shakai-shugi: Sano Manabu and the Limits of Marxism as Cultural Criticism," in *Culture and Identity*, ed. T. Rimer (Princeton, 1990), 168–86.

32 S. Tanaka, *Japan's Orient: Rendering Past into History* (Los Angeles, 1993).

33 L. Hartz, *The Founding of New Societies* (New York, 1964); S. N. Eisenstadt, "The

Axial Age – The Emergence of Transcendental Visions and the Rise of Clerics," *European Journal of Sociology* 23 (1982): 294–314. On some discussions about the unity and diversity of the historical experience of the Americas see L. Hanke, ed., *Do the Americas Have a Common History? A Critique of the Bolton Theory* (New York, 1964).

34 A. de Tocqueville, *Democracy in America* (New York, 1966).

35 Freiherr Alexander von Humboldt, *Personal Narrative of Travels to the Equinoctial Regions of America during the Years 1799–1804*, trans. and ed. Thomasina Ross (London, 1851); von Humboldt, *Ensayo Politico Sobre el Reino de la Nueva España* (Mexico: Compania General de Ediciones, 1953).

36 See, for instance, Octavio Paz, *The Labyrinth of Solitude: Life and Thought in Mexico* (New York, 1961); Paz, "A Literature without Criticism," *The Times Literary Supplement* (August 6, 1976): 979–80; R. M. Morse, "Toward a Theory of Spanish American Government," *Journal of the History of Ideas* 15 (1954): 71–93; R. da Matta, *Carnivals, Rogues, and Heroes – An Interpretation of the Brazilian Dilemma* (Notre Dame, IN, 1991).

37 Eisenstadt, *European Civilization in a Comparative Perspective*; A. D. Lindsay, *The Modern Democratic State* (Oxford, 1962); H. Luthy, "Calvinism and Capitalism," in *The Protestant Ethic and Modernization: A Comparative View*, ed. S. N. Eisenstadt (New York, 1988), 87–109; L. Kolakowski, *Chrétiens sans Eglise* (Paris, 1973).

38 J. H. Elliott, *Imperial Spain, 1469–1716* [1963] (London, 1969); A. Dominguez Ortiz, *Sociedad y estado en el siglo XVIII español* [1976] (Barcelona, 1988); J. H. Elliott, *Spain and its World, 1500–1700, Selected Essays* (New Haven, 1989); H. Kamen, *Spain in the Later Seventeenth Century 1665–1700* (London, 1983); M. Menendez y Pelayo, *Historia de los Heterodoxos españoles*, 8 vols (Madrid, 1946), Vols 3 and 5; C. F. Gallagher, "The Shaping of Hispanic Intellectual Tradition," *Fieldstaff Reports*, West Europe Series 12 (1976), 1:1–16; Gallagher, "Culture and Education in Spain, Part II: Absolutism and Liberalism in Bourbon Spain (1780–1860)," *Fieldstaff Reports*, West Europe Series 12 (1977), 1:1–16.

39 Rainer Baum, "Authority and Identity: The Case for Revolutionary Invariance," in *Identity and Authority*, ed. Roland Robertson and Burkart Holzner (New York, 1979), 61–118.

40 N. O. Hatch, *The Sacred Cause of Liberty: Republican Thought and the Millennium in Revolutionary New England* (New Haven, 1977); Perry Miller, *The American Puritans* (Garden City, NJ, 1956); see also A. Heimeart and A. Delbanco, eds, *The Puritans in America: A Narrative Anthology* (Cambridge, MA, 1985); R. Kent Fielding and Eugene Campbell, *The United States: An Interpretative History* (New York, 1964); Richard Hofstadter, *The Structure of American History*, 2nd edn (Englewood Cliffs, NJ, 1973).

41 B. Siebzehner, "Patterns of Incorporation of the Enlightenment in Spanish America, Mexico and Argentina, 1790–1825," Ph.D. thesis, Hebrew University, Jerusalem, 1990; H. Wiarda, *Politics and Social Change* (Boulder, CO, 1992).

42 Wiarda, *Politics and Social Change*; Siebzehner, "Patterns of Incorporation of the Enlightenment"; Elliott, *Spain and its World*, especially Part I, pp. 7–27; C. H.

Haring, *The Spanish Empire in America* [1947] (New York, 1963); J. H. Parry, *The Spanish Seaborne Empire* [1966] (London, 1973).

43 M. Gongora, *El Estado en el derecho Indiano: Epoca de fundación* (Santiago, 1951); Wiarda, *Politics and Social Change*; S. H. M. Harrell, *The Hidalgo Revolt* (Westport, CT, 1966); B. R. Hannef, *Roots in Insurgency: Mexican Regions 1750–1824* (Cambridge, 1986); W. B. Taylor, *Banking, Homicide & Rebellion in Colonial Mexican Villages* (Stanford, 1979); J. L. Phelan, "Authority and Flexibility in the Spanish Imperial Bureaucracy," *Administrative Science Quarterly* 6 (1960): 730–60; S. A. Zavala, *Las Instituciones juridicas en la conquista de America* [1935] (Mexico, DF, 1971); T. E. Anna, *The Fall of the Royal Government in Mexico City* (Lincoln, 1978).

44 Zavala, *Instituciones juridicas*; M. Gongora, *Studies in the Colonial History of Spanish America*, trans. R. Southern (Cambridge, 1975).

45 J. H. Elliott, "Introduction: Colonial Identity in the Atlantic World," 3–15; S. B. Schwartz, "The Formation of Colonial Identity in Brazil," 15–51; A. Pagden, "Identity Formation in Spanish America," 51–95; in *Colonial Identity in the Atlantic World*, ed. N. Canny, N. and A. Pagden (Princeton, 1987); see also S. N. Eisenstadt, "The U.S. and Israel, a Chapter in Comparative Analysis," in Eisenstadt, *Jewish Civilization – The Jewish Historical Experience in a Comparative Perspective*.

46 "Still, reintegration was precisely what happened in the distant past in some key regions of the sub-continent. Take the case of Mexico on the morrow of the Conquest. At that time, several uprooted Indian cultures experienced cultural reintegration thanks to Christianization. The Spain-bashing of nationalist rhetoric would not acknowledge it, but the facts speak for themselves. Octavio Paz writes: 'Thanks to the Catholic faith, the Indians, once in a condition of being cultural orphans, their links broken with their ancient cultures, their Gods dead as well as their towns, find a place in the world.' Out of this fruitful acculturation was born what the Westernised Indian, the liberal Ignacio Altamirano, so aptly called 'equality before the Virgin.' The Virgin, it goes without saying, of Guadalupe ..."

"... In Central/South Mexico there happened what historian Enrique Florescano has dubbed the 'pulverisation' of the Indians' ethnic memory. Subject to a triple separation – territorial, legal and economic – their writing and calendars abolished, thrown into the impossibility of articulating autochthonous messages of more than a strictly local reach, Mexicas and Zaporecas stopped speaking of their nations as such. A chasm was cleft between their past and their present.

"But into that chasm was poured the mythogonic energy of missionary Catholicism. Its crowning achievement was, of course, the Creole elaboration of the Guadeloupian cult, already afoot by 1600. The myth and worship of the local Virgin Mary became the hub of a Creole Catholicism which, though deprived of Messianic bent, presided over a large Mexicanisation of Christianity by translating sundry Indian myths into the Roman rite." Merquior, *On the Historical Position of Latin America* (London, 1982), 153–4.

47 A. Heimeart, *Religion and the American Mind* (Cambridge, MA, 1966); C. Becker, *The Declaration of Independence* (New York, 1958); G. Haskins, *Law and Authority in Early Massachusetts* (Lanham, MD, 1960); D. Little, *Religion, Order and Law* (New York, 1969); Fielding and Campbell, *The United States: An Interpretative History*; R. Hofstadter, *The United States* (Englewood Cliffs, NJ, 1972); see also A. Seligman, "The Failure of Socialism in the United States, A Reconsideration," in S. N. Eisenstadt, A. Seligman, and L. Roniger, *Culture Formation, Protest Movements and Class Structure in Europe and the United States* (London, 1982), 24–56.

48 R. N. Bellah, *Beyond Belief* (New York, 1970), especially chapter 9; and Bellah, *The Broken Covenant* (New York, 1975); Martin Marty, *Religion and Republic – The American Circumstance* (Boston, 1987).

49 R. da Matta, *For an Anthropology of the Brazilian Tradition* (Washington, DC, 1990); see also S. N. Eisenstadt, A. Seligman, and B. Siebzehner, "The Classic Tradition in the Americas: The Reception of Natural Law Theory and the Establishment of New Societies in the New World," in *The Heritage of the Classical World*, ed. B. Haase (Berlin, 1992).

7 Time, Space, and Prescriptive Marginality in Muslim Africa

1 Arthur Darby Nock, *Conversion* (Oxford, 1933).

2 Jeli Banna Kanuté, Banjul, July, 1988. Kanuté once led the Senegalese Instrumental Ensemble in Dakar, and was active for many years in Bamako, Mali, where he turned professional.

3 The Muslim historian, Bayhaqí, declaimed such a mechanistic approach to history thus: "These stories may be far from history, where one usually reads that such and such a king sent such and such a general to such and such a war, and that on such and such a day they made war or peace, and that this one defeated that one, or that one this one, and then proceeded somewhere. But I write what is worthy to be recorded." Cited in *Islam: From the Prophet Muhammad to the Capture of Constantinople*, trans. and ed. Bernard Lewis, 2 vols (New York, 1987), vol. I.

4 Victor Turner, *The Ritual Process: Structure and Anti-Structure* (Ithaca, 1982), 132. Turner describes *communitas* as: (a) existential or spontaneous *communitas* with its ad hoc character; (b) normative *communitas*, which is a social system marked by social control; and (c) ideological *communitas* of utopian radicalism. This pattern is reflected in the phases of historical marginality as discussed here.

5 The term is that of Arnold van Gennep, *The Rites of Passage*, trans. Monika B. Vizedom and Gabrielle L. Caffee (Chicago, 1960), 15–25, 192. See n. 17 for details.

6 John Locke, *A Letter Concerning Toleration* (Amherst, NY, 1990), 50.

7 Muhammad Bello's correspondence with al-Kanemí, in Bello, *Infáq al-Maysúr*, ed. C. E. J. Whitting (London, 1957), 131. Also cited in J. Spencer Trimingham, *A History of Islam in West Africa* (London, 1962), 199.

8 Al-Bakrí, *Kitáb al-Mamálik wa'l Masálik*, ed. and trans. J. F. P. Hopkins and N.

Levtzion, *Corpus of Early Arabic Sources for West African History* (Cambridge, 1981), 82–3.

9 A fourteenth-century Spanish pilgrim, cited in *Islam*, trans. and ed. Lewis, Vol. II, 30.

10 *The Autobiography of Malcolm X, with the Assistance of Alex Haley* (Harmondsworth, 1966), 441, 442, 458–9.

11 Ibid., 482, 483.

12 Stewart Crawford as cited in Arthur Jeffrey, "The Mecca Pilgrimage in the Life of Islam," *International Review of Missions* 14 (1925): 77.

13 Ibn Jubayr, *Al-Rihlah* ["The Travels"], trans. R. J. C. Broadhurst, in *Anthology of Islamic Literature: From the Rise of Islam to Modern Times*, ed. James Kritzeck (New York, 1964), 218.

14 Jeffrey, "The Mecca Pilgrimage," 77–8.

15 For the application of liminality analysis to the history of Muslim Africa the interested reader should see Humphrey J. Fisher, "Liminality and Hijra," in *Rural and Urban Islam in West Africa*, ed. Nehemia Levtzion and Humphrey J. Fisher (Boulder, CO, 1987).

16 William James, *The Varieties of Religious Experience* (New York, 1958), 164.

17 Van Gennep makes a similar point when he says of ritual enactment that "sacredness as an attribute is not absolute; it is brought into play by the nature of particular situations. A man at home, in his tribe, lives in the secular realm; he moves into the realm of the sacred when he goes on a journey and finds himself a foreigner near a camp of strangers." *The Rites of Passage*, 12.

18 See note 4 above. Also Turner's *Dramas, Fields and Metaphors: Symbolic Action in Human Society* (Ithaca, 1983).

19 *Shari'a in Songhay*, trans. John Hunwick (Oxford, 1985), 66–7.

20 Turner, *The Ritual Process*, 166.

21 So said al-Ghazálí. Duncan Black Macdonald, *The Religious Attitude and Life in Islam* [1909] (London, 1985), 222–3.

22 Cited in Mervyn Hiskett, *The Sword of Truth: The Life and Times of the Shehu Usuman dan Fodio* (New York, 1973), 66.

23 Cited in ibid., 67.

24 Van Gennep, *The Rites of Passage*, 192.

25 'Uthmán dan Fodio, *Bayán wujúb al-hijra 'alá 'l 'ibád*, trans. and ed. F. H. El-Masri (Khartoum; London, 1978), 52.

26 Hannah Arendt, commenting on the phenomenon of the Boer sense of isolation as "the first European group to become completely alienated from the pride which Western man felt in living in a world created and fabricated by himself," argues that rootlessness is characteristic of race organization, of the hatred of territorial limitation. Rootlessness inspired in this instance "an activistic faith in one's divine chosenness." Hannah Arendt, *The Origins of Totalitarianism* (Cleveland and New York, 1964), 194, 196–7.

27 Boubacar Barry, n.d., "L'Expansion du Fouta Jallon vers la côte et les crises politiques et sociales dans la Sénégambie méridionale au cours de la première moitié du XIX siècle," unpublished manuscript, 14–15.

28 E. W. Blyden, *Islam, Christianity and the Negro Race* [1887] (Edinburgh, 1967).

29 Ibid., 206.

30 The Shádhiliyáh, the first such religious order in North Africa, was founded by Núr al-Dín al-Shádhilí (1196–1258), although the order was organized by a later disciple of his. An early leader of the order, Shaykh Abul-Qásim, wrote of the order: "Whoever stands at the door of our *taríqa* [order] and enters it for one or two days has the happiness of this life and the life hereafter … He, too, secures the life of his heart … because it [our *taríqa*] is a living *taríqa* which hears, sees and moves. It grows out of the spirit that has entered it. By the name of God it never penetrated into the constitution of any man but shook his life, destroyed his actuality through bringing out his reality, and set him free from hell after rebuilding his disintegrated self." Cited in Nicola A. Ziadeh, *Sanúsíyah: A Study of a Revivalist Movement in Islam* (Leiden, 1968), 6.

31 See L. Sanneh, "Tcherno Aliou, the *walí* of Goumba: Islam, Colonialism and the Rural Factor in Futa Jallon, 1867–1912," in *Rural and Urban Islam in West Africa*, ed. Levtzion and Fisher.

32 L. Sanneh, *The Jakhanke Muslim Clerics: A Religious and Historical Study of Islam in Senegambia* (Lanham, MD, 1989).

33 Ibn Khaldún, *al-Muqaddima*, ed. and trans. Franz Rosenthal, Bollingen Series XLIII, 2nd edn, 3 vols (Princeton, 1967), II, 335, text II, 295–6.

34 Ibn Khaldún, *al-Muqaddima*, text II, 304, in *An Arab Philosophy of History*, trans. Charles Issawi (London, 1963), 69.

35 Ibid., I, 225, trans. Issawi, 66–7.

36 Ibid., I, 228, trans. Issawi, 67–8.

37 Ibid., II, 304, trans. Issawi, 69.

38 Cited in Nehemia Levtzion, "'Abd Alláh b. Yásín and the Almoravids," in *Studies in West African Islamic History: Vol. I: The Cultivators of Islam*, ed. John Ralph Willis (London, 1979), 85–6.

39 G. E. von Grunebaum, *Classical Islam: A History: 600–1258* (London, 1970), 175.

40 Cited in Levtzion, "'Abd Alláh b. Yásín," 87.

41 Cited in von Grunebaum, *Classical Islam*, 183–4.

42 The Sanúsíyah movement was founded by the Grand Sanúsí, Sayyid Muhammad ibn 'Alí al-Sanúsí (d. 1859), of *sharífian* descent. The Grand Sanúsí made a pilgrimage to Mecca, where he developed his ideas of reform. He founded a *záwiya* in Mecca in 1837, and preached widely in the Muslim world, in Arabia as well as in Jordan, the Sudan, Tunisia, and Libya, where he established the mother *záwiya* of his movement, in territory hospitable only to those disposed to austerity and physical privation. It was a grandson of his who became a king of Libya. Ziadeh, *Sanúsíyah*, 44ff.

43 Barbara Daly Metcalf, *Islamic Revival in British India: Deoband, 1860–1900* (Princeton, 1982), 92.

44 Ibid., 97.

45 Text of the foundation charter, cited in ibid., 98.

46 Ibid., 105.

47 Ibid., 239.
48 Ibid., 146. The classic textbook on Anglo-Muhammadan law is by Asaf A. A. Fyzee, *Outlines of Muhammadan Law* [1949] (Delhi, 1974). Also Fyzee, *Cases in the Muhammadan Law of India and Pakistan* (Oxford, 1965).
49 Metcalf, *Islamic Revival in British India*, 151.
50 Ibid., 153, 253.
51 Ibid., 253–4.
52 Turner tries to salvage his use of "anti-structure," but not completely successfully. *Ritual Process*, 125f., 166–7.
53 Ibid., 132–3.
54 Ibid., 133.
55 Martin Buber, *Between Man and Man* (London, 1961), 51. Buber's thought here is akin to Emmanuel Levinas's ethical teachings, though Levinas lacks Buber's clarity.
56 Cited in Macdonald, *Religious Attitude*, 232.
57 The testimony is that of Kazem Zadek, who made the pilgrimage in 1910–11. Cited in Jeffrey, "The Mecca Pilgrimage," 78.
58 Jeffrey gives some examples: three Sumatran pilgrims from Indonesia were making the *hájj* in 1803 when the Wahhábís struck. When the Indonesians returned they formed Padri sects in the highlands of Padang from where they declared *jihád* on the infidel Bataks. It was in Mecca, too, that the radical nineteenth-century Indian reformer of Oudh, Sayyid Ahmad, came into fateful contact with Wahhábí ideas which he embraced and took to India, opening a corridor of violent encounters with the Sikhs from 1826 to 1846, and with the British in 1854 in the Frontier War, which lasted until 1868. A third example was the 1837 Sanúsíyah movement of Shaykh Sanúsí, who received the inspiration for his movement while visiting Mecca. Mecca struck fear in the hearts of European colonial powers for whom change was tantamount to political sedition. Jeffrey, "The Mecca Pilgrimage," 79–82.
59 Shiháb al-Dín al-Suhrawardí, *al-'Awárif al-Ma'árif*, trans. and ed. Wilberforce Clarke (Calcutta, 1891); reprinted as *A Dervish Textbook* (London, 1980), 26.

8 HISTORY'S FORGOTTEN DOUBLES

This is a revised version of the Opening Address at the World History Conference, organized by *History and Theory* at Wesleyan University, March 25, 1994. I am grateful to Giri Deshingkar and the participants in the conference for their criticisms and suggestions.

1 A creative variation on the same response is in works like Gananath Obeysekere's *The Apotheosis of Captain Cook: European Mythmaking in the Pacific* (Princeton, NJ, 1992). Obeysekere argues that history can be part-mythic and myths part-historic, that is, there is no clear discontinuity between the two. His narrative, however, seems to suggest that he dislikes the mythic-in-history and likes the historical-in-myths. The young scholar Shail Mayaram pushes

Obeysekere's argument to its logical conclusion in her "Oral and Written Discourses: An Enquiry Into the Meo Mythic Tradition," unpublished report to the Indian Council of Social Science Research (Delhi, 1994), 6: "No civilization is really ahistorical. In a sense, every individual is historical and uses his/her memory to organize the past. ... The dichotomy between history and myth is an artificial one. History and myth are not exclusive modes of representation."

In this essay I reject formulations that impose the category of history on all constructions of the past or sanction the reduction of all myths to history. I am also uncomfortable with formulations that do not acknowledge the special political status of myths as the preferred language of a significant proportion of threatened or victimized cultures.

2   Speaking of the Partition of British India and the birth of India and Pakistan, Gyanendra Pandey ("Partition, History and the Making of Nations," presented at the conference on State and Nationalism in India, Pakistan and Germany [Colombo, February 26–8, 1994]) asks: "Why have historians of India (and Pakistan and Bangladesh) failed to produce richly layered, challenging histories of Partition of a kind that would compare with their sophisticated histories of peasant insurrection; working class consciousness; the onset of capitalist relations in agriculture; the construction of new notions of caste, community, and religion, ... and, indeed, the writing of women's autobiographies ...? Or, to ask the question in another way, why is there such a chasm between the historian's history of Partition and the popular reconstruction of the event, which is to such a large extent built around the fact of violence?"

Pandey goes on to answer: "The answer lies, it seems to me, in our fear of facing ... this history as our own: the fear of reopening old wounds. ... It lies also in the difficulty that all social science has faced in writing the history of violence and pain. But, in addition, it inheres ... in the very character of historian's history as 'national' history and a history of 'progress.'"

Could Pandey have added that, when faced with a trauma of this magnitude, when the survival of communities and fundamental human values are at stake, popular memories of Partition have to organize themselves differently, employing principles that are ahistorical but not amoral? Do the historians of South Asia have a tacit awareness that they are in no position to supplant memories which seek to protect the dignity of the one million or so who died in the violence and the approximately five million who were uprooted in ways that would protect normal life and basic human values?

3   On the fear of ambiguity as a gift of the Enlightenment, see Donald N. Levine, *The Flight from Ambiguity: Essays in Social and Cultural Theory* (Chicago, 1985). On the psychological and cultural correlates of ambiguity, once a popular subject of research in psychology, see, for instance, Anthony Davids, "Psychodynamic and Sociocultural Factors Related to Intolerance of Ambiguity," in *The Study of Lives: Essays in Honour of Henry A. Murray*, ed. Robert W. White (New York, 1963), 160–78.

4   For instance Paul Feyerabend, *Against Method: Outline of an Anarchistic Theory of Knowledge* (London, 1978); and *Science in a Free Society* (London, 1978).

5   For a pithy critique of postmodernism's anti-history from the point of view of the non-West, see the series of essays by Ziauddin Sardar, "Surviving the Terminator: The Post-Modern Mental Condition," *Futures* 22 (March 1990): 203–10; "Total Recall: Aliens, 'Others' and Amnesia in Post-Modernist Thought," *Futures* 23 (March 1991): 189–203; "Terminator 2: Modernity, Post-Modernism and the 'Other,'" *Futures* 24 (June 1992): 493–506; and "Do not Adjust Your Mind: Post-Modernism, Reality and the Other," *Futures* 25 (October 1993): 877–94.

6   Actually, history has thrived on such impersonality – according to some a core value of modernity. On the role of impersonality in modern knowledge systems, see Tariq Banuri, "Modernization and Its Discontents: A Cultural Perspective on Theories of Development," in *Dominating Knowledge: Development, Culture and Resistance*, ed. Frédérique Apffel Marglin and Stephen Marglin (Oxford, 1990), 73–101.

7   Alvin W. Gouldner, *The Coming Crisis of Western Sociology* (London, 1971); and Stanislav Andreski, *Social Sciences as Sorcery* (London, 1972); Rollo May, *Psychology and the Human Dilemma* (Princeton, NJ, 1962); Abraham Maslow, *Toward a Psychology of Being* (Princeton, NJ, 1968); Roland Laing, *The Divided Self: A Study of Sanity and Madness* (Harmondsworth, 1970); Thomas S. Szasz, *The Manufacture of Madness* (London, 1971); and *The Myth of Mental Illness* (London, 1972).

8   N. Georgescu-Roegen, *Energy and Economic Myths* (New York, 1976); J. Schumacher, *Small is Beautiful: Study of Economics as if People Mattered* (New Delhi, 1977); and *Roots of Economic Growth* (Varanasi, 1962); Ludwig Wittgenstein, *Tractus Logico-Philosophicus*, trans. C. K. Ogden and F. P. Ramsay (London, 1922); and Richard Rorty, "The Priority of Democracy to Philosophy," *Objectivity, Relativity and Truth: Philosophical Papers* (Cambridge, 1991), I, 175–96; and "Philosophy as Science, as Metaphor, and as Politics," in *Essays on Heidegger and Others* (Cambridge, 1991), II, 9–26.

9   So much so that in anthropology, I am told, graduate students in some universities are more keen to do cultural critiques of anthropology than empirical studies of other cultures.

10   William Irwin Thompson, *At the Edge of History: Speculations on the Transformation of Culture* (New York, 1972), 179–80.

11   Ananda K. Coomaraswamy, *Selected Papers*, ed. Roger Lipsky (Princeton, NJ, 1977), vols 1 and 2; Frithjof Schuon, *Language of the Self*, trans. M. Pallis (London, 1968); and *Logic and Transcendence*, trans. M. Pallis (New York, 1975); René Guénon, *The Reign of Quantity and the Signs of the Times*, trans. Lord Northbourne (Baltimore, 1972); Seyyed Hossein Nasr, *Introduction to Islamic Cosmological Doctrines* (London, 1978); and *Islamic Life and Thought* (London, 1981).

     I hope the rest of this essay will not now be read as a convoluted plea for perennial philosophy, though I have obviously benefited from the critique of history ventured by such philosophy. Mine is primarily a political-psychological argument which tries to be sensitive to the politics of cultures and knowledge.

12   For instance, Anthony Giddens, "Structuralism, Post-Structuralism and the

Production of Culture," in *Social Theory Today*, ed. Anthony Giddens and Jonathan Turner (Cambridge, 1987), 194–223; 212–13:

> The methodological repression of time in Saussure's conception of langue is trans-lated by Lévi-Strauss into substantive repression of time involved in the codes organized through myths. ...
>
> Foucault's style of writing history ... does not flow along with chronological time. Nor does it depend upon the narrative description of a sequence of events. ... There is more than an echo of Lévi-Strauss in Foucault's view that history is one form of knowledge among others – and of course, like other forms of knowl-edge, a mode of mobilizing power.

13 Keith Jenkins, *Rethinking History* (London: Routledge, 1991). See especially pp. 5–20.

14 Gyan Prakash, "Writing Post-Orientalist Histories of the Third World: Indian Historiography is Good to Think," in *Colonialism and Culture*, ed. Nicholas B. Dirks (Ann Arbor, 1992), 353–88; and Dipesh Chakrabarty, "History as Critique and Critique of History," *Economic and Political Weekly* (September 14, 1991): 2262–8; and "Post-Coloniality and the Artifice of History: Who Speaks for the 'Indian' Pasts," *Representations* 37 (Winter 1992): 1–26.

15 Vinay Lal, "On the Perils of History and Historiography: The Case, Puzzling as Usual, of India," manuscript, 1988; see also his "The Discourse of History and the Crisis at Ayodhya: Reflections on the Production of Knowledge, Freedom, and the Future of India" (1994, unpublished manuscript). The latter goes further in its critique of history as a cultural project and its relationship with violence in the context of the Ramjanmabhumi movement in India, something to which I turn towards the end of this essay briefly and from a slightly different point of view.

Is it merely an accident that so many of the critics of history I have mentioned in this paper are South Asians or have a South Asian connection? Is it only a function of my own cultural origins? Or is it possible that, pushed around by pow-erful traditions of both modern history and the surviving epic cultures in their part of the world, many South Asians are forced to take, sometimes grudgingly, a more skeptical stance towards history?

16 Chakrabarty, "Post-Coloniality and the Artifice of History," 19.

17 David Lowenthal, *The Past Is a Foreign Country* (Cambridge, 1985).

18 Paradoxically, that debate, centering around Cyril Burt's ethical lapses, only con-solidated the status of the tests as *the* measure and operational definer of intelli-gence.

19 The moderns like to build their selfhood on the past that looks empirical and fal-sifiable. But it can be argued that the unsatiated search for a touch of transcen-dence in life is, as a result, only pushed into weird psychopathological channels and finds expression in using or living out history with the passions formerly elicited by myths, without the open-endedness and the touch of self-destructive-ness associated with myths. Later on in this essay I shall give an example of this from the backwaters of Asia, but the reader can easily think up similar examples from his or her surroundings.

20 Nikos Papastergiadis, *Exile as Modernity* (Manchester, 1993).

21 Robert Jay Lifton, *The Protean Self: Human Resistance in an Age of Fragmentation* (New York, 1993), 131.
22 Gayatri Singh, "Displacement and Limits to Legislation," in *Dams and Other Major Projects: Impact on and Response of Indigenous People*, ed. Raajen Singh (Goa, 1988), 91–7; see 91.
23 Robert Sinsheimer's certainty principle, which he proposes as the inverse of Heisenberg's uncertainty principle, is particularly relevant to this argument. The uncertainty principle has to do with the effect of observation on the observed; the certainty principle with the effect of observation on the observer. Robert Sinsheimer, "The Presumptions of Science," *Daedalus* 107 (1978): 23–5.
24 Hannah Arendt, Interview with Roger Errera, *New York Review of Books* (October 26, 1978): 18.
25 Richard Pipes, "Seventy-Five Years On: The Great October Revolution as a Clandestine *Coup d'Etat*," *Times Literary Supplement* (November 6, 1992): 3–4; see 4.
26 Ibid., 3.
27 Erik H. Erikson, "Youth: Fidelity and Diversity," *Daedalus* 1 (Winter 1962): 5–27; see 22.
28 Girindrasekhar Bose, *Purāṇa Praveśa* (Calcutta, 1934).
29 Christiane Hartnack, "Psychoanalysis and Colonialism in British India" (Berlin, 1988; unpublished Ph.D. dissertation); Sudhir Kakar, "Stories from Indian Psychoanalysis: Context and Text," in *Cultural Psychology*, ed. James W. Stigler, Richard A. Shweder, and Gilbert Herdt (New York, 1990), 427–45.
30 Lal, "On the Perils of History," 1–3.
31 Ibid., 2. Could it be that things looked different in the Islamic cultures for a while to some historians of India because for a long time the ruling dynasties of India had been Muslim? Was the earlier reading of South Asian Islam as historically minded based on the assumption that dominance and successful statecraft required a "proper" sense of history?

I am not the right person to answer this question but it is pretty clear that the new sense of history spread unevenly in India. It became a deeper passion among the Brahminic castes – after all, history did require written texts at a time when oral histories were not fashionable – and castes aspiring to a Brahminic status (such as the Bhadraloks of Bengal, traditionally considered peripheral to the mainstream Brahminic culture but now closer to power in the pan-Indian scene due to their colonial connection). History also became a passion with those Brahminic communities that had opted for the Kṣatriya vocations of statecraft and bureaucracy, which previously contributed to one's power but not to caste status. These vocations now contributed to one's status because of the revaluation, under the colonial regime, of the Kṣatriyas as martial and masculine and therefore, as true indigenous rulers of people in India. Two examples of communities gaining from their non-traditional vocations and opting for history with a vengeance in colonial times are the Chitpāvan Brahmins of Maharashtra and the Nāgar Brahmins of Gujarat.

32 Surendranath Banerjea handled the situation the way many modern Indian his-

torians would like to handle it. After asking whether it was imaginable that a great civilization did not have proper histories, he concluded that histories did indeed exist in India but could not survive the social upheavals in the country, the carelessness of the Brahmins, and the tropical climate. Ibid., 6.

33 It was certainly not an accident that the new enthusiasm for history in India was accompanied by a fear of a return to the Indian past. While the new acquaintance with history created an awareness of and a tendency to celebrate some aspects of the European past – especially the legitimation of modern science in India, as in Europe, proceeded on the basis of a systematic invocation of the beauties of Europe's Hellenic traditions – any similar attempt to invoke the Indian past immediately triggered and continue to trigger accusations of retrogression or atavism. Gradually the idea that some pasts were more equal than other pasts came to be successfully institutionalized in India's westernized elite's new-found historical consciousness.

34 Bose, *Purāṇa Praveśa*, 212–13.

35 For instance, among the interpretive principles Bose deciphered was *atiyukti vicāra*, analysis of *atiranjana* or the stylized exaggerations of the Indian epics which put up the back of James Mill, as a part of the narrative mode of the *purāṇas*.

36 Ivan Illich, "Mnemosyne: The Mold of Memory," in *In the Mirror of the Past: Lectures and Addresses 1978–1990* (New York, 1992), 18:

> For the historian, the script is a vehicle which allows him to recover the events or perceptions that the document was meant to record. For the student of pastness itself, the script has a more specific function. For him, the script is a privileged object which allows him to explore two things: the mode of recall used in a given epoch, and also the image held by that epoch about the nature of memory and therefore of the past.

37 Bose, *Purāṇa Praveśa*, 179.

38 Rama himself, though a venerated deity in much of South and Southeast Asia, has been open to diverse forms of veneration and recognition within Hinduism itself. The two main sects of Hindus, Vaiṣṇavas and Śaivites, see him differently, with the former only granting him full divinity. There are versions of *Ramayaṇa*, the epic that tells the story of Rama, where he is the villain and there are even temples dedicated to the demons Rama fought against.

39 Almost all the main leaders of the movement have come from modernist sects that explicitly attack Hindu idolatry. Till the movement succeeded in bringing to power a party committed to their cause in the state where Ayodhya is located and the new cabinet made a symbolic appearance at the Ayodhya temple, almost none of the major leaders had found time in seven years to visit the temple. For details of the Ayodhya case I have depended on Ashis Nandy, Shikha Trivedy, Shail Mayaram, and Achyut Yagnik, *Creating a Nationality: The Ramjanmabhumi Movement and Fear of the Self* (New Delhi, 1995).

40 See, for instance, S. Gopal, Romila Thapar, and others, *The Political Abuse of History* (New Delhi, n. d.), pamphlet; also, Romila Thapar, Harbans Mukhia, and Bipan Chandra, *Communalism and the Writing of Indian History* (New Delhi, 1969), pamphlet.

41   See, for instance, Arun Shourie, Harsh Narain, Jay Dubashi, Ram Swarup, and Sita Ram Goel, *Hindu Temples, What Happened to Them (A Preliminary Survey)* (New Delhi, 1990); Koenraad Elst, *Ramjanmabhumi Versus Babri Masjid: A Case Study in Hindu–Muslim Conflict* (New Delhi, 1990); and *Negationism in India: Concealing the Record of Islam*, 2d edn (New Delhi, 1993).

42   I found out from a local leader of the Vishwa Hindu Parishad during a field trip to Ayodhya that the local Shia leaders had offered, at least twice, to relocate the mosque and the local Hindus were willing to accept the offer. But the all-India leadership of both the Hindu nationalists and important sections of the Muslim political leadership refused to countenance such a compromise. The local Hindus and Muslims had no right to decide what was an issue that involved all the Hindus and Muslims of India, some of the latter said.

43   Ashis Nandy, *The Intimate Enemy: Loss and Recovery of Self Under Colonialism* (New Delhi, 1983).

44   Ramchandra Gandhi, *Sītā's Kitchen: A Testimony of Faith and Inquiry* (New Delhi, 1992), 10.

45   Ananda K. Coomaraswamy, *Time and Eternity* (Bangalore, 1989), 71.

46   See, for instance, Gyanendra Pandey, "Modes of History Writing: New Hindu History of Ayodhya," *Economic and Political Weekly* 29 (June 18, 1994): 1523–8.

47   Krishna Mohun Banerjea, "Discourse on the Nature and Importance of Historical Studies," in *Selection of Discourses Delivered at the Meetings of the Society for the Acquisition of General Knowledge* (Calcutta, 1840), Vol. 1, quoted in Lal, "On the Perils of History," 1.

9 IDENTITY IN WORLD HISTORY: A POSTMODERN PERSPECTIVE

1   William McNeill, "The Rise of the West as Long-Term Process," in *Mythistory and Other Essays* (Chicago, 1986), 51.

2   Ibid.

3   Theodore Von Laue, *The World Revolution of Westernization: The Twentieth Century in Global Perspective* (New York, 1987), xvii.

4   Ibid.

5   Erik Erikson, *Childhood and Society* (New York, 1963), 261.

6   Erik Erikson, *Insight and Responsibility* (New York, 1964), 92.

7   Stephen A. Mitchell, "Contemporary Perspectives on Self: Toward an Integration," *Psychoanalytic Dialogues* 1 (1991): 136.

8   See Heinz Kohut, *Self Psychology and the Humanities*, ed. Charles Strozier (New York, 1985), for a collection of Kohut's writings on history, society, and culture.

9   Kohut, "Self Psychology and the Sciences of Man," in ibid., 82.

10   Kohut, "On the Continuity of the Self" (conversation with Charles Strozier), in ibid., 236–7.

11   Donald Spence, *Narrative Truth and Historical Truth* (New York, 1982), chapter 5, "Formal Interpretation," 137–73.

12   Roy Schafer, "Narration in the Psychoanalytic Dialogue," *Critical Inquiry* 7 (Autumn 1980): 30.

13 Roy Schafer, *Retelling a Life: Narration and Dialogue in Psychoanalysis* (New York, 1992), 56.

14 Evan H. Bellin, "The Psychoanalytic Narrative: On the Transformational Axis between Writing and Speech," *Psychoanalysis and Contemporary Thought* 7 (July 1984): 9.

15 Ibid., 28.

16 Ibid., 11.

17 Humphrey Morris, "Introduction," in *Telling Facts: History and Narration in Psychoanalysis*, ed. Joseph H. Smith and Humphrey Morris (Baltimore, 1992), xiv.

18 Erik Erikson, *Young Man Luther* (New York, 1958) and *Gandhi's Truth: On the Origins of Militant Nonviolence* (New York, 1969).

19 See Lewis D. Wurgaft, "Erik Erikson: From Luther to Gandhi," *Psychoanalytic Review* 63 (Summer 1976), for a more detailed discussion of the relationship between these biographies.

20 Erikson, *Young Man Luther*, 231.

21 Ibid., 267.

22 Ibid., 252.

23 Erikson, *Gandhi's Truth*, 242.

24 Ibid., 396.

25 Ibid., 406.

26 In 1967, two years before the appearance of Erikson's *Gandhi*, Robert J. Lifton published an essay on Protean Man, another identity construct for contemporary society that incorporates the fluid boundaries and adaptability that Erikson attributes to Gandhi. See *Boundaries: Psychological Man in Revolution* (New York, 1967), 37–63.

27 Robert May, "Concerning a Psychoanalytic View of Maleness," *Psychoanalytic Review* 73 (Winter 1986): 181.

28 See Betty Friedan, *The Feminine Mystique* (New York, 1963) and Kate Millett, *Sexual Politics* (Garden City, NY, 1970).

29 See Nancy Chodorow, *The Reproduction of Mothering* (Berkeley, 1978) and Carol Gilligan, *In a Different Voice* (Cambridge, MA, 1982).

30 Virginia Goldner, "Toward a Critical Relational Theory of Gender," *Psychoanalytic Dialogues* 1 (1991): 254–5.

31 Ibid., 250.

32 Jacqueline Rose, "Introduction-II," in *Feminine Sexuality*, ed. Juliet Mitchell and Jacqueline Rose (New York, 1982), 30.

33 Ibid.

34 Goldner, "Toward a Critical Relational Theory of Gender," 257.

35 Muriel Dimen, "Deconstructing Difference: Gender, Splitting, and Transitional Space," *Psychoanalytic Dialogues* 1 (1991): 343.

36 Ibid., 339.

37 Jessica Benjamin, "Sameness and Difference: Toward an 'Overinclusive' Model of Gender Development," *Psychoanalytic Inquiry* 15 (1995): 138.

38 Ibid., 126.

39 Ibid., 128.

40 Christopher Bollas, *The Shadow of the Object* (New York, 1987), 9–10.
41 Mitchell, "Contemporary Perspectives on Self," 145.
42 Malcolm Slavin and Daniel Kriegman, *The Adaptive Design of the Human Psyche* (New York, 1992), 204.
43 Mitchell, "Contemporary Perspectives on Self," 145.
44 Benedict Anderson, *Imagined Communities* (New York, 1990), 14.
45 Ashis Nandy, "From Outside the Imperium: Gandhi's Cultural Critique of the West," in *Traditions, Tyranny and Utopias* (Delhi, 1987), 153.
46 Eric Hobsbawm, "Introduction: Inventing Traditions," in *The Invention of Tradition*, ed. Eric Hobsbawm and Terrence Ranger (New York, 1993), 1.
47 Ibid., 12.
48 Ibid., 14.
49 Ernest Gellner, *Nations and Nationalism* (Ithaca, NY, 1983), 125. Another work which focuses on the heterogeneity of national formations is Etienne Balibar and Immanuel Wallerstein, *Race, Nation, Class: Ambiguous Identities* (London, 1991). In particular see Balibar's chapter, "The Nation Form: History and Ideology," 86–106.
50 The phrase is taken from the title of a collection of essays by Ashis Nandy. See *At the Edge of Psychology: Essays in Politics and Culture* (Delhi, 1980).
51 Tom Nairn, *The Break-up of Britain* (London, 1977), 359. Quoted from Anderson, *Imagined Communities*, 14–15.
52 Anderson, *Imagined Communities*, 144.
53 Ibid., 36–40.
54 Anne McClintock, "Family Feuds: Gender, Nationalism and the Family," *Feminist Review* 44 (Summer 1993): 64.
55 Ibid., 66.
56 Homi Bhabha, "DissemiNation: Time, Narrative, and the Margins of the Modern Nation," in *Nation and Narration*, ed. Homi Bhabha (London, 1990), 292.
57 Ibid., 297.
58 Ibid., 300.
59 Homi Bhabha, "The Third Space" (interview with Jonathan Rutherford), in *Identity, Community, Culture, Difference*, ed. Jonathan Rutherford (London, 1990), 211.
60 Bhabha, "DissemiNation," 313.
61 See Robert Young's *White Mythologies: Writing History and the West* (London, 1990) for a treatment of postcolonial discourse within the broader framework of the meaning of history for the West since Hegel and Marx.
62 Ashis Nandy, "The Psychology of Colonialism," in *The Intimate Enemy: Loss and Recovery of Self under Colonialism* (Delhi, 1983), 32–3.
63 Ibid., 38.
64 Homi Bhabha, "Remembering Fanon: Self, Psyche, and the Colonial Condition" (foreword to Frantz Fanon, *Black Skin, White Masks* [London, 1986], xiv, quoted from Young, *White Mythologies*). Young's book contains a useful critical treatment of Bhabha.
65 Homi Bhabha, "Signs Taken for Wonders," in *Race, Writing and Difference*, ed. Henry Louis Gates (Chicago, 1985), 173.

66   Ashis Nandy, "The Uncolonized Mind," in *The Intimate Enemy*, 77.

67   Ashis Nandy, "Towards a Third World Utopia," in *Traditions, Tyranny and Utopias*, 43.

68   Ashis Nandy, "The Psychology of Colonialism," in *The Intimate Enemy*, 55.

69   Ashis Nandy, "The Uncolonized Mind," in *The Intimate Enemy*, 107.

70   May, "Concerning a Psychoanalytic View of Maleness," 180.

71   Jane Flax, *Thinking Fragments* (Berkeley, 1990), 219.

72   Mitchell, "Contemporary Perspectives on Self," 138.

73   Ibid., 139.

74   Benjamin, "Sameness and Difference," 136–9.

75   Anderson, *Imagined Communities*, 14.

76   Ibid., 18.

77   Ibid., 19.

78   Bhabha, "DissemiNation," 310.

79   Ibid., 308.

80   Octave Mannoni, among others, has made this argument in the framework of colonial relations. See *Prospero and Caliban: The Psychology of Colonialism* (New York, 1964). For a recent treatment of the psychology of international relations that revolves around the mechanism of projection, see Vamik D. Volkan, *The Need to Have Enemies and Allies* (Northvale, NJ, 1988).

81   Most contemporary commentators writing on colonialism draw this perspective from their readings of the master/slave paradigm in Hegel's *Phenomenology of Mind*. For an interesting recent treatment of this paradigm, see Paul Gilroy, *The Black Atlantic* (Cambridge, MA, 1993), 46–58.

82   See *Projection, Identification, Projective Identification*, ed. Joseph Sandler (Madison, CT, 1987) for a series of essays that deal with projection and related defenses in both a clinical and a political context.

83   Gilroy, *The Black Atlantic*, 45–6. This is also an important perspective in Edward Said's *Culture and Imperialism* (New York, 1993).

10   REFLECTIONS ON *THE END OF HISTORY*, FIVE YEARS LATER

This article was originally published as a chapter in *After History? Francis Fukuyama and His Critics*, ed. Timothy Burns (Lanham, MD, 1994) and is reproduced here by permission.

1   I do not like the word "normative" because it implies that there is a multiplicity of "norms" or "values" among different societies, or within the same society, about which there can be no rational consensus and no rational discourse, as opposed to "empirical" facts, about which consensus can, through application of the proper method, be reached. However, my meaning will probably be clearer, particularly to social scientists, if I use the term "normative" rather than, for example, "theoretical."

2   Gregory B. Smith, "The End of History or a Portal to the Future: Does Anything Lie Beyond Late Modernity?," in *After History?*, ed. Burns, 1–21.

3   That they are arguably fairer does not mean they are actually fairer; equal distri-
    bution of economic gains would be fair only if people were equally deserving of
    them.

4   For a more extended analysis of *Capitalism, Socialism, and Democracy*, see Francis
    Fukuyama, "Capitalism and Democracy: The Missing Link," *Journal of Democracy*
    3 (July 1992): 100–10.

5   For a review of the extensive social science literature that confirms this point, see
    Larry Diamond, "Economic Development and Democracy Reconsidered,"
    American Behavioral Scientist 15 (March–June 1992): 450–99.

6   See, for example, Samuel Huntington, *The Third Wave* (Lexington, KY, 1992).

7   Peter Fenves, "The Tower of Babel Rebuilt," in *After History?*, ed. Burns, 226.

8   The principle's inability to make rational moral distinctions makes it therefore
    perhaps not surprising that Rorty compares the Serbs to Thomas Jefferson. See
    his "Human Rights, Rationality, and Sentimentality," in *On Human Rights: The
    Oxford Amnesty Lectures 1993*, ed. Stephen Shute and Susan Hurley (New York,
    1993), 111–34.

9   This problem I alluded to in *The End of History and the Last Man* (New York,
    1992), 296.

10 Tom Darby, "Technology, Christianity, and the Universal and Homogeneous
    State," in *After History?*, ed. Burns, chapter 11.

11 Timothy Burns, "Modernity's Irrationalism"; Victor Gourevitch, "The End of
    History?"; and Peter Augustine Lawler, "Fukuyama versus the End of History," in
    After History?, ed. Burns.

12 I owe this formulation to Charles Griswold.

13 See Theodore von Laue, "From Fukuyama to Reality: A Critical Essay," in *After
    History?*, ed. Burns, 23–37.

14 Fenves, "The Tower of Babel Rebuilt," 229.

15 In his formulation, I "proclaimed the end of history"; in fact, I never proclaimed
    anything but merely raised the *question* of the end of history.

16 Susan Shell, "Fukuyama and the End of History," in *After History?*, ed. Burns, 45.

11 WORLD HISTORY, CULTURAL RELATIVISM, AND THE GLOBAL FUTURE

This essay is an expanded version of my article "Heretical Ruminations about
World History" published in the *World History Bulletin* 10, no. 1 (1993). It also
draws on ideas expressed in my book *The World Revolution of Westernization* (New
York, 1987).

1   In 1725 the archbishop of Goa, Ignacio de Santa Teresa, said: "God has deliber-
    ately chosen the Portuguese out of all other nations for the rule and reform of the
    whole world, with command, dominion, and Empire, both pure and mixed." C.
    R. Boxer, *The Portuguese Seaborne Empire, 1415–1825* (New York, 1969), 374.
    The Portuguese set the pace for other European imperialists.

2   For a convenient survey, interested readers may consult William McNeill, *The
    Rise of the West* (Chicago, 1963).

3   For additional insights to McNeill, *The Rise of the West*, see F. C. Jones, *The European Miracle: Environment, Economics, and Geopolitics in the History of Europe and Asia* (Cambridge, 1981), and his subsequent book *Growth Recurring: Economic Chance in World History* (New York, 1988).

4   This statement is bound to be disputed as a product of Eurocentrism. Examining the defense of non-Western traditions by anti-Western intellectuals, we find that their arguments are derived from Western analysis. Anti-Western intellectuals implicitly Westernize their own non-Western cultures, none more so than Afrocentrists. Yet while questioning the validity of the refutations, we have to honor their search for a source of creativity-promoting pride, a major challenge to the Western (and American) state of mind (as discussed below).

5   Seth K. Humphrey, *Mankind, Racial Values and the Racial Prospect* (New York, 1917).

6   *The Lenin Anthology*, ed. Robert C. Tucker (New York, 1975), 83.

7   For my analysis of the Soviet system based on the criteria here suggested, see *Why Lenin? Why Stalin?* (New York, 1971).

8   *The China Reader: Republican China*, ed. Franz Schurmann and Orville Schell (New York, 1967), 180.

9   "Charter of the United Nations," *Yearbook of the United Nations 1993* (Dordrecht), 1335.

10 *Yearbook of the United Nations 1993*, 1333–4.

11 See his essay "The Clash of Civilizations?," in *Foreign Affairs* 72 (1993).

12 See also Robert D. Kaplan, "The Coming Anarchy," *Atlantic Monthly* (February 1994).

13 Especially as described by Nicholas Kristof and Sheryl WuDunn, *China Wakes* (New York, 1994).

14 *Yearbook of the United Nations 1993*, 777.

15 Salman Rushdie, *Imaginary Homelands* (New York, 1991), 394.

Index